More Advance Praise for
One Blade of Grass

"Lovely prose . . . This memoir will resonate most with readers wanting to understand the slow, rocky process of practicing Zen."
—*Publishers Weekly*

"This is the book Shukman was born to write—I've been waiting a long time for someone to write this—a record of how we evolve, from ignorance and suffering as a young boy, tracking his accidental awakening, discovering in fits and starts his way-seeking mind to peace and the ground of being. So beautifully written, the reader immerses along with the author on his stumbling path to wholeness. In parts hilariously funny, I cannot say enough—I love this book." —NATALIE GOLDBERG, author of *Writing Down the Bones* and *The Great Failure*

"It is a marvelous book . . . Anyone interested in writing, anyone interested in Zen, and anyone interested in writing in Zen—the book is marvelous, and also you can read it just for fun. It's a really interesting book about [Henry Shukman's] life, which has been extraordinary, leading into [his] Zen practice."
—ABIGAIL ADLER, *The Last Word*

"What a wonderful and generous book this is, Roshi Shukman sharing so openly his particular path into the depths of Zen, and sharing also those depths themselves. If you've ever wondered how a messed-up kid like you or me might master the wisdom of Zen, *One Blade Of Grass* is the adventure for you. It's great company—and after reading it, you might recognize that you're further along than you imagined."　　　　—DAVID HINTON, editor and translator of *The Four Chinese Classics* and author of *The Wilds of Poetry*

"There's no two ways about it. Henry Shukman has a seductively natural style of writing. And the story he tells is both informative and inspiring. Shukman grew up in a culturally rich but physically and emotionally painful situation. Upon encountering the writings of Zen Master Dogen, he was fortunate to have an early experience of the reality that mountains dance. This planted a seed which eventually bore the fruit of happiness at the deepest level—happiness independent of conditions. Read and be encouraged."　　　　—SHINZEN YOUNG, author of *The Science of Enlightenment*

"Henry Shukman's autobiographical journey from childhood trauma to healing teacher, from the glamorous life of a successful young writer to the quiet of the meditation cushion, from the torment of eczema to the ecstasy of no-self, fascinated me all the way, in part because Shukman can articulate both inner and outer experience with poetic precision and nuance. He manages to capture here how one might have a profound experience just this side of ineffable, and how it might become central to a person's life. There is Zen wisdom here for those who want to learn more about Zen, presented in the most unpretentious way possible, with writing that resonates in the heart and mind long after it is read. You will meet in *One Blade of Grass* many great teachers, and one more who stands among them and shines with them all." —RODGER KAMENETZ, author of *The History of Last Night's Dream* and *The Jew in the Lotus*

"Henry Shukman is a wonderful and brilliant teacher who has affected me deeply. His journey from a troubled kid to a widely respected Zen master is a fascinating story in which everyone can find inspiration. *One Blade of Grass* is a must-read for anyone interested in human spirituality and gaining practical wisdom about how to navigate this thing we call life."

—KIRSTEN POWERS, CNN political analyst and *USA Today* columnist

ALSO BY HENRY SHUKMAN

POETRY

In Doctor No's Garden

Archangel

FICTION

Darien Dogs

Mortimer of the Maghreb

Sandstorm

The Lost City

NONFICTION

Sons of the Moon

Travels with My Trombone

Savage Pilgrims

One Blade of Grass

FINDING THE OLD ROAD

OF THE HEART

A ZEN MEMOIR

Henry Shukman

COUNTERPOINT
Berkeley, California

One Blade of Grass

Library of Congress Cataloging-in-Publication Data
Names: Shukman, Henry, author.
Title: One blade of grass : finding the old road of the heart / Henry
    Shukman.
Description: First paperback edition. | Berkeley : Counterpoint Press, 2019.
Identifiers: LCCN 2019002952 | ISBN 9781640092624
Subjects: LCSH: Shukman, Henry. | Zen Buddhism—Biography.
Classification: LCC BQ986.U555 A3 2019 | DDC 294.3/927092 [B]—dc23
LC record available at https://lccn.loc.gov/2019002952

Cover design by Alex Camlin
Book design by Jordan Koluch

COUNTERPOINT
2560 Ninth Street, Suite 318
Berkeley, CA 94710
www.counterpointpress.com

Printed in the United States of America

10 9 8 7 6 5

For my teachers

꣠

Joan Rieck Roshi,
John Gaynor-roshi,
Ruben Habito Roshi,
and Yamada Ryo'un Roshi,
abbot of Sanbo Zen of Kamakura, Japan

I sought and I found.

CARLO CARRETTO

CONTENTS

Part Three
Calf Born of a Bull

One Blade of Grass

Prologue

I T WAS THE THIRD OR fourth night of the retreat. Rain was
lashing down, pinging against the dark windows and sometimes clattering as if a handful of shingle had been thrown
at the panes.

Rain is a blessing in the desert, and rare, and the meditation room was growing pungent with the thick scent of wet dust,
along with an invigorating cool that had crept in from outside.

I was aware of all that, but mostly I was conscious of having
slipped into a state of calm and clarity at last. That was a welcome relief. All day I'd been having a hard time of it. Long trains
of difficult, distressing thoughts had been grinding through my
mind—about life choices, about having moved back to New
Mexico, abandoning a good life in England, and the many ways
I hadn't been as good a father as I'd have liked, or as attentive a
husband. Finances, work challenges, difficult conversations over
the past weeks or from decades ago, all had been erupting in

my mind just when I most wanted—and felt I needed—inner quiet. There were all kinds of ways I could torment myself when I was helplessly stationary in meditation, and even though I knew most of them by now, knowing them didn't seem to make much difference.

The retreat center was in the hills above the remote town of Gallup, in western New Mexico. Gallup was a small sprawl on the desert, dusty and quiet, except for its trains. It happened to be a major railroad junction, and all day long, any time I had started to feel my mind settle down, inevitably just then a long, sonorous blast on a train whistle would come hooting up the hillside and yank me out of the slowly gathering calm. Once again, pangs of unease and remorse would move through my mind, accompanied by tensions and stresses in my innards—like the storm clouds that must have been moving through the night sky outside.

But now all that had changed. Instead, in the cooling room fragrant with the chalky smell of desert rain, a glowing calm was seeping up through me, like an incoming tide rising through wet sand, making me highly alert, very still, deeply relaxed. As if the whole body were enjoying the simple fact of existing. I could feel my sense of the world opening wider and wider, like the aperture on an old camera expanding. At the same time, I was starting to get an odd sensation, such as can sometimes happen in meditative absorption, where I felt like I was being squeezed from both sides, becoming thinner and taller by the moment, until I was slender as a flower's stalk, so thin and tall I felt I might topple over at any moment.

Then my gaze fixed on the wall in front of me—a wall of adobe, glowing in the light of a lamp. An intense love for the wall welled up, almost as if I were falling in love with it, and it with me. All of a sudden, with what felt like a seismic jolt, the room seemed to blow wide open, the whole scene became an infinitely broad expanse, and it was as if I was sucked into that expanse myself and became part of it, so that the desert hills outside, which reached down to Gallup, in the valley two miles away, and on beyond, were my very own body.

An intense energy was moving all through me and through the world, and I could feel tears streaming down my face—tears of love, of joy, of gratitude. It was true, as the Buddhists said: I was one with the world. I was one with everything. The whole world was my body, my mind. And because of that, I was beloved, I belonged, I was healed in all possible ways. All had been well, secretly well, all along.

The bell rang for the end of the period, and things quietened down and became normal again, except that I was left with a tingling sensation in my limbs and a sense of great spaciousness, as if my mind had been extinguished and replaced by a boundless peace.

Then I had to go and set up the interview room for the teacher, and the evening went on, and the rain was still thrashing down on the little retreat center, drumming on the roof, filling the air with its thick scent of promise. But I knew: this Zen, I could trust it. In some ways it was the best thing. It was real, and it worked. In spite of many occasional doubts, I was on a true path.

❧

I ONCE HEARD THE ENGLISHWOMAN Tenzin Palmo give a talk about the twelve years she spent in a remote Himalayan cave. The isolation had been part of her Buddhist training. An audience member asked how it had felt to get ready to come out again.

"Fine," she said. "Either you're cooked or you're not."

"How do you know if you're cooked?" the questioner wanted to know.

"You just know. You're done."

She paused, then added that she'd heard of people who had done the same twelve-year cave training and not been cooked by the end. But if you were, you were—that was all there was to it.

You can get this impression in the world of meditation: people go in ordinary; then something happens in the middle, inscrutable, ineffable, not castable in language mere mortals can grasp; then they reemerge new, different, "done."

I used to live near Stroud, in Gloucestershire, England. A local café had a print on the wall, a triptych of three images of mountains. The first picture was plain and simple, an iconic triangular mountain, with these words beneath: BEFORE ZEN, A MOUNTAIN IS A MOUNTAIN. The second was confused, with several mountains superimposed at odd angles over one another, above the words DURING ZEN, A MOUNTAIN IS NOT A MOUNTAIN. The final image was the same as the first, simple and plain, and the phrase beneath read, AFTER ZEN, A MOUNTAIN IS A MOUNTAIN.

So whatever the cooking did, however disorienting it might get in the middle, it wasn't supposed to lead to some otherworldly result, at least not in the Zen approach. But in a way, that only made it more confusing. If everything ended up just the same, what was the point? Or perhaps things were the same but you saw them differently afterwards?

This book hopes to demystify the cooking process, to cast it in ordinary language, and to show how it can work in normal life. And to convey why it matters. For even though we may continue to lead ordinary lives, it offers the possibility of a change in the way we experience them that is not at all ordinary. Some claim it is the most radical thing we can do for ourselves and our fellow beings. After all, it can show us that we are not and cannot be alone, no matter how lonely we may sometimes feel. Instead, we are all part of one single existence. If this is right, the implications are mind-boggling.

THE NINTH-CENTURY MASTER GENSHA (HARD g, as in "get") had a sudden experience of this single life when he was thirty years old. He grew up the son of a fisherman in China, and while still a boy he watched his father get swept to his death by a surging river. He became a fisherman himself, but as a young man, troubled by the transience of life, he entered a monastery and took up meditation. After several years, feeling he didn't have what it took to penetrate the mysteries of the practice, he strapped his traveling case to his back, stepped into his sandals, and headed off he knew not where.

On his first day out, while ambling up a hillside, he stubbed his toe on a rock. It was bad. Some records say a lot of blood appeared, others that his toe "exploded." As he clutched his foot in agony, a profound epiphany befell him, and his sense of being a separate person moving through the world vanished. He is said to have cried out, "There is no body. So where does this pain come from?"

Dizzy with relief in spite of his painful toe, he limped back the way he had come.

"Why are you back so soon?" his old master asked. "What about your pilgrimage?"

Gensha replied, "Not a single step was taken."

Apparently the master liked this statement and welcomed him back. Then he asked what had happened, what he had seen.

Gensha's response was, "This whole universe is one bright pearl."*

This little story suggests a few things. One is that sometimes it's true: no pain, no gain. Another is that sometimes we make more progress when we give up. *Reculer pour mieux sauter*, as the French say: to retreat in order to leap better. And sometimes we'll find what we're looking for only when we stop looking. If what we're looking for lies outside of imagination or calculation, we can't know what it is until it hits us.

WE ARE LIVING IN AN extraordinary window. On the one hand, our situation is perilous, with climate change and the nuclear arsenal hanging over our heads. On the other, even as global society becomes more polarized between the wealthy few and the rest, unprecedented numbers are turning to the practice of meditation, which can not only steer us toward kinder, wiser ways of living, but also happens to be more or less as free as the air we breathe. Ancient teachings—of esoteric Tibetan Buddhism, of the early Buddhist canon, of Zen koan training—are readily accessible, often all in a single city.

At the same time, the contemplative traditions are being subjected to the scrutiny, invention, and utilitarianism of West-

---

* I have taken liberties in editing and compressing this story, and I use Japanese forms of Chinese masters' names throughout. Here, Gensha is the Japanese name for Hsuan-sha, or Xuansha, who lived from 835 to 908.

ern science: how can we extract the most useful parts and adapt them to modern needs? The most widely known result has been the mindfulness movement, pioneered by various teachers, notably the Harvard doctor Jon Kabat-Zinn, who began his meditation practice as a Zen student. There is debate about the wisdom of divorcing mindfulness meditation from its roots, but there is little doubt it is taking Western society by storm. While half a century ago perhaps ten thousand Westerners might have tried it, today the number is over thirty million and counting in the United States alone.

Neuroscientific research keeps yielding new evidence for its positive effects on brain function, suggesting that it can indeed lead us out of stress, anxiety, and self-absorption, toward peace, creativity, and compassion, as its adherents have claimed for millennia. Yet along the way, as its popularity grows and it becomes ever more mainstream, sold as a cure-all for many modern ills, it's possible that the kind of training I have been through, young as it is in the West, may be lost. In our quest for efficiency, the old ways of proceeding through a slow, patient training over many years under an experienced guide may go the way of the dinosaurs, replaced entirely by short-term methods, even surgery or new, as yet unknown neurological interventions. Will something be lost? Is meditation merely an instrument to induce desired changes?

For one thing, in its paradoxical way, it tends not to work so well if we are too directly seeking its benefits. For another, the chance to apprentice with a teacher, to entrust ourselves to an authentic guide, is a privilege like no other. And if the modern approaches end up supplanting the ancient, transformative insights into what it means to be human, they will have lost their true power to help our world.

THIS BOOK IS ABOUT HOW I found a path when I didn't even know I was looking for one. For a long time I didn't know where I wanted to be; I just knew I wasn't there.

I tell this story not because it holds any special interest. Far from it; my challenges have been unremarkable. It's a tale of everyday desperation, such as many know, that healed through meditation practice. That's why I hope it may be helpful: to show that the practice can steer and jolt even a common dolt into kinder, better ways of living, without divine intervention though with moments of grace. For those who feel, as I once did, like giving up on life, perhaps this little narrative may incline them to think again.

It's also for people who have lived a long time with indeterminate unease, inwardly taking up residence at a fork in the road, following neither the more nor the less traveled path. Sure, life shakes us down and sweeps us along. It's hard to shirk the currents of our nature and culture, and we find ourselves in lives that more or less make outward sense. But inside we know there is more. We sense a more real investment of our powers still waiting.

"Late and soon, getting and spending, we lay waste our powers," said the poet William Wordsworth. Too right. A more real engagement must be possible. But with what? Of that we may not be so sure—but at least with the bare fact that we exist for a while, in a world full of other beings who also exist. Is there a way to get closer to that before we die? Yet if we don't, isn't our life somehow wasted?

Part One

One Bright Pearl

Speedy's Dog

IT HAS TAKEN A FEW years to get this Zen center rolling again. Founded in 1985 but abandoned by its teacher in 1986, this husky adobe haven on the edge of Santa Fe, New Mexico, has been barely surviving for decades. Rented out to different groups, its identity all but dissolved back into the earth on which it stands, and out of which it is made, Mountain Cloud Zen Center somehow kept going through many lean years, and now it's starting to hum.

This is the eighth retreat in a row to which more than thirty people have come. Thirty is just about our maximum. And these are the dog days of June, days that come early here in the mountains of northern New Mexico, when summer has barely stolen into the land yet the heat is as fierce as it gets: noon till six every day, the thermometer stands in the mid-nineties. Later, in July, the rains will roll in and things will cool down. But not yet. Not even the thick mud walls of our zendo can keep out the heat.

Dressed in the lightest clothes, trickles of sweat inching down our bodies, we slowly bake as the afternoon creaks, twitches, hisses, clacks, or flutes by, according to the sounds of our nonhuman cohabitants on the land.

Early mornings as night is paling, we sit out on a deck. There is basically no dew, but the air is rich and cool. The boards have a sweet resonance as people step about, finding places to settle. Up the hillsides, the piñon trees are still dark.

The timekeeper rings the bell. It sounds matter-of-fact in the outdoors, and the day's first period of silence begins.

At first there's the usual uncertainty—like, what? What are we supposed to do? But quickly the mind settles into the body, and the body settles into the surroundings, as the sense of boundaries dissolves. An ease of belonging in the world, a gratitude for existing, emerges from the flesh.

As the week wears on, we start to appreciate more and more where we are and what we're doing: walking over the dry earth, on little river-falls of pebbles, on paths that wind among the frugal trees; steeping in the quiet. Here we are, perched on dry land amid stands of juniper and piñon, which eke out their lives from the red-baked earth. Beautiful ferrous rocks mark the land. On hot days the shade of the old ponderosa pines is a balm. This is a place of kindness, where human beings don't have to prove themselves or strive to be anything they are not already. We learn a lot here by sitting still. But this collection of mud buildings among the trees is a home for exploration too.

It reminds me of an exploratory impulse that woke in me long ago, in the city and valley where I grew up, in Oxford, England. The warm air here, the dry soil and baking afternoons, when the trees hiss with a thick life whose pleasure only they know—it's something personal to them. Then the light thickening, the clock slowing, the trees resting after their long secret union with the sun, as evening begins to show in the form of a blue hue to the foliage—it all reawakens sensations from my youth, taking me back to summer in my early teens, when there was a long ease in the land, a promise in the very earth. There was the thrill of looking out early mornings and seeing, yes, once again, not a cloud in the summer sky. It's all somehow sweetly familiar, and stirs a memory of a particular evening long ago.

⊰⊱

ONE NIGHT AT THE TAIL end of summer, when I was twelve years old, there was a thudding on the back door of our family home, a dilapidated cottage up the Cherwell Valley. Our mother opened up, and we heard her cry out in surprise and delight. It was a rainy night, and we gathered round to see what was going on.

"Come in, come in," Mum called, and out of the weather stepped a windswept heap of a man wrapped in a damp, hairy overcoat, with two dogs at his heels. I guessed it must be Speedy.

We'd all heard of Speedy, and even caught glimpses of him on the far sides of fields, in his shaggy greatcoat, the same color as his spreading ginger beard. Staff in hand, he'd be pressing along, his two dogs weaving in and out of hedgerows in his wake. But I'd never seen him up close before, face-to-face.

He appeared in the valley each spring, putting up in the ruined mill two miles away downriver, hidden in its lonely stand of giant willows. That place had an atmosphere. On sunny evenings it was enchanting. On dark afternoons it was ominous, with the long willow wands stirring at cross-purposes, hissing like the ocean.

Speedy spent his winters on the south coast of England, where it was warmer. No one knew how it was he'd started coming to our valley, but every spring he would show up. No one minded, not even the farmers, even though he used his dogs, a terrier and a lurcher, for hunting rabbits and moorhen. He was a dab hand at smoking pike, which he hooked from the canal, and he buttered up the village women by bringing them yellowish sides of oily, smoky fish. Mum was thrilled when he brought her some.

This was the mid-1970s, when there were still bona fide tramps stalking the byways of England, old-school "men of the road" such as had been beating the footpaths for at least a century, or maybe much longer. We'd heard of tramps, with a mixture of fear and fascination.

The autumn evening Speedy rapped on our door, rain was lashing down. He stood under the little porch, his hairy coat dripping. He brushed himself down, opened up his front, and pulled out a little puppy.

"Well, you did say," he said to Mum, and wheezed out a laugh.

"Oh, yes," she cried, with a mix of delight and nerves, and ran off to the kitchen to put together a bag of food, beer, and tobacco for him, as well as a banknote from her wallet.

While she was gone, Speedy looked down at us kids. We'd never seen a face like it. First off, hidden between his beard, hat, and hair, it was hard even to see his cheeks. Then when you realized you were looking at them, it was a shock to see skin so brown and ruddy. It looked more like animal hide. Then you landed on the eyes, shimmering, alive. They shocked you when you stole a glance at them, there was so much life and light in them. It was like having a wild animal in the room. Only when I did did I realize he was smiling.

"So then," he asked, "which one of youse's she going to be?"

At first we didn't know what he meant. His voice was a growl somewhere under his coat, and we couldn't make head or tail of his accent—it was more like thunder heard two valleys off than speech.

"Eh, then?" he prompted us.

"Wha-at?" my sister asked hesitantly, and giggled.

"Oose's she gonna be? Yours or yourn?" he asked in a singsong.

"Oh," we said as we both got it.

He was holding out the sweetest little puppy, yellow-brown, with a dark, shining snout, like a baby African hunting dog, and gleaming black eyes that gazed at us eagerly.

"Everyone's," I said. "No one's in particular."

"It's a she, is it?" my sister asked.

"Course it is. Like yer mum said. 'If she 'as pups, bring us a bitch,' she told me."

Even now that we were understanding him, Speedy's voice still sounded strange and muffled, yet the words rang clear in his body. You could understand him better if you listened to his chest.

"Who's gonna yold her first, then?"

My sister and I glanced at each other and laughed nervously.

"Reckon it'll be you," he said, handing the puppy to my sister.

Mum came back in with the bag for Speedy, and he said, "Much obliged, ma'am."

We'd never heard anyone call her *ma'am* before.

"Thank *you*," she said politely, and we sensed that he was somehow important.

He opened up the bag and peered in. "Look at that." Then he stood up stiffly. "Well, just like you said, she's a bitch, and a right sweetie."

And he was off, into the night and the rain, his dogs at his heels.

BY THE TIME SPEEDY WALKED away that night, I realized there was another way of being human. It was unlike anything I'd known. It was as if the room itself had just been shocked, and a stunned peace fizzed among the furniture. An aliveness that was new, and not my own, welled up inside me.

FOR THE FIRST WEEK WE had the puppy, every day at some point the mother would appear at our back door and trot into the house to find her daughter, who would jump up, tail quivering, and greet her. The bitch was a beauty, a terrier like a small fox, but white. All that summer, she had cavorted with our dog, a larger terrier, and both our mother and Speedy had surmised there might be puppies.

Each day, she stood there in the kitchen suckling her pup a moment, then gave her a lick round the ears and scampered back out of the house, toenails clicking on the linoleum. The pup would stand watching her go.

It fascinated us kids. The mother hadn't forgotten her; she knew where to find her. She came by herself. How did she know the way? It was two miles from the old mill. Could she read the land like a map?

Then one day when she came, the puppy didn't get up. The

bitch trotted in and stood still, looking across the floor at her offspring, who sat quiet and glum where she was. The mother walked out and never came back.

NOT LONG AFTER, IT WAS back to the ivory tower for us, to Oxford and the school term.

It was September by then, and back in the city the annual funfair of early autumn had come to town. The night the fair began, I was at my window, looking out over the rooftops, seeing faint stars low in the sky, when I realized I was also seeing the far-off lights of the carnival rides, and I couldn't tell the lights and the stars apart.

I fancied myself a young poet, so when a phrase came to mind, I grabbed paper and pen. After a while a new kind of poem, different from any I'd written before, was on the page, something that knew the scene better than I did, as if produced by an energy that had come in from outside, which left me trembling with excitement. I felt closer to the world than I ever had. The poem had been written not by my normal mind but by that other part Speedy had woken up.

THAT WINTER WE READ *As I Walked Out One Midsummer Morning*, Laurie Lee's luminous account of wandering around Spain with a fiddle, a blanket, and a handful of pesetas earned from busking. We read *The Dharma Bums*, by Jack Kerouac, and learned about the Beats, who had lived working odd jobs and writing poems, inscribing their trajectories across America. We read the Imagist poets of the 1910s, who had admired the Chinese poets of the eighth century, who wandered the mountains and rivers of the "Middle Kingdom," losing themselves in the precipitate landscapes, writing poems about friends they missed, about their love of wine, and about the natural scenery around them. We met in coffee shops and smoked roll-ups, comparing poems we had come across, sharing scraps we had written. Poetry was our way to get closer to life.

An idea bloomed: the land itself could be your home. We were earthborn creatures, autochthonous, as Plutarch called it. Why shouldn't one be at home anywhere? Just like Speedy and his dogs?

THE NEXT YEAR HAPPENED TO be 1976, a legendary year in England. Barry Sheene and James Hunt became world champions in motorcycle and Formula One racing, Lynyrd Skynyrd toured the UK, but more than anything, from June to September, England baked. It was a summer that would go down in history, when hay trucks spontaneously burst into flame and traffic backed up for hours on the roads, when reservoirs ran dry and, around our valley, the fields hardened into rustling savannas, the cattle-trod earth either side of gates becoming African watering holes, their moisture long since gone. The woods turned dark and serious under the dome of natural sky, as if for the first time tasting a maturer life long denied them.

It was also the summer we got to know Speedy for real. He befriended us, and taught us some of his tricks. How to make a rabbit snare out of garden twine and set it on secret rabbit paths. How to catch and smoke fish. He told us of his winters on the south coast, his life on the open road. Roped in his hairy overcoat, stringed into his boots, he liked to sit still and watch things, he said. You could learn a lot if only you just sat yerself still. Everybody else, the whole world, is rushing about all day long, they don't have time to learn nothing, if they just stopped still a moment they'd be amazed what they'd learn.

He also talked of old roads that crossed the length and breadth of the land. These days people didn't know how to find them, but they were plain as a pikestaff if you knew what you were looking for, he said. "Most people can't see the ghost roads"—another name he had for them. "They only show they-selves once you been walking a lot."

We didn't know what to make of that. But the open road was real. Hedgerows, bushes, woodland, ruined sheds, old rail-way signal boxes: Speedy loved a signal box, he told us, being shaken to sleep at night by coal trains coming down from the Black Country. There were lots of places a man could rest if he just had a sleeping bag and a sheet of plastic. And with a hook and line he could pull perch and tench from the brown waters. Speedy didn't have a home, or a kitchen, or a bedroom. He basi-cally just had himself, that was all. That and the land. He was at home anywhere. He *was* his home.

We imitated him, slinging on backpacks stuffed with sleep-ing bags, sausages, tea, and bread and wandering the valleys and hills, sleeping rough under the stars night after night, drinking sweet tea made with stream water over open fires. There was a small, changing group of friends who would join us. We felt we were starting to live, and thought our dreams of becoming wan-derers, vagabond world lovers, were coming true. You could drift like the old poets of the Chinese mountains, losing your old life, finding every day a new life in the contours of the land, chasing the scent of a fulfillment always just out of reach.

We lit cigarettes from the embers of our fires, drank bottles of local ale, and began to discover a force inside us that wanted to

live. Something happened that summer. In the swells and cam-
bers of fields that we got to know as well as our own bodies,
in the rambling farther and farther from home, in the village
shops where we stocked up on supplies, in the gullies and copses,
clambering over wooden fences bleached by the sun, splashing
through streams, we found ourselves, as people with our own
relationship to the land and its creatures.

The young dog would always come with us when we slept
out. She couldn't resist the pull of the old fields she'd known as
a puppy. She would disappear into reeds by the riverbanks. We'd
hear her thrash through them, then burst out in excitement. She
came alive on the land. This was the life she had been made for:
tramping the fields, rivers, and woods of her native territory. She
didn't have to think why. She was made for it, and it for her. At
the end of a day she would sit at the foot of my sleeping bag, a
pale triangle, looking out across the dark land into the night, and
not curl up until everyone else was asleep.

Skin Deep

ALL THE ABOVE—THAT'S ONE STORY, one version. But there is another. Often I felt my body and skin weren't made for this world at all.

I WAS BORN INTO BURNING skin, a nettle shirt.

At school we learned about the mythological beast Typhon, who lived under the volcano Etna. That was me. I lived in a volcano. Or else a little Typhon lived inside me, belching sulfurous steam that worked its way out through my skin.

They called it eczema, which meant "boiling out." Bubbles appeared under the dermis and epidermis and broke open into the air, and the itching, weeping, bleeding, and so on followed.

Actually, I wasn't born into it; I was born just fine. The problem started when I was six months old. My father, a historian in Russian studies at Oxford University, was offered a fellowship in Helsinki and took his family with him.

From Helsinki, Russia was less than a day away by boat, across the Gulf of Finland. It was the Cold War, and when a message came through from Cambridge Circus that my father was to travel to Leningrad on urgent business, he didn't hesitate. Although he was a quiet Oxford man, like many Russianists at that time he also did occasional work for "the Circus"—namely, MI6. He was a part-time spy.

Mum and Dad went together. They disappeared across the water into the Soviet wastes, leaving the kids in the care of a Finnish au pair. Apparently my four-year-old brother did fine while they were gone, but I didn't. I don't know what happened, but when they came back some days later, they found the baby— me—red and raw all over, covered from head to toe in eczema.

"He looks like he's been flayed," my father reportedly said, frowning over the hot little bundle in his arms.

What had happened? Was it the au pair girl? What had she done? My mother cursed herself for having weaned the child so abruptly, simply leaving him—and in a foreign country, too— with only a teenage girl to look after him. The au pair thought it was an allergy to the Finnish pines. My father scratched his head and mused that once they returned to Oxford, all would be well, so they'd better not dwell on it. But Finland was just the start.

BACK HOME, MY SKIN RAGED and seethed. Over the years the doctors often sent me to the Radcliffe Infirmary, where I'd lie on crisp sheets through days of lonely relief, feeling numb and safe. When I was home, the district nurse came daily to lay me on a towel and bathe me in antiseptic solution, which smelled like toffee, then wrap me in coal-tar bandages of gray, wet clay, which smelled like chalk.

While I specialized in eczema, my little sister, when she grew into childhood, specialized in asthma. She had inhalers and pills and sometimes went to hospital, too. Apparently they traveled together: eczema, allergies, asthma. Some mothers might fuss over such kids, drag them to specialists and quacks. Others, like middle-class postwar British mothers, were more apt to say, "Stop making a fuss." Our mother wasn't sure which way to go. Sometimes she believed in them, sometimes she didn't. Perhaps we were exaggerating and only wanted attention. But on the other hand, it was terrible to see us suffer like that. Meanwhile my sister gulped on her inhalers, and I scratched my way through childhood.

I WAS ALSO BORN INTO privilege. We lived in ancient Oxford, in its broad depression among low hills, where clouds congregated and drizzle was common. The rain made the streets shine and the faces of the old colleges dark. When the sun came out, the stone facades, hewn from local hills, glowed the color of peach.

Both our parents taught at the university. Our parents' friends taught at the university. So did our friends' parents. My brother and I went to a local private school that thought itself progressive because the boys wore corduroy bomber jackets rather than blazers. They drilled us in French, Latin, and Greek from the age of eight.

We were privileged, but it was complicated. Mum's family had been lawyers for generations on one side, Northumbrian coastguardsmen on the other. A century before, one of the coastguardsmen ran away to sea as a cabin boy, and returned home a shipowner. He built up a merchant fleet, most of which he lost in the course of the two world wars. But the ghosts of former glories hung over the wider family.

Dad's family, on the other hand, had been tailors down to the last man and woman. Penniless refugees, they'd escaped the pogroms of Eastern Europe and arrived on the Tilbury docks with a couple of cardboard suitcases between them, believing they'd reached America. So they got off the boat and stayed.

We didn't exactly belong in the middle classes, but nor did we belong in the working classes. Nor among the Jews, since our mum wasn't Jewish.

Rather than tailoring like everyone else, Dad went into electrical engineering, but when he was drafted into his national service, at the age of eighteen, he was sent to the "Joint Services School for Linguists," a Russian crammer dreamed up in 1950, when Britain found itself entering the Cold War short of Russian speakers. Dubbed the Spy School, it offered a route out of the working classes for many bright young men, Dennis Potter and Alan Bennett among them—and our dad, raised in a London tenement, later an Oxford professor. Part of the training involved a term in the Russian Department at Cambridge University, where he met our mother.

We were hothouse kids. Our academic parents didn't have great wealth, but they had educational resources, so that was what they heaped on us. We were brought up to excel, in humanities, sciences, literature, languages, music—something, anything, so long as we excelled.

DAD LOOKED LIKE INSPECTOR MORSE, the TV detective. Flowing seventies hair, darker than Morse's until it turned silver. Darker-skinned too. A heavy-cheeked, Jewish face, with a decisive blade of a nose. He would scowl like Morse at foolish ideas. "A Kashmiri spice merchant," he once appraised, staring at a picture someone had taken of him: a dark-skinned man with heavy sideburns and eyes that bore into the viewer, hard as hailstones. "No," he corrected himself. "A Lebanese jewel trader."

We laughed, because of course he was neither. He was our dad.

☙

"ATOPIC ECZEMA HAS A MULTIFACTORIAL etiology," says the *British Medical Journal.* Meaning many things may cause it.

The underlying condition, atopy, from the Greek meaning "placelessness," is a maternally transmitted genetic disorder that generates allergic reactions. A cat's whisker, a mite's detritus, a speck of pollen: these harmless guests, drifting into nostril, brushing against ankle, are taken as lethal intruders, and the body goes into overdrive to be rid of them. But though eczema is linked genetically to allergies, it needs no allergen to kickstart it. And it sticks around chronically, unlike allergic reactions.

The life cycle starts with vesicles: mini-blisters that emerge in slow motion. They were the *zema* part, the boiling. Greek was what my studies gravitated to later: perhaps because of my brand, which was Greek: *ek-zema.* The language claimed me early and dragged me down into Typhon's cave, where he articled me, apprentice to his noxious arts.

"Atopic" or "placeless" was an odd designation, given that the sores would stick to their places tenaciously. On me, some would pass the three-decade mark in the fullness of time, never moving, just rolling through the seasons of their life cycle: first the mini-blisters like blackberry nodules, then the moist gashes of the middle cycle, then the dried-out gulches of the parched later phases, as well as the knots and gnarls of the final state. Then starting over again, like fruit trees in the tropics that bloom, fruit, and shed their leaves all at the same time.

There were pavements from my childhood gashed by the force of rising tree roots that transfixed my gaze when we walked past them, so exactly did they resemble the slow eruptions in my skin.

But all these stages met in one furnace called *itch*. As if it weren't enough of a mess, often there was no choice but to tear the whole geothermal process to shreds, destroying all delineation of the stages of the "natural history" in one frenzied rapture—scraping over trouser seam, tearing across table edge, or down and dirty fingernail ripping—anything to quench the ancient fire of the forges within with a draft of blood and lymph and tears.

Yet "placeless" was right, too. It was a Jewish condition, they said. We were placeless people. From England and Scotland, yes, but Russia too. Except not Russia, because our people hadn't been allowed in Russia proper, only its annexes: Ukraine, Poland, Belorussia. We were the placeless tribe.

WESTERN MEDICINE HAD TWO OPTIONS: antibiotic ointments, which had no effect beyond annoying the eczema, and steroid creams, which were the holy grail because they worked, at least the strong ones. But the doctors were wary of them. They "burned" the skin, thinned it, caused cancer.

Eczema doesn't mark only the skin, but the psyche as well. The shame runs deep, clever at reinforcing itself. A stranger's glance across the street, a brush-off by a nursery teacher—shame looks for shame. There's despair too, because in spite of the doctors' predictions, it never ends. Year after year you keep passing the landmarks by which time the doctors said it should have left: learning to ride a bike, going to school, making friends, playing games.

The doctors say don't scratch. But they don't understand. Whether you scratch or not is immaterial. Not scratching doesn't make it go away. It just evolves differently, a spreading subcutaneous intrusion, whereas if you scratch, at least the sores generally stay put.

In 2007 the Center for the Study of Itch at Washington University, in St. Louis, discovered a receptor in the spinal cord that was specific to itch, thus establishing that itch and pain travel by different neural pathways. The big payoff of itching is that when you scratch, the neurological reward centers offer the brain a bath of endorphins. But with eczema, to scratch to the point of overwhelming an itch means tearing the skin open, so the pain receptors fire, too, canceling out the rush of endorphins.

THAT WAS ONE PROBLEM: THE interface between the world and me, my vivid skin. There were others. Like Dad. And the divorce.

The "family meeting" (our first and last) happened in the little-used sitting room. One morning Dad summoned us all, and we slouched disconsolately into the room and sat nervously on the stiff upholstery, wondering what was going to happen.

Mum had a ball of tissue clenched in one hand. Dad said something I didn't understand and started to laugh. My sister looked at him and burst out crying. Through his laughter Dad said, "You didn't know Daddy could cry, did you."

So he wasn't laughing.

My older brother wailed, "Oh, no, you're not getting divorced?"

So he knew what it was, and it wasn't good.

Soon all four of them were sobbing, while I perched on the edge of the sofa, transfixed by an itch on the back of my knee, and now on the webbing between the index and middle finger of one hand, then the other—except in my case it wasn't webbing, it was scaly hide.

Eczema has a way of trumping all other concerns. While an itch is going on it's hard to turn the mind to anything else at all. It has no space for anything that might not help its constant endeavor—to escape the present itch.

Then Dad was down the hall with his navy suitcase, and down the slapping stone steps to the street, and into the little Fiat, with its fragrant blue smoke, and me clinging to the back bumper shouting, "I'm pushing you, Dad!" still not understanding what was happening, and the world all glassy and watery and uncertain in its shapes, and Dad calling from his open window, "Let go, dear, let go," a choke in his voice, and driving off with the aroma of his little tail of smoke hanging in the air.

THEY USED TO SAY THEY had got on each other's nerves. But we all got on one another's nerves.

As a child our mother hadn't known a stable home, her childhood having been decimated by the Second World War. Her mother had been one of a very few women who flew for the war effort, the first woman to fly a Spitfire. She worked as a ferry pilot in the Air Transport Auxiliary, delivering battle-scarred planes from airfields along the south coast to factories farther north, where they could be refitted. She died in a plane crash in 1944. But even before the war, she had been largely absent, making pioneering transcontinental flights in her De Havilland Gipsy Moth biplane.

Perhaps Mum imagined life would be simpler without a husband, not bargaining on the weary slog of raising three children alone. Yes, we went to Dad's for one night every two weeks, but that wasn't enough relief. The remorseless round: breakfast, dinner, laundry, tucking into bed, shopping, overseeing homework, feeding the pets, round and round, day after day.

Mum didn't want to be single, but she hadn't wanted to stay married either. Marriage was a torment. She never could relax. She came from a lineage of divorces, and perhaps divorce was in her genes. The best relief was boozy dinners with university friends where the wine flowed and the talk grew outrageous. We kids loved those evenings. We'd sneak out of bed and listen through the banisters to the hubbub down at the bottom of the house, and feel blessed, sprung into a fairy tale where the adults were happy. But those nights were too rare.

After the divorce, Mum threw herself into work and study with a vengeance. She hired the cleaner more often so that he, a sweet Scottish Lowlander, could help with the children while she plunged into writing a book on Soviet literary theory. She taught us kids how to make beans on toast so we could feed ourselves, and packed us off to school as soon as possible after breakfast so she could settle down to work in her study.

DAD WASN'T EXACTLY REMOTE AFTER the divorce. He lived only a mile away, and we saw him every two weeks. But that one mile of the Banbury Road in Oxford separated us for the rest of our lives.

At first the arrangement was fine. In his new flat we got to play on the rolling office chair and sleep on bunkbeds while he cooked chicken with soy sauce and Chinese cabbage, and after supper we'd curl up on his modern corduroy sofa and suck mint imperials while he read to us: American books mostly, like *The Adventures of Huckleberry Finn* and *Catcher in the Rye*, his voice radiating through us, warming us with happiness. At bedtime he would strip me down on my bunk and apply the creams and ointments that were part of my daily routine. As his hands moved over me in their calm, measured way, I'd feel a hope that someday the eczema might really end.

It was sad when we had to leave on Sunday afternoon, but at least we knew the place would be waiting for us just as we had left it.

It didn't last. One night a year or two after the divorce, as Dad was driving us, so we thought, to his flat, he made another announcement.

It was October, my sister and I in his new car. Our brother was already away at boarding school. We clamored, as usual, for the sunroof; it was the first car we'd had with a sunroof. The autumn evening drizzled, but Dad groaned and agreed, and we watched in delight as the large, pale sycamore leaves moved across the open roof above our heads.

Out of the blue he said, "You'll never guess who's moving here."

Before we could ponder any guesses he said, "Your auntie."

The mood in the car changed.

My sister said, "*Who-o?*" in a long English intonation. "Our *aunt*ie?"

"That's right," Dad declared. "Your auntie."

Our auntie wasn't really our auntie; she was our mother's cousin. I loved her. She lived in Canada, so we rarely saw her, but she was kind and treated us like adults. She was an artist, and that made her different. She was frank and free, and we kids could feel it. Yet at the news Dad had just divulged, neither my sister nor I felt good. Something strange was in the air.

It turned out she wasn't moving; she already *had* moved. She was here, in Oxford, with her children. But no one had mentioned it. Even at the ages of six and nine my sister and I knew that was odd.

Not only that, but we were on our way to her house now. Not to Dad's beloved flat, with its soft carpet and sweet scent of soy sauce and rolling chair, but to a house we didn't know, to a family we did know but only as our cousins in Canada.

It ought to have been good news, yet some dread hung in the car. We tried to get him to turn round and take us to his flat, but he wouldn't. Our nights alone with him were over.

MUM HADN'T SEEN THIS COMING: her first cousin returning to England with her children and her belongings in tow—and not just to England but to Oxford, to move in with our dad.

It was unthinkable. Her cousin. Her ex-husband.

She tried not to think about it, and threw herself harder than ever into work and study, avoiding contact with the people who had once meant so much to her.

She never spoke of it, but we knew what she was going

through. I could tell. Some mornings I'd find her in the kitchen, frozen in the act of opening the fridge or of putting a pan on the stove. She'd be hunched in her dressing gown, face tipped into her palm, cheek wrinkled like an old apple. I would try to comfort her. But what could my little arm do? I'd try anyway, put the arm round her and feel her shudder.

It was embarrassing—to me and to her. She didn't want me to see her like this, and I didn't want to be comforting her. Yet in some secret way, I *did* want to. Ravaged by eczema, I felt like a disgrace to my father, in spite of his occasional ministrations to my skin. It was easier to be with my mother. Perhaps in a way I had wanted him gone. And he had gone. Perhaps secretly I had contrived it, and it was all my fault. And now I had the consequences on my hands.

MEANWHILE OUR FATHER'S REMARRIAGE WAS a union of true love. A photo taken soon after the nuptials smolders like Burton and Taylor, the communion of body and soul palpable in the old image.

It was hard not to imagine Dad washing his hands of us after the wedding, saying, "Lovey, don't worry about a thing—their mum will take care of the kids. They'll be no trouble at all."

At night back home in Mum's house, after administering the various creams and ointments myself, I'd lie awake fantasizing about our parents. Mum was trapped in a ditch, and a wicked witch whisked Dad away across the night sky, and I had to rescue them both, one after the other, and bring them home.

I woke one night at Dad's from a nightmare. A witch had been standing at the foot of my bed, sticking out her tongue and humming at me. In the dream I realized who she was: a child killer who had been stalking the city, killing children. And this was how she did it—by what she was doing with her tongue. She was in the middle of murdering me. One glimpse was enough, Gorgon-style.

I woke, screaming and wailing, to see the curtain stir as if someone had just slipped out.

Perhaps some part of me was killed then, something I would have to reclaim many years later.

MY HEART SEETHED. I HATED the remarriage. I sulked savagely. One evening Dad sat me down in his office at the top of his house and told me I just had to accept it—he loved our stepmother and that was the end of it, and he didn't want to hear anything more about it.

Thereafter, he didn't. Instead the two of them had to endure my stony silence. I dug my heels in and refused to speak to my stepmother at all.

BUT THERE WAS SCHOOL TOO: I threw myself into academics, putting the time in, slowly accomplishing the grades expected.

"You see?" said the skin doctor. "He's top of the form. They always make up for it in other ways."

Who these "they" were—these other eczematics—I didn't know. There were none at our school.

So academic performance was the payoff. Like the woman in one of Chaucer's tales whose otherworldly beauty is paid for by a pair of sores hidden on her thighs, I had to pay for my academic performance with my skin.

In class I'd swaddle my hands in a handkerchief, or sit on them to suppress the conflagrations, imprinting them with ribs of corduroy. The school made no concessions on health grounds. Mud-heavy rugby balls, games shorts, changing rooms, showers, holding pencil or hockey stick or cricket bat, riding a bike home, washing up, making my bed—all were fraught with fear. Water was pain. *L'eczème craint l'eau*, I heard an Algerian doctor say many years later: eczema fears water. It was true. But it also feared life. Life was a litany of things you couldn't do without skin. Skin was there, whatever you did. A hug could light up a bodywide incandescence.

The doctors pretended they had all angles covered. Different creams for different purposes. Every morning, Aureomycin, a yellow antibiotic ointment. Then coal-tar paste from a big brown jar, then a "barrier cream" slapped on knees and calves, leaving them daubed with white clay. It was an ordeal, especially in school shorts, the skin simultaneously hot and exposed. At night, Tri-Adcortyl, a green ointment; or Graneodin, cold and gray. Then Oilatum, E45, Nivea, any of which made the skin livid.

I grew up in silent resentment, sheathed in a landscape of volcanic fissures. And in my heart a stone of shame, a stubborn despair at the loss of our family. The magma slid into me and hardened.

✿

THAT WAS THE DEPTH OF life. So I lived out on the surface, hobbling up there as best I could. The surface served me fine. Academic kudos, poetry, landscape wanderings with a few friends. We aped our older siblings, sitting cross-legged round a scratchy gramophone stacked with Van Morrison and Creedence, a joss stick burning in a vase. I tacked an Indian shawl to my bedroom wall and stole two colored lightbulbs from the funfair: blue or orange, depending on mood.

Fuck the parents, fuck the skin, gimme a roll-up of Old Holborn and a glass of ale.

I GREW TO LOVE OUR city.

O Oxford,

wrote my fourteen-year-old hand,

let me take your dark syrupy air
and pour it through my fingers
from hand to hand
and soak up the immense
impassiveness
of your old stone.

I could have used some impassiveness myself. Not to feel, not to itch.

(And I didn't like commas.)

Sometimes I achieved a blessed state where I did feel nothing. At night on the slab of pruritus, after a bout of itching had kept me awake long into the night, I'd enter a strange condition of numbness, where I'd float with my limbs feeling huge, like inflated barrage balloons or blimps, and where the world was held at bay, far out at the fringes of sensation. It was blissful. It felt as if I had become a cloud myself.

My mother had a book on her shelves called *The Cloud of*

Unknowing. Was this what that title referred to? I didn't know but guessed it just might be.

THEN GUSTAVO CAME TO TOWN.

Gustavo was a Colombian priest. One summer he came through Oxford on his way back to his home country after a year at a radical Marxist seminary in Belgium.

I had seen priests before, with their stale breath and rancid robes, intoning from pulpits into the empty gloom of churches. Gustavo was different. He had long black hair and a straggly beard. He wore flared jeans and went barefoot. He looked like Cat Stevens. Or Jesus.

He was a Liberation theologian, and the summer he passed through, he enchanted a group of us kids. We sat on sunny lawns under elms in back gardens and listened to him. He wanted to be with the children, he said.

He told us stories of enlightened masters in the Himalayas who meditated and could make themselves die then come back to life, of indigenous shamans in his homeland who could talk with jaguar and deer, of street children who ran taxi services, bakeries, coffee stands. Kids could do many things adults did, he told us.

He was going back to Colombia to help the poor. The world was ruled by greedy men who stole from the poor, and as a priest it was his mission to help them.

He offered to read our palms. I held back. Basically no one touched my hands. No one wanted to, and I didn't want anyone to if I could help it. But eventually he noticed that everyone else had gone except me, and he turned his lambent eyes on me. I couldn't say no.

He held my hands gently, turning them over. He smiled at

them. Then at me. He said my life would be full, like a medieval painting, with all kinds of things crammed into it—a ship sailing by, farmers plowing, children playing, a couple getting married, a blacksmith at work.

He asked us if we had ever been in love. We were only kids, but we were rapt, and looked inside and gave our answers.

Had we ever hated? he wanted to know. He said how hate could be strong—like love in some ways. It made you think about the person all the time.

My face flushed, sitting on the lawn in the shade of the leafy trees. But his warm eyes and bearded face, and the bare soles of his feet, gave off such an air of easy acceptance that it was like sitting with some holy man, and my need to hide melted. I told him that, yes, I had hated.

Instead of telling me off, he nodded. "Why don't you say a little about it?"

When I finished explaining our parental situation he paused, looking deep into my eyes, and said, "Of course you didn't want to lose your father. I bet you hoped your parents would get back together."

He was right, and it was good to hear someone say it.

"It's only natural," he said. "Do you think about them a lot?"

"I suppose so," I said.

He nodded, and a weight lifted off me. Perhaps I was not bad, and my wishes, impossible to give up, were not wrong.

He smiled. "It's not their fault, you know. Your stepmother has only been loving your father. Maybe one day it will be possible to forgive them. Let them have their life, and you can have yours."

My mind reeled. I had revealed my deepest secret, my

still-festering rage and misery at what had been done to our original household, and instead of feeling ashamed, I felt understood and forgiven.

"Of course you want your mother and father to reunite," he said again. "Anyone who stands in the way—how could they not seem an enemy?"

There was something about his eyes: dark, more or less black. Yet they shone, and had a softness that seemed infinite. They gave and gave. He'd brush long strands of hair aside, and a half smile would dimple his cheeks, and he'd turn those eyes on you and you'd feel a body blow of warmth.

The conversation moved on, but his comment kept coming back: *You can let them have their life.* Eventually it all became clear; the penny dropped. I could forgive my dad and stepmum. They loved each other. It was actually nice. And it was their life, not mine. Why not release them?

The world expanded. I sensed new possibilities, unknown horizons. There was more to life than I knew.

There was more than Gustavo knew, too. Two years after he got home, one morning in the marketplace of a small mountain town where he had been helping the poor, the authorities shot him dead.

MY LIFE WENT ON. MY friends and I spent our teen years in the rain and, once we looked old enough, in the pubs. Beer was our sunshine—yeast, hop, and barley grown in the rain that gave them life—the roll-up and ale jar our sacraments. I just had to keep my cuffs pulled low, and sit on my hands when they itched. I took to wearing a lot of Band-Aids on my fingers, and sweaters with long, dangling sleeves, so I could pick up a glass without revealing too much.

In cloistered Oxford, in our ivory tower, poetry was still our renegade activity. We got into T. S. Eliot and Ezra Pound, then Ted Hughes and Elizabeth Bishop, and clung to poetry as the pursuit of something unnameable that could make even the rain beautiful.

Dripping willows, raindrops wrinkling the river, old stone walls looking drab and dull in the fog, buses' headlights glinting on puddles: that was Oxford and what we wrote about, and that was the daily bike ride to and from school. I wore gloves. There were rare weeks in May when a heat wave struck and the pastures along the river baked hard so you could ride a bike without skidding in mud, when the towpaths were smooth as cement under your tires, when the benches outside pubs were bone-dry, and the girls wore dresses so slight you could sense the camber of every muscle under them, when the grass was green as lettuce and the oaks stood alone in meadows, lost in their smoke-blue foliage like medieval monks too drunk to take a step.

BUT GUSTAVO WAS RIGHT: I did still have my life, and my horizons were soon to expand beyond anything I could imagine, and something outside all calculation would show itself.

The Gap

There is nothing of me that is alone and absolute except my mind, and we shall find that the
mind has no existence by itself, it is only the
glitter of the sun on the surface of the waters.

D. H. LAWRENCE

I T'S TOO BAD IT HAD to happen on a tropical beach. It
may give the impression it required a special location. But
it could have been anywhere: on the London Underground,
driving down a motorway, making supper in the kitchen. It was
only a minute, or a second—it's hard to say. But at the end of my
teens, five thousand miles from home, out of the blue I was visited by something that turned my world upside down.

When I was eighteen I went away on a gap year. I remember

the afternoon my friend Rory and I, breathless with terror, stood our backpacks upright on his bedroom floor and packed them with everything we thought we needed. We laid it all out on his carpet: kerosene stove, army surplus sleeping bags, tent, pen-knife, canteens, two changes of clothes. The next day we flew off into an unknown land across the ocean, to the continent where Gustavo had lived.

Thanks to Gustavo's old friend at my father's college who arranged it all, we went to work on an estancia far into the northern hills of Argentina. We were put to work weeding bean fields, feeding cattle, clearing saplings. We helped rebuild miles of remote fencing with a couple of farmhands, getting up in the dark, spending all day out under the sun, and returning to the bunkhouse as evening drew in. Then came the day when we headed down the farm track with our packs on our backs, a fat wad of pesos folded in our pockets, to hitch our way north, riding in the backs of trucks across the empty mountains and plateaus of the Bolivian Altiplano, an impossibly remote and magical land. We crossed salt lakes, climbed volcanoes, befriended village *corregidores*, ate alpaca and unleavened bread, staggered on foot to stone-age villages and unvisited ruins, put up in simple adobe houses under straw roofs.

I kept a journal I hoped might one day become a book. Rory was an aspiring photographer, and we planned to use his pictures in the book. (In time he did become an acclaimed photographer.) Meanwhile the simple food, the fitness, the hard work, the trekking, the mental work of recording it all changed me. It was all so different in South America. To be among people who had grown up in close contact with the mountains, streams, llamas, potato fields, and earthen homes where they lived—it seemed to make them more at peace with themselves. The infants were constantly on someone's back, whether an older sibling, aunt, or mother—a bundle in a blanket, eyes gleaming at you from over a shoulder. What would it do to a child to live unseparated from a human body the first year or two of its life? What kind of security in its own being would a child imbibe, growing like a tree in the mulch cultivated by generations of its own kind? Was that the difference? These people had less irritability and anxiety. They were calm. They had a depth you could feel. They were friendly and hospitable. Occasionally we'd meet someone unfriendly, but even then you'd sense they had deep roots in their own humanness.

It was all new to me. Where I came from, most people just didn't seem to have that kind of innate self-possession.

Along the way, from time to time I'd hole up in a hostel to work on the book. Often I'd fast during these writing sprints. I'd heard years before from my older brother about a hike he had done during his own gap year, when they trekked with only chocolate and milk powder for food. Apparently you could live off the two. I tried it once, surviving for a whole week on nothing but cigarettes and pints of chocolate milk. It was a weird kind of arcadia, the ink flowing from the nib of the pen like smoke from the cigarette tip, as Walter Benjamin fantasized. At the end of these sprints I'd stagger out to drink a beer and eat a plate of stew.

My fantasy of being a writer and wanderer, someone who explored the world and wrote hymns to it: it seemed to be coming true. And to top it all, my skin cleared up. I'd brought a tube of steroid cream with me, finagled from the doctor before we left, and had distantly worried about what I'd do when it ran out. But I hadn't needed it. The ancient scabs vanished, the gashes closed, the roughnesses smoothed over. I became well. I was healed. It was a miracle: half a year of hale heart, healthy body, a book forming under my hands, and completely clear skin.

TOWARD THE END OF THE trip I was staying in a fishing village on the coast that had a few cheap cabanas for gringos. Rory had already flown home, so I was alone. One afternoon, I walked a few miles up the lonely shore to a small, remote beach, arriving at the hour when the sun was growing big and low. A glow was beginning to fill the air, and out on the sea a path of white-hot light, too bright to look at, led out to the horizon.

There was no one else around. As I stood gazing at the light on the water from the lowering sun, which broadened as it stretched farther away, I felt uncommonly good. I had been far from my hometown, enfolded in its green English hills, for long enough that it had become a memory. That alone felt like an accomplishment. And in a few days I was flying home, and that, too, was exciting. And I had been writing hard lately and believed I had now finished the book. (I didn't yet know the first draft is just the beginning.) And I was all alone on that beach.

The author of *The Cloud of Unknowing* says the "work of God" is the "work of an atom," which for fourteenth-century Christians meant their smallest unit of time, one sixty-fourth of a second. This was like that: one blink, one fall of an eyelash, and everything was new.

I've tried to describe what was about to happen many times. When I broached the subject with friends, they'd ask what I had been on, to which the answer was an embarrassing nothing. Stone-cold sober. Apart from the odd beer now and then, I always was those days. Had I not been, it probably wouldn't have become a defining moment in a life.

Here is my earliest attempt at writing it down. A youthful coyness made it easier to frame in third person, as if it had happened to someone else.

It was late afternoon, the hour when the sun lowered a dazzling path onto the sea. As he gazed at it he started to feel unaccountably happy.

He had the little beach all to himself. It felt like he'd put down a burden he didn't know he had been carrying. Something in him rose by itself as your arms do when you set down a heavy weight. All his life he had been trammeling his mind, he realized, keeping it in channels so it could communicate with others. Now he didn't have to. He was free, totally free, in a way that felt so good he wanted it always.

A large old fishing boat was anchored off shore. As he stared into the blinding light on the sea the boat vanished, swallowed by the brilliance. Then it reappeared for an instant, a black shape, then disappeared, a ghost-hull flickering on and off like a stain on the retina. It seemed so beautiful he could hardly comprehend it. And suddenly all the past months of travel seemed like nothing more than a dream-like series of images that had passed before his eyes.

A young man, a beach, a boat on the water: there was nothing to tell him what year it was. He could have been any young man in any century, gazing over any water.

And the water was fascinating, blindingly white yet completely dark. Scales of brilliance slid over darkness, so it alternated between thick matt black and blinding light. But water was transparent, so was air, yet there the surface was, the sea's skin, thick as elephant hide. What was he actually seeing?

As he pondered this question, suddenly the sight was no longer in front of him. It was inside him. Or he was inside it, as if he'd stepped into the scene and become part of it. He could no longer tell inside from outside. At the same instant the whole world, around, above, below—the sand, the sea, the light on the water—turned into a single field of sparks. A fire kindled in his chest, his fingers tingled, in fact everything tingled. The fire was not just in his chest but everywhere. Everything was made of drifting sparks. The whole universe turned to fire. He was made of one and the same fabric as the whole universe. It wasn't enough to say he belonged in it. It was him. He was it. The beginning and end of time were right here, so close his nose seemed to press against them.

Suddenly he knew why he had been born: it was to find this. This reality. His life was resolved, the purpose of his birth fulfilled, and now he could die happy. He could die that very night and all would be well.

Two arms of black lava enclosed the little beach. They lay like lazy iguanas with their noses to the water, and they too were implicit in this truth. That it was true he knew beyond doubt. It was more true than anything else. This was the way things always had been and always would be.

It was like an explosion of beauty, bliss, joy. But it was much more. I had seen into some kind of invisible truth hidden in the heart of all existence. As I walked back down the shore afterwards, I felt as though I weighed nothing. I drifted, I floated—the world floated, too. Palm trees, cactuses, the lapping waves of the heavy, slow Pacific, the muscular surface of the sea, the light in the western sky, which was turning luminous orange, and the moon hanging in it like a chip of chalk—it was as if we were all in one and the same movie, or dream, which no one could ever intrude on.

Back in my cabana, I lay on my bunk in the gloom with the wooden ceiling just overhead while a flame burned in my chest like the flame of my kerosene camping stove, which was fierce but ghostly. It was a fire of love, and it kept pouring out of me. I'd never known anything like it. Yet somehow it was familiar, as if it had been with me all my life, just unnoticed.

The walls of weathered plywood gleamed in the dark. I lay listening to the rustle and murmur of water outside. Previously there had always been a limit to beauty, but now it was everywhere. Nothing was left out. All I had to do was lie here, with love pouring out of my breast in a swift, silent stream, like a Roman candle. I felt like I'd been claimed by immemorial love.

That night I lay awake a long time, the watch fire in the heart burning long into the night. It seemed I would never need to sleep again. I'd found something larger than the world, and didn't need to.

But what on earth was it? What had just happened?

✿

FAST-FORWARD: FIVE DAYS LATER. A steel table in an outdoor café in a city.

The café is deserted. Midmorning and I'm back in the modern world, waiting for a bus to the capital later in the day.

By now the fire in the midriff has dulled to a warm glow, but it is still there. Ever since that mystic afternoon I've been living in a transfigured world. Worries and hopes about the future have evaporated. I'm interested only in what is before me. As I glide down concrete avenues, under the shadows of casuarina trees and palms, passing through the exhaust fumes and growl of traffic, I feel insubstantial as the shadows themselves.

At the table in the streetside café I sip a coffee, light a Winston, and open my exercise book. I want to write about that wondrous afternoon. I want to try to understand what happened. I had thought I wanted to go out and see the world. Instead it was the other way round: the world opened its arms and pulled me in. What did it all mean? I was only nineteen, and everything I'd ever thought life was had just been pulled out from under me.

Yet I didn't mind.

If I'd been brought up a Christian, I might have thought I'd encountered the "godhead," whatever that is. If I'd been a Hasidic Jew, I might have believed I'd seen the *hitlahavut*, the holy fire for which "each hour is its footstool and each deed its throne," as Martin Buber put it. If I'd been a Buddhist, I might have wondered if it had something to do with "Buddha-nature." If I'd heard of the New Age, I might have dabbled with the notion that I'd dropped into an encounter with the quantum field. But I wasn't interested in anything like that.

I hadn't just been brought up a rationalist; I had been raised in Oxford, the epicenter of logical positivism. My parents were academics. Soon I was heading to a good university and, who knows, toward a life in academia one day myself. The word "spiritual" wasn't in the vocabulary. I didn't even know what "mystical" meant. Yet within a few months of leaving school, where I had been reared in classical humanism, during the gap between my school days and my college days, something outside imagining happened.

As far as I was concerned, that afternoon must have been about the nature of consciousness. It was something I had never seen before, which nothing in my schooling had prepared me for, yet which felt familiar. It was baffling, but it didn't mean you had to become a religious maniac.

AS I START WRITING ABOUT it in the café, or trying to, it comes easier as fiction, and before I know it ten pages disgorge themselves. I feel like I've just written the first chapter of a novel. Aha. Whatever else it may have been, that experience was the seed of a novel, I decide—the siren call of a literary vocation. It was about a book.

Over time, the numinous grace on the beach turned into a compulsion. Dad had always dreamed of being a popular novelist, a "paperback writer." While sitting at the wheel of our old Renault, hissing through the Oxford rain, he'd talk wistfully of writing blockbusters and driving a white Rolls on the Riviera. I decided I would set out to fulfill his dreams for him, by writing, by perhaps even one day matching his own remarkable accomplishments with a writing career of my own. At least that gave me a handle on the strange afternoon.

If I had known more about psychology, I might have called it a peak experience. But in Oxford we didn't learn about psychology. We learned how to write hexameters in Greek and Latin, how to parse any part of speech, how to write a literary essay. The task of life as I'd absorbed it was to cultivate your eye and ear for literature. What else could the experience do as it faded but turn into a literary calling?

But still: was that really what it had been?

THESE THINGS HAPPEN. THROUGHOUT TIME, humanity has sought "awakenings" and "realizations" by sitting under trees, fasting, praying all night, making holy pilgrimages. Sometimes they happen randomly, while doing the washing up or riding a bike to work—or staring at the ocean. Sometimes they have launched religions or cults, while other times they lead to a more ordinary path.

It might have just been a random moment, a stray visitation of "grace." I could have put it behind me with gratitude and got on with the rest of my life. But during the gap year, far from home, several things had changed. I'd been at a pitch of health, physical and mental, with miraculously clear skin, when the mysterious moment struck.

In the weeks and months that followed, as I tried to understand it, I couldn't help clutching after other explanations: it had been an ecstasy upon finishing the draft of my first book, on the gap year coming to its end, or an aesthetic orgasm like "Stendhal syndrome," or an explosion of narcissism or solipsism. But if so, why had its power come from being so freed of my ordinary self, with its cravings and complaints? And why the sense of belonging, of having been claimed by some great love that included all things? It had swept all concerns aside, it didn't care how undeserving one might be, it offered such a new perspective on what life was.

I could never have imagined then that not only might a

means exist for opening up to it further—into a new kind of life, in which one was grounded in it, part of it, living from it—but one day I would find myself in deep need of that means.

I WISH THIS COULD HAVE been a shorter story. There are fly-by-night snake doctors who promise "enlightenment" in a weekend, or through a four-week online course. But they are not offering the old paths, the ancient roads that have spent thousands of years taking the measure of a human being. And this is not just a story of "spiritual awakening."

In the end I did become a writer. But over time the experience on the beach turned into the start of something else, something different and much longer: a reluctant journey of healing. Ultimately, many years later, it would lead to the last thing I would have anticipated: to my becoming a Zen teacher, and not in England but in New Mexico.

Everything took a long time. Some things, especially good things worthy of the fact that we live and die, can't be rushed.

A few days later I was sitting in the airport of the country's lonely upland capital, waiting for my flight home. It had rained. The runway was silvery. A few miles away, a mountain range rose along the skyline.

I had mixed feelings: back in England I'd be starting at university soon, where I hoped to live a studious life. I'd crossed a mountain range, I'd earned enough money to take care of myself, I thought I'd written a book, and I'd had an epiphany. I believed I'd grown up and found myself. I thought my life had come right. But I was about to go home, and there was sadness, too, that this extraordinary period was coming to an end.

The damp runway shone, and between the mountains and

a tarnishing of clouds a strip of sky showed, silver-bright. Puddles gleamed on the wet tarmac. It all looked rather English, and reminded me of what I was going home to. I couldn't have said why, but I felt a queasy misgiving as I walked toward the departure gate.

Homecoming

IT WAS A DRAB MORNING at Heathrow. Not quite raining, but not quite not raining. Everything hissing—cars, buses, baggage wagons putting up fringes of spray.

I followed signs for the bus station, crossing vast, glossy floors. At WHSmith I bought a pack of cigarettes and a box of matches. Everything seemed swollen. The cigarettes were insanely fat, and the matches thick as kindling compared with the spindly wax-paper splints I'd grown used to in South America. Even the newspapers, announcing the death of another hunger striker in Belfast, seemed lavish in their thick folds.

When I found what I thought was my bus and asked for a ticket to Oxford, the driver tutted and scowled. "Stop wasting my time. You want the X70."

Stung, I got off and waited.

The right bus came, and while it lurched round the lanes of the airport to the whine of the windshield wipers, collecting more passengers, for a second I forgot why I was here. I had come back to go to college, of course, to resume my life, but as the bus gurgled through the rain, my sense of purpose, which I had enjoyed feeling curled up in my midriff while away, failed me.

In Slough, the people on the high street moved stiff and slow through the rain, and I got the first inkling that the new me, the person I'd become while abroad, healthy in mind and body, might not belong here. On buses in the Andes, people talked, shouted, laughed, slept, and whistled, and radios played. Here, people sat in a pall of silence, as if they knew some terrible, numbing truth. I could feel my brain flipping through its files, trying to understand. Was it the IRA bombs and hunger strikes? Mrs. Thatcher's policies? The shadow of lost empire? Meanwhile, with their strict curbs and white lines, the roads forced back the fields of grass into sullen obedience. Cars paused at junctions— correctly, dutifully—with turn signals pulsing large and emphatic in the gloomy day. Where I had just been, there weren't cars, only trucks, which didn't bother with indicators. They just lumbered and growled where they wanted to go.

DAD MET ME AT THE bus station in Oxford. He was standing behind his car with the trunk open, wearing his corduroy car coat sewn by the hand of his dead tailor brother.

He didn't say anything, but held my temples in his gloved hands and warmly kissed my cheeks.

"Cold? You're not cold?" he asked, after a pause.

I wasn't. At least I hadn't been. But now I wondered. Perhaps I was and hadn't realized it. I was wearing my cords and a stiff shirt of blue Bolivian cotton. I considered this my cold-weather outfit. I loved that shirt, and wore it until it smelled so bad I'd have to give in and wash it, then wait bare-chested while it dried in the Andean sun, and pull it back on reeking of bitter lye soap.

I must have hesitated. Dad asked, "Need a hand?"

I swung my pack into the back of the car, saying, "Course not. I just carried it the length of the Andes." A brag I regretted instantly, an exaggeration I didn't know why I'd said.

I couldn't believe how small the shops on the streets were. Nor how it felt to be sitting beside Dad in the car. Except it wasn't just the shops' smallness. They seemed plump, like the cigarettes I'd bought at the airport, yet toy-size too, like a model village. It was pretty, almost cozy, but weird.

On St. Giles' and the Banbury Road, the big Oxford horse chestnut trees were thick with five-fingered leaf, the gutters strewn with their gleaming conkers. When I saw them I felt guilty, and memories stirred of the autumn term, another school year beginning, as we rode over the thick asphalt of the Banbury Road, thoroughfare of my childhood.

Dad and I had exchanged letters while I was away. One of the thrills of travel was to find the poste restante in a new city and wait in line, then anxiously present our passports as the official flipped through a stack of letters. Would there be one or not?

Both my parents wrote to me, and I loved receiving their letters. Mum's were handwritten on special fold-up airmail letters, and talked about the house in the country, the new book she was writing, the latest Soviet dissident writer who had come to stay. My father's were single-spaced and long: he typed them on extra-long foolscap and generally went to two sheets, even while typing on both sides. I'd never received letters like them. I cherished them, and reread them many times. Nor had I ever received such undivided attention from him. He was a historian, a lecturer, a translator, an editor—and a spy—and in the days before he left our home, he was often out, at college or the university, giving lectures, seminars, tutorials. I'd see him at supper and briefly at bedtime. Then, after he'd moved out, the visits to his flat had been blessed events, numinous with safety, but brief and too rare. Now I was longing to talk with him about everything that had happened—the work, the travel, and the revelation on the beach. Our relationship had changed while I was away. I was a young man now, a son who'd left home and come back.

AT DAD'S HOUSE I LEFT my backpack in the hall and we sat in the sitting room, I on a wicker chair, Dad sunk in the sofa.

"So," I said, and tried a smile. "I guess I'm back."

"Yes," he agreed. "Quite. You're back."

His tone was strange, as if it weren't exactly a good thing either that I'd gone or that I was back.

Perhaps we were both embarrassed, sitting opposite each other on either side of the small brass coffee table. I had written long letters to him, too, mostly about what I'd been doing at work on the farm, then about the travels, and the book I was writing, sharing my thoughts, impressions, hopes with him. He had done the same. We had got to know each other on the page, free of complaint and disgruntlement. I had felt his hand on my back as I traveled. In the years before the trip, I had become a disgrace to him, drinking, smoking, skipping school, my skin livid and cracked. Worse, toward the end of my schooling I'd fallen in with a debauched crowd all older than myself, which centered round a gifted artist whose studio seemed a paradise of sophistication, an Olympus of small-town worldliness. Worse still, I'd gone through a phase in which I adopted a dandified garb of jackets and ties bought in thrift stores with money I earned from tutoring. I wanted to look the part in the artist's studio.

My father, the rare times I saw him, had watched these affectations with dismay. I could hardly bear to look into his dark eyes, exaggerated behind his glasses.

But at work in the mountains on the other side of the world, I had shed that youthful folly and become strong and lean. Here I was now, fresh-skinned, healthy, and home.

So, boychick. You're back.

His voice sounded strangely normal, with no recognition of where I'd just been. Nor of our letters. Nor of how I'd changed.

"So how was it?" he asked, then chuckled, as if acknowledging the question's inadequacy.

I laughed, too, but half of me was watching what was going on with growing horror. I felt like I was perched on the edge of a cliff, with the carpet below me moving farther and farther away. At the end of the laughter was silence. *How was my time away?* He was waiting for me to answer.

I sat paralyzed. I had just spent months becoming a person worthy of him, who could chat in a friendly way with all manner of people. More than anything, I wanted to ask him about the moment on the beach. I wasn't sure he'd know what it had been, but at least he might have some take on it, some pointing toward a way to follow up on it. But now it seemed impossible to speak at all, about that or anything else.

I forced myself to take the plunge. "Actually, something amazing happened," I began.

But as soon as I started, I felt it wasn't going to work.

"Ye-es?" he chuckled. "I'm sure a lot of amazing things happened."

I nodded and tried to say "Yes," but the word came out in a croak. It was as if he and I, who had written so copiously to each other these past months, were suddenly strangers.

"Go on," he said.

An abyss opened. There was a lump in my throat. Everything in front of me—the red carpet, the table, Dad in his gleaming glasses—became misty, remote. What was happening? Was I ill? Going mad?

Then his wife, my stepmother—also my mother's cousin, and my own cousin, it was complicated—walked in.

"Hel-*lo*," she said with a laugh.

An unfamiliar sensation woke in my midriff, half itch, half churning. I got up and the room tilted a little. We came toward each other and embraced.

She stepped back. "You look *older*. Doesn't he look older, lovey?"

Dad grunted.

She looked me up and down. "Look at you. You've become a *man*."

I couldn't help smiling. I loved her for saying that.

Dad chuckled, neither agreeing nor disagreeing.

"Sit, sit," she said. "What can I get you? Juice? Tea? Coffee?"

At this I came alive. Coffee, national fuel of South America, lubricant of social intercourse, held out a friendly hand.

"Coffee, please," I said.

It would be instant—it always was in England—not the shots of sweet black jet fuel that boys hawked on trays on Andean streets, but it was still coffee.

"Milk? Sugar? How do you like it these days?"

Her solicitous questions acknowledged that I might have

changed. That was nice, too. Yet I stumbled over the answers. How did I want my coffee? I couldn't remember. I blurted out, "Milk and sugar, please," hoping that would resolve it.

"How many sugars?" she asked.

I had to think again. But I didn't know how many. My head was all fog. She was standing there waiting. For a second I forgot where I was; there was just this utterly strange scene: standing on a red floor, someone waiting for me to speak, and in my belly a seethe of sensations like eels in a bucket.

Then I had a thought: *Three.* Then another: *Or four.* I said out loud, "Four, please."

There was a pause. Dad said, "Four?" in a high, incredulous voice. "Since when did you have *four* sugars in your coffee?"

Since when had I? I didn't know. I usually had one spoon, but I couldn't remember that now. I felt like I didn't know anything.

I said, "Well—er—what's right?"

Dad looked at me from the sofa and laughed. "What's *right*? There *is* no right. What you *like* is what's right. If you *like* four, then four is right."

And they both laughed.

"Okay," I said to get past this stumbling block, and went and sat down.

After another pause Dad said, "So. You were saying. Something *amazing* happened." He put an ironic emphasis on the word, and smiled.

Another dizzying silence opened, as if the room itself were yawning.

He was normally a talkative man and would have taken up the slack, but something—me, presumably—had flummoxed him.

"Aren't you hot?" he asked finally.

I hadn't noticed.

"You must be hot in that sweater. And I can see you've got a vest on under that shirt."

I never wore vests these days, but I did have a T-shirt on. The word "vest" caused a plunge of panic. Vests were a uniform of the past. I had had to wear them as a child. Was I going to have to once again?

I unpeeled my sweater.

At which Dad laughed and said, "Phaw! I can tell *you* haven't had a bath in a while."

He waited for me to respond.

"I haven't," I said with a nervous smile.

He rolled his eyes. "Well, have a bath *now*. Of course. It will be *nice*. Wash off the dust of the *road*."

My father was pulling out all the stops. In our family a good mood was indicated by irony. He was trying to amuse me.

When my stepmother returned with a mug of coffee so sweet it made my gums tingle, we all sat listening to me sip and slurp, until he said, "Lovey, I'm going to run him a bath. I'll pop up and you sit tight."

Dad handed me a towel at the door to the bathroom; I noticed two towels already hanging over the radiator inside, but they would have been my stepbrother's. I felt vaguely guilty at the sight of them.

The taps thundered and the room filled with steam.

"Okay?" he said, glancing back at me. "Okay, boychick?"

A lump came to my throat and I nodded, pulling the door to.

I CAUGHT SIGHT OF MY pale brown skin in the bathroom mirror and realized I hadn't seen myself naked in a mirror since leav-

ing home. The hot water scalded. I didn't mind. I brushed a fizz
of bubbles off my legs and lay back. In South America hot baths
had been rare. I tried to enjoy it. During the months away, I
thought I had learned that how one accepted discomfort was the
measure of a man. But a frightened squirrel was darting around
inside my skull, and that squirrel was my own mind.

I heard pipes whistle deep in the house's masonry. I recognized their changing pitch. Then, dimly, I heard my father and
stepmother talking downstairs. I had forgotten how well I knew
the timbre of their voices. The sound of their talking triggered
something, and it was like finding myself back in an old dream—
in a nightmare, in fact, one I had forgotten, a long state of affairs
that had been how things used to be.

I reached for the soap to try to break the spell. As soon as
I sat up, my mouth tightened into a grin and the room filled
with gold-yellow light. I could feel the filaments in the lightbulbs
glowing like stars, milky as asteroids, bloated like glowworms, I
heard them hiss and fizz, and the ceramic shelf round the bath
glared like an indoor swimming pool. Then I couldn't see anything, and a sound forced its way out through my teeth: a hiss, a
pant. Suddenly I was crying.

I hadn't cried in years. All through childhood, I could hardly
remember having cried. I tried to shut the feelings down and
stifle the sobbing. Home after six months away, after becoming
a man, and now this—blubbering like a baby in the bath. *What's
the matter? Hold it together, man.*

Something gave way in me. The part that held me together,
the new self I had built up over the gap year, broke up and dissolved into the water. At the same time, a terrifying truth presented itself: my time away was over. I had come back.

My mind was spinning, and where it spun was down into a terrible dread. It was as if, along with my new robust, hard-working, world-loving self, all hope spun away down the plug hole.

I quivered like jelly when I climbed out of the tub. I felt like cellular plasm stripped of its genetic code. I curled up on the bath mat with a big towel pulled over me and crouched in the dark in terror—terror of the world outside, and the world within.

It was emotion in excess of the facts, in T. S. Eliot's phrase. All I had done was have a good gap year and come home to go to a good university. I was moving from one good fortune to another. Yet in between the two, the center gave out.

IT SURELY DOESN'T SOUND LIKE much: the guy got home and cried in the bath. But I was so sensitized, so disoriented—by coming home, by the weird moment on the beach—that I felt I had slipped right back into some kind of hell and the gates had clanged shut again. They'd never let me out a second time.

HOW NICE IT WOULD BE if this were merely the tale of some undeserving clod having a random revelation on a beach and letting it transform his life. But it's not. I could present it that way, I guess, as some traditional spiritual narratives might do, but it wouldn't be true.

I didn't know it then, but I was entering a minor breakdown.

Panic attack. Late onset of adolescent depression. Acute anxiety. Reactivitaion of childhood trauma. Various diagnoses landed in years to come.

This is a story not only of awakening but of healing. Perhaps the two can't, or shouldn't, be separated. No healing without a wound.

COLLAPSES, BREAKDOWNS, PSYCHIC RIFTS COME in different guises. This is how mine came. The level of dread was new to me. I felt instinctively that something was going wrong, and wouldn't easily be fixed. Sure enough, over the coming weeks, months, years, I sputtered along like a car with only half of its cylinders firing.

I washed my face again and again at the sink, trying to wipe away the stain of the tears. Eventually I dressed, checked my face a final time in the mirror, and drifted downstairs, feeling like a walking ghost.

"Good," my father said. "Ready? I spoke to your mum and she's expecting us. I'll run you out."

❧

IT WASN'T RAINING, BUT DROPLETS misted the windshield as we drove. The countryside was shades of a color without a name, between gray, green, and brown. The color of England. Every weekend we'd driven through it—my sister, mother, and I—to our semi-ruin in the countryside, a terminal building project, to days of allergies and DIY. Mum was living there full-time now.

"You'll have to get your feet back on the ground," Dad said beside me.

So the months abroad might really have been one long fantasy. But if so, why had they felt so right? I'd learned what the word "happy" meant. It meant there was no weight in your belly, and if you asked yourself how you felt, the answer spontaneously came back: *good*. And what about my skin? Had its clearing up been an aberrance, a mistake?

The drizzle became rain. We turned in, past my mother's old iron gate, long since collapsed against a bed of nettles, past a pebble-dash garage that a drifter/builder had erected from a kit and got wrong, so there were gaps in its walls, past the chestnut with its trunk black in the damp day.

When I saw the stone house I felt a surge of raw love.

Dad gave me a one-armed hug from the driving seat, meaning he wouldn't be getting out. But the dogs came sniffing at his door, wagging their tails, and he wound down his window to greet the old one, saying, "Look, he remembers me."

The front door of the house opened.

"Okay," Dad said with a nervous laugh, and put the car in gear.

It wasn't Mum but my brother who stepped out onto the porch. He raised his arm in a wave, hunched and ran out through the rain.

"Here, here," he called, rushing over, taking my backpack out of my hands.

"It's okay, I'm fine," I said, and couldn't help smiling.

"Long-lost traveler," he said. "Come on, let me carry your bag, for chrissake."

He stood with my bag over his shoulder, talking to Dad. "Wow, I can hardly believe it. He's back."

"Yes," Dad agreed, and let out a growling chuckle. "He really *is*," as if just now realizing it.

I felt a flush of relief. My brother would understand. He, too, had been away at my age.

I wasn't sure whether to lean down to give my father another farewell hug. He was buckled up in his corduroy coat, gloved hands on the wheel, ready to be off. Here my brother and I were, out in the rain on our mother's drive, and there he was, in his car, which he hadn't switched off, about to drive back to town. And I hadn't managed to say a thing about the beach.

That was the start of clamming up about it. Years would pass before I mentioned it to another soul.

The rear lights glared red in the rainy day as Dad drove away.

IT FELT STRANGE WALKING IN without my pack, but my brother was insistent, generous, welcoming.

My sister came up to me, laughing, and we hugged. I saw Mum beyond, in the sitting room, getting up from an armchair. There was laughter around the room. Then it died away and here I was, standing on the carpet, open door behind me, sofa and window facing me, cold autumn day outside, and the two dogs, now getting old, at my feet with their tails sawing back and forth, panting up at me, the tips of their noses periodically making contact with my trousers, and the three members of my family looking at me.

Once again, I was speechless. They were waiting for me to say something. But I didn't know what to say. Before I knew it, another sob was coming. I wasn't speaking; I was crying. Not again! I was about to put my face in my hands but instead ran out of the room, up the stairs, along the landing, up the ladder to my room in the attic.

Here I was, nineteen, home on my bed, sobbing. The months of maturing, of finding my way in life—ripped away, lost!

I felt a hand on my back: my brother.

"What's *wrong*?"

I tumbled into more billows of weeping.

He didn't give up but stayed in the room. Eventually I rolled onto my back to try to say something, to wipe my face. It was then that I saw two cards pinned to the beam over the bed.

WELCOME BACK!!!! they said. One from my sister, one from my mother.

Eventually my sister came upstairs, then Mum, and a kind of reunion happened. We all lay on the bed, and while the three of them mused, chatted, joked, I was painfully aware of failing to live up to their good humor. Sorrow rang through me like a bell.

But why?

I had come back. *I should never have come back*, I kept wailing at myself. What had I been thinking? I hadn't thought; I'd just dumbly returned like some migratory bird to its nest. And to go away again wouldn't work, because I was broken now.

FROM A DISTANCE OF DECADES, maybe it was natural. I'd started to grow up while abroad, working, earning, developing some independence, attempting to write a book. Now I was back, with family, where different resources were called for. It never occurred to me that maturity might even need a little forging in grief.

But grief over what? It was too unaccountable, too untrustworthy. It undid me—I was all undone by that tearful downpour in the bath, and the grief short-circuited into despair.

I didn't realize I had held a lot of feelings at bay during childhood. Now that I'd come home they jumped me, wanting to be remembered, and floored me. It was too much. Yet it was me. It was who I was, it was my pain. But right then I couldn't accept it, and it was easier to break.

They asked me about my trip. *So tell us about it.*

I was stymied, and again the brink yawned.

And there was still the moment on the beach. Where had it gone now? Another *me* still existed somewhere, a drifter, writer, poet, journeyman, with stubble on his jaw and a pack on his back. I could see him waiting at a roadside for a truck across the next sierra. He glanced back at me as I shuddered on my soft bed at home. The only shuddering he knew was of a truck bed on a dirt road. He swung up his dusty pack and headed off to the next junction, where he might have better luck with a ride.

What about *this* me? He had stumbled into a morass. The most precious thing had just been lost. Somehow he had to recover it. But how? And what was it, anyway?

WE ALL WENT OUT FOR a walk with the dogs. My brother and I chopped wood, a task we normally relished. But as we stood under the black trees in the smoky English autumn afternoon, swinging ax and sledge, splitting drums of wood, my arms went weak. Worse, in the house I began to sneeze. Then my forehead started to itch. Instinctively I scratched, hoping to get rid of the itch, but it only spread. By the time we congregated for dinner round the kitchen table that night, I was itching all over.

Home half a day and already the eczema was back.

The Alternatives

THE NEXT FEW YEARS—IT'S HARD to know what
to say. They were a mess, a blur, a bog, something to
get out of. All direction gone. In its place, skin trouble, shame, intoxication, despair. The eczema reoccupied its old
outposts, and I hid myself away in my college room, inexpertly
nursing it, fearful to go out.

Something was wrong: not just the skin but my mind,
my heart. Something had broken. I knew it but didn't know
what. From morning to night I tried to put it right even without knowing. For months I hardly spoke, lest a random outburst of tears befall me. I couldn't study. I was too bereaved,
walking around in a cold, white daze while my sulfurous core
steamed.

I got caught once again in the other version of the story,
where, bereft of the seeker, the wanderer, there was no trail. Life
was a sump, and I was the sludge on its bed. Too ashamed to

seek help, convinced of my constitutional wrongness, I dragged myself through further education hobbled by the breakdown, scarred by the skin, inhibited by enduring shame.

ONCE, EARLY ON AT CAMBRIDGE, I called Mum from a chilly autumnal phone box: waiting for the beeps on the line, the signal to push the coin in.

She picked up, I said hello, I heard her say hello.

Then I couldn't speak. I stood with my cracked hand hurting as it held the receiver, my rash-riddled face feeling as stiff as a towel left to dry outdoors. The silence gaped. The beeps came on again and I couldn't get a coin out of my pocket quick enough. Then she was gone. Two of my knuckles bled from the tussle with the jeans pocket.

What should I do? It was a cold gray morning. I should have been at a lecture, a tutorial, a seminar, something. Instead, as happened every morning, I was lost, searching for refuge in a phone box, trying to call home.

I called again, and managed to push in a coin and blurted into the phone that everything had gone wrong.

"Don't be silly," she replied. "You're at *Cambridge*. You'll have a whale of a time."

I tried my dad.

"How many people would give their right *arm* to be there," he told me.

I knew they were right. I was fortunate. Yet I felt like a crustacean, armor-plated with eczema, mind a fog, and no idea why. Somehow, I thought, I had to find a way to get used to this. If I wanted to be here, this was how it would be. Who I had felt myself to be while away was wrong. This was life, this was England, this was me.

I COULD GO ON AND on.

It was like an amputation and I was the severed limb. Porridge Face, they called me. The thing from *Doctor Who*.

I guess I was picking up my life challenges, the things I would have to reckon with—dybbuks who sat on my shoulder whispering in my ear to stray from the road, or that there was no road to begin with. It was my responsibility to address them, but I had no resources. I didn't even recognize they were there. And I couldn't trust the sorrow. It might have been the pledge of an authentic wound, but I couldn't accept that—I didn't know how to have a wound. It all just pointed back to the catastrophic bathtub: it was true, it had been my undoing. Damnation was what it meant. Having discovered inviolable belovedness on the beach, in the tub I was damned once again to the corridors of hell, which only now did I sense had been my old haunts. No way out. If anyone mentioned therapy, counseling, help, it was only further proof of my cursedness.

For someone who hasn't had it, it may be hard to imagine the extent to which eczema is not about the skin. The itching, for example, doesn't happen just on the surface but in the belly. The diaphragm convulses. Emotions seize the heart: frustration, despair. *Not this again. How long this time?* It's hard to have perspective when you're in the grip of an attack. Time and space close down. The eczematous mind fixes on one thing only: the present itch.

The shame, the withdrawal, the idiosyncratic thinking—you

think differently, you can't help it. The fuming skin brands the soul. Zelda Fitzgerald's famously dire skin would flare at the same time as her psychosis. She'd be checked into her Swiss sanatorium with mind and skin both on fire. Eczema may be a genetic disorder, but there's the stress factor too, which works both ways: stress exacerbates the skin, but the ruinous skin itself causes stress.

I listened to old records in my room, swigged Smirnoff from the bottle, brooded over unwritten essays, and agonized over not studying what I wanted, incapable of taking on the medieval university statutes that would not allow me to switch courses, wasting my time but seemingly unable not to, wondering how I could leave yet terrified at the prospect. *Leave Cambridge?* I'd think with a gulp. My parents, uncles, aunts, grandparents had all excelled at Cambridge. And I was a scholar, a linguist, a would-be writer.

That was another thing: the book. It felt like a calamity now, lying sheathed between the covers of its notebook in my cupboard. I had fondly imagined that at college, between essays and lectures, I would revise and type it and it would get published. I wasn't in a state even to open it.

Obviously, many people face far harder challenges. But to my skin-skewed mind, having the skin reignite just as I started out on adulthood seemed disastrous, especially after the months abroad. I thought I had grown up while away, outgrown my childhood issues. All I had done was temporarily escape them. And then made the fatal, irreparable mistake: coming home.

Diligent study was out the window. The only reason Cambridge didn't throw me out was my understanding tutor, who repeatedly kept my essay failures to himself.

BUT IT WASN'T ALL BAD. For one thing, the issues I struggled with probably made me a reasonable test case for the kinds of practice I would later find. My suffering was "sticky" as any, full of barbs to keep the unwary specimen well hooked. If I could pick my way out of it, there was hope for us all.

Even at the time I figured there had to be ways out. Buckets of ale, for example, were easy to reach for, and bottles of vodka, and fat, weak joints of red Leb: they all offered temporary relief, even if they did aggravate the skin and make the head throb the next day. But even while lit up, I wasn't much fun to be around, and the friends I'd known when I arrived at university soon dwindled. New friends came and went, too, mostly barroom philosopher types who liked to see the vanity of things in the bottom of a whiskey glass.

Briefly I joined the gymnastics team. Gym had been my sport for a while at school. I pulled various muscles immediately, and even before the injuries it was hard to sustain the effort needed to train. It was as if something else more pressing was always crying out to be attended to—I just didn't know what it was. I'd walk under wintry trees alone, hands jammed in my pockets, trying to figure it out.

Sometimes a kind old friend from school days would drag me out of my lairs into his network of conviviality, where I would skulk and long for the events to be over. Or else quaff potations and think I was the soul of the party. In time, alongside Mr. Morbid I evolved another personality: Mr. Fun, who was flirtatious and gregarious, but brittle and oversensitive, and emerged during bouts of drinking, arranging his clothing and hair to hide any ailing skin to the point where he could banish it from consciousness, and despise it almost as someone else's blight.

My friend introduced me to a series of achingly desirable young women, reared at expensive schools, after whom I'd hanker. But in spite of Mr. Fun's bonhomie, they picked up an untrustworthy shadow of oddness on their radar. They could tell something was off, they just weren't sure what.

I developed a hobby: plugging myself into headphones to disappear into the lilting rhythms of world music, especially calypso and soca from Trinidad. The horn lines played by trumpets and saxophones sizzled and dazzled, scintillating like light on an ocean. They'd bring to mind a sunlit sea on the far side of the world, and a beach, and a moment of surpassing peace I'd once tasted.

HALF OF ME LONGED TO be an anchorite, half to be a suave man of the world, and each had no idea how to engage with the other.

Perhaps I was just a classic young Jew, like a character from Bashevis Singer or Amos Oz: nervous, indecisive, eczematous. There was a provenance, a heritage. I just couldn't recognize it.

I TRIED OTHER AVENUES.

One autumn evening, damp and chilly but not raining, I rode my bike out to the Gog Magog Hills, seven miles from town. I was yearning to feel different. I padlocked the bike to a sapling, walked up among the tall beech trees that covered the small rolling hills, and lay on my back under the lofty, hissing canopy. It was slightly scary. Recent winds had stripped the trees bare of leaves, and their latticework of twigs and boughs was illuminated by an eerie sheen from the dusk sky.

The hills were said to be a prehistoric site. Some believed them to be a Neolithic hill fort, others an ancestral shrine. Some said there was a chalk figure of a mother goddess hidden among the beech roots, and that it was a "power site" capable of shifting consciousness.

I didn't really care what it was, so long as I came away feeling a bit better.

Mostly I was too anxious to engage with where I was. But then something happened. As I lay on my back, a last leaf up in the branches detached itself and began to fall. I watched it coming down. It was strange. Time seemed to slow down. The leaf spun and twirled, and normally I would have lost its flickering track, but somehow I managed to keep my eye on it. It flickered as it fell, becoming pixelated, freeze-framed like a cartoon. I was spellbound, seeing it twirl and descend, coming closer and closer, when, with a start, as if some stranger in a crowd were suddenly reaching out to touch me, I realized it was coming right at me. An urge to dodge, move, get up, roll away. Instead I lay still and briefly surrendered, and the leaf landed right on my chest.

There was a superstition that to catch a falling leaf brought good luck. I had caught this one with my heart. I couldn't help feeling that I had somehow been met. The leaf had transfixed me, then chosen me for its landing.

For a while I went quiet inside, stunned into inner silence, then I put the leaf in my pocket and rode the dark miles back to college, with the beam of my bike light quivering over the road and the sky still pale as the world darkened around me.

It probably meant nothing, but that strange encounter touched me.

ॐ

SOMETIMES WHEN I FELT UP to it I launched into "skin cures." These could often be more traumatic than the eczema itself. Herbalism, bioenergetics, kinesthesiology, macrobiotics—in spite of their scientific-sounding names, they were all highly alternative, but since the doctors had no cure bar the cancer-causing steroids, sooner or later you had to try them.

The herbalist operated from a farmhouse outside Cambridge. He was an imposing man, big and bearded, with a bearing, a presence. I liked him, though his herbs scared me. Herbs were like hay, and hay made you itch. He sat among his walls of shelves, lined with baskets and jars of dried leaves, and asked me how I was enjoying university.

I told him.

He asked why I was doing it, and I repeated what others said—that you needed a safety net in life.

He didn't respond, but asked me to remove my shirt and trousers and examined me.

"Well, you're burning up, aren't you?" he said. "If there's this much heat coming out through your skin, what do you think is happening inside? Something's making you burn."

From the golden time in South America, I knew my skin did not have to burn. But that was the burning question: Why had I been so free of eczema while away?

He looked at me through his glasses and shrugged. "Anyway. We need to cool you down." He sold me two sacks of dried herbs that weighed nothing and told me to make tea with them and drink many cups each day. They would cool me down.

Chamomile, verbena: I followed his instructions, but the only effect I noticed was my face heating up and tingling.

The "kinesthesiologist" was a tall, brisk woman with curly gray hair. She wanted to know if there was tuberculosis in our ancestry.

"My grandfather," I told her, "had TB."

My mother's father had been a promising young barrister until consumption took him down. He didn't die but lost a lung, as well as his career as a king's counsel in London. And his first wife, my mother's mother, flew out of the dreary, disease-ridden marriage in her biplane, to glamorous adventures in the Orient.

"Ah," said the kinesthesiologist. "That's it, then. The skin's the third lung, you know."

"I have TB of the skin?"

"In a way. Whatever your grandfather left unhealed he passed down to your mother, who passed it on to you. Tuberculosis is like a fire in the lungs," she added, as if to explain it all.

So eczema was a fire of the "third lung," the skin?

It was one of many diagnoses.

"Remember, we're looking for the source of the *dis-ease*," she said. She always pronounced the word that way, in two distinct syllables. I found it disconcerting. Eczema was surely more than a lack of ease.

Then she had me hold my thumb and index finger in a ring while she asked "it"—the ring—questions. If the ring was weak, that meant we had identified a weak point, an "aspect" of the dis-ease.

"Henry's mother?" she asked.

The ring crumbled.

Another test was to hold my arm out straight while she pressed down on it. If my arm collapsed, that was a telltale sign.

"Henry's father?"

The arm gave way.

"Okay! This disease is connected to your relationship with your mother and father! And don't forget to leave a check at the door."

Mum and Dad. They fuck you up, said the poet Philip Larkin.

Had they fucked me up? It was weirdly hard to contemplate. Surely my problems, if I had them, were mine. Could others be involved? Even blamed?

The bioenergeticist was a handsome woman from the Territorial Army who offered treatments on Wednesday afternoons. It was all about the feet, she explained as she dug into my soles. The feet were a map of the body, and it was like pursuing enemy forces over disputed territory. She had to chase the disease to an "exit point."

She was delighted when a rash developed on one foot. But it turned out only to be athlete's foot.

One time I got on a macrobiotic diet cure. The "doctor" was convinced that in South America it was simply not drinking milk that had cured me. I told her I wasn't consuming dairy products now either, but that didn't sway her. It wasn't enough to avoid the allergen; we had to cure the disease, not the symptom. The source of the allergy had to be chased out, as if by exorcism. The right diet could do it.

At the time, an old friend had asked me to join his calypso band. Peter and I had known each other long ago, at school in

Oxford, where we had met in music classes and played in the same brass group. Like him, I had been a trombonist. A talented composer, he had gone on to excel in music and now had some gigs lined up at the Cambridge May Balls. I started on the "diet cure," hoping to get better in time for the concerts.

Only certain things could be eaten. No dairy, of course, and no wheat, and nothing processed. Plenty of brown rice and oats. And steamed vegetables. And no tap water. Only pure, bottled water.

I hardly knew how to cook, and it was all beyond me, but I did my best. The skin rebelled at the cure, and soon there was hardly an inch of me that wasn't rippling red.

The macrobioticist told me the flare-up was good news: sure enough, the disease was coming out. But I must keep it clean.

So every day I had a bath and toweled off afterwards, distressing the skin yet further, no matter how gentle I tried to be. Afterwards, shaken, I'd withdraw to my attic digs, feeling like I was made of wet rags, and pull on my headphones for the one relief: filling my skull with the tidal rhythms of tropical music, a sun-filled dose from far away.

One day I happened to run into my medical doctor in a store. He took one look at me and marched me to the nearest pay phone, where he called the hospital.

"You have highly infectious impetigo," he snapped. "Why on earth aren't you on the ward?"

No! You don't understand! I'm in the middle of a cure. It has to get worse before it gets better.

He was having none of it, and ended up driving me to the emergency room himself.

Which was lucky. It meant I scored more steroids, and got better just in time for the May Balls.

The wounds had a strange way of healing under the chemical onslaught. They gathered into sheets of bark that seared away to reveal soft new skin, unblemished as sheets fresh from the laundry. But once the tube ran out, the old guard soon moved back.

WHEN I WENT HOME DURING the holidays I'd have lunch with Dad in his college.

"So, boychick. How's it going? Good term? Tell us about it."

I'd be stumped. I wouldn't know what to say. Dictionaries had never felt so heavy, nor libraries so intimidating. But I couldn't tell him that. Cambridge had changed his life. His world revolved around academics. Mum's, too. In one of my second-year finals I managed to write only half a page, so paralyzed had I been in the exam hall: an unprecedented failure for a youth bred to be a scholar. I couldn't let them know.

I'd mumble something, and he'd growl a noncommittal laugh.

"You've been okay?" he'd ask, to check, and I'd try to find an answer while my stomach turned to mush.

Next thing I knew we'd be buttoning our coats, trotting down the steps out of his study and into the damp Oxford air, and making our way over to the dining hall for a first-rate lunch. As we walked under the old houses and dark elms, for a moment I'd feel a strange relish in his presence, a shared relief, a sense that life could be okay and my misery had been imaginary. I'd have a fresh sense of who we were. Indeed we were sturdy rationalists, thinkers, straightforward, healthy souls. Misery wasn't the kind of thing for us, surely.

In some part of my scrambled psyche I knew my reactions were exaggerated, my situation must be manageable, tractable, and indeed was fortunate. But that only worsened it: I had no right to feel as dismal as I did.

Yet around Dad I'd be dazzled, unaware of any feeling, as if a portcullis had rattled down between me and my life and made me numb and mute. It wasn't just that I couldn't explain myself; I'd no longer remember the previous weeks and months. There'd be a vague anxiety covered by a skim of strange excitement; that was all.

We'd finish up our plates in the echoing hall, deposit them at the hatch, where a college scout waited, and clip back out into the Oxford weather.

"Going back to Cambridge soon?" he'd ask.

I'd nod. Or else mumble that I was heading to Mum's.

He'd take my cheeks in his hands and plant a kiss on my forehead. The feel of his stubble on my brow would send a tingle through me.

"Thanks, Dad."

"What for?"

And I'd be stumped for words again. Then would remember: "Lunch."

"Right you are."

And he'd be off down the road in his overcoat and cap, broad back swaying a little as he went. I'd watch him go, feeling a wave of sadness at another lost opportunity.

DAD'S WORK WAS TO SIT in his study and advise graduate students. He was a homebody. But he admired men of action. Not the lowly artisans and wage slaves among whom he had grown up, but wheelers and dealers. He'd gaze out his study window longingly, as academics do, toward a world where real people did real things, dreaming of bestsellers and a Rolls on the Riviera.

Where we came from, it was all about the book. Whoever it was—had they done a book? Without a book, no person was complete. There was our parents' brilliant friend at All Souls College, for example, who frittered away his brilliance on dinner talk. He wrote the odd article, but no book.

The problem of the book came closer to home. As a young man Dad had won a series of competitive fellowships and written a doctoral thesis that became a book, and he wound up a precocious young lecturer at Oxford. Greater things would surely come. Yet fifteen, twenty years on, the greater things—the books—hadn't come. Planned books dissipated into lectures. He edited books, translated books, but that wasn't the same.

I had written a book as soon as I could: two hundred pages in that old notebook, fruit of the gap year, languishing in my cupboard, reproaching me, telling me I was living wrong. Just the thought of it could tip me into a tailspin.

DRUNK, LONELY, IN LOVE WITH Caribbean music, I somehow left college with a good enough degree to continue my studies on Homer in London, with a major state scholarship to fund me, and limped off to the great city.

Tired of London, Tired of Life

ALL THROUGH MY EARLY TWENTIES, living in London, I wore a shapeless, bushy beard that hid half my face. Sometimes I would rather have had no face at all. I slouched into a shapeless anorak each morning, bought for four pounds from a street stall, and betook my body from library to library under the overwashed linens of the London sky.

I was going through the motions of researching a PhD thesis. I had a marvelous topic—palpable, authentic vestiges of shamanism in Homer—but I didn't want to do it. I didn't really want to do anything. Now that I was an adult, I didn't want to be part of the human race.

Meanwhile I read the Bible cover to cover, in search of some kind of answer. Sunday mornings I started shambling into different churches, seeking relief or redemption. In the depths of despair I sometimes had a vague, superstitious notion that I might be possessed: that a sprite from the East Anglian Fens might have hitched a ride on me and was running me like a puppet. Maybe I did need an exorcism. I wasn't a believer in the supernatural, but I was desperate enough to try anything, even the old miracle worker of Galilee.

Once I asked an evangelical pastor if Jesus could help with my skin. He said of course, but not the way I thought. I had to let Jesus into my heart first. Once I had done that, it wouldn't matter if I had eczema or not.

"So he might *not* heal me . . ."

He nodded.

"But why would he withhold his help?"

"It would be up to Jesus what to do," said the pastor.

Another time I heard a Pentecostalist explain Satan. He wouldn't appear as himself, she said. Oh, no, he didn't come showing his red tail. More likely he'd come as a beach boy with a six-pack and an oiled body. She proceeded to describe this imaginary, buff Adonis with such relish you could feel the tension rise in the hall.

I had read too much D. H. Lawrence to buy this. Hadn't we been vilifying our healthy urges for centuries? Wasn't it the great Judeo-Christian fallacy to despise the God-given body? The Jew in me, the scholar, writer, poet, rationalist, just couldn't go there. My skin was a mystery. It had energies and battles all its own, and truths and histories. It knew more about me than I did. Its life was mine, only truer. When I surrendered to it, I found mine. When I ignored it, I lost mine. It tried to remind me, but I didn't understand. I only wanted it to be quiet, no trouble.

I was searching for something authentic that addressed troubles, and didn't sweep them aside in a tide of conviction, as the preachers did. I wanted eczema and despair to be allowed a fair hearing. They must lead the healing.

Then one day Dad called out of the blue and announced he would be in London next week, and why didn't he come round.

I WAS DEEP IN A "marigold cure" at the time. I had been saving it for the long summer vacation, when it would matter less if I was debilitated. Someone had told me that the time to read Proust was when you had a broken leg. My limbs were fine, but my skin was broken, so I stayed in and read Proust. He felt sympathetic to an eczematous neurasthenic. He had been one, too, after all.

The skin had been going wild every time I smeared on the marigold tinctures. The marigold doctor, a young Indian man with a thick black beard who operated his clinic from a bungalow in North London, where he had greenhouses and flower beds full of different healing marigold species, had run his fingers over my hands the last time I saw him and congratulated me on the result.

"Really?" I asked.

"Oh, yes, the pathology has to come out. Look at it coming out."

We both gazed at my livid hands, glistening like roasts fresh from the oven.

My father rarely visited. He had only ever come once before, and that he happened to arrive this time when I was at a pitch of sensitivity, in the middle of a cure and in the middle of Proust— well, that's just how it was.

As soon as he sat down on the sofa in the flat that summer night, removing his light jacket and hanging it on the back of a chair, then settling in and crossing his knees, he sighed and started talking about the difficult time my stepbrother was having.

My stepbrother, a couple of years younger than me, was an undergraduate. I liked and admired him, but just then he wasn't what I wanted to hear about.

I had been on the marigold tinctures a month, and somehow the treatment, along with the heavy dose of Proust, had turned me into an ever more febrile neurasthenic, to use Proust's word, even though I wasn't sure what it meant. As I listened to my father talking I started to tremble. Suddenly I heard myself ask, in a breaking voice, "You're talking about your stepson and his troubles. But what about your *own* son?" Next thing I knew I was raising my voice: "Do you have any idea what *I'm* going through?"

A deafening silence followed. I had never said anything like that to him. Neither of us had any idea what to say or do next.

Dad glanced at me. I didn't see his eyes—there was too much glare on his glasses—but I could see the shock in his body as he sat immobile, legs crossed. After a moment he cleared his throat.

"Well, what can I say?" he said, and let out a cough.

I calmed down enough to talk rather than shout, and began trying to explain, more heatedly than I meant to, how for years he had neglected his own children in favor of his stepkids.

He grew defensive. "What else could I do? You know the situation," he said in a kind of whine.

I wasn't sure what he meant. "But we're your kids," I said.

"I know, I know, of course I know that," he responded, his voice going up and down.

Then we were at another dead end. I was shocked by my

outburst, already sensing it couldn't help. It was all a dead end, there wasn't anything to say, and now that I'd raised such a long-repressed grievance, what could be done? He didn't deny it, yet the subject was too big to address.

Had I been frozen for years? Had we all? Incapable of moving on, of feeling, of adjusting. That day long ago when Mum and Dad had announced their separation: while everyone else cried, I had sat in a glassy daze. And when we learned that Dad and our stepmum were getting married, I dug my heels in, refusing to accept it. And meanwhile Mum closed her study door, and Dad said nothing.

These days psychologists say a traumatic event can trigger not only the fight-or-flight response but also a freeze. We go into lockdown, all the more likely in the case of a nervous system already debilitated by an ongoing stressor, such as a chronic ailment.

Finally Dad shrugged his shoulders, uncrossed his legs, and said, "Well, maybe you just have to accept it. Your dad's a bastard."

MY SKIN WAS LIKE WET canvas. Where it tore, the flesh was granulated like sausage meat. My PhD thesis was a sail flapping in a gale, too large to get the measure of. I was having to read scholarly articles in five languages, and recently my supervisor had thrown out that I needed German too—you couldn't pursue a career in classics without German. Did I want a career in classics? Was that what I was pursuing? But I was also still trying to get something going as a writer, trawling for freelance work, and fretting over the old book—the two hundred pages penned on tabletops in the Andes, which through my inaction had evolved into a permanent thundercloud. That book was the measure of my life: it was what I wasn't doing. Dawn to dusk, day by day, year by year, I did not finish it. The task wasn't unmanageable; I could see that. The problem wasn't capacity or even ability. It was on another level. More like self-trust, or basic competence at functioning. How to move from imagination to action without getting stuck in preemptive remorse on the way.

And now this. Dad was a *bastard*. He had said so himself. All along I had understood that *he* was the good guy, the *mensch*, and I, his son, was the one failing us. Dad was a *good* man, active, productive, friendly, encouraging, beloved of his colleagues, his students, his friends, devoted to his professional life. How had the son of such a man fallen so far from the tree? How did he turn out confused, eczematous, troubled, rapturous, a misfit, a poet, a despondent, a failure? (Too much failure all round: the skin, the book, the thesis, no job, no girlfriend—that last was another thing. How to find time for that, and what to do if I ever did, because who would want a sulfurous old hermit on her arm?)

Did Dad mean it? *He* had let *me* down? But he was admirable. He had decided on his priorities, that was true, but fair enough: a peaceful home came first, whatever that called for.

THAT EVENING WITH DAD LEFT me bereft, and feeling mean besides.

I heard the door thud downstairs, in the bleak, musty London hallway. I heard two lonely footfalls out on the pavement, and he was gone.

He had been wearing a pale linen suit. It was summer. He had been at an art opening before coming over, and had arrived full of the pleasure of his evening in the city. And I had whipped him, and he had cowered and said it was his own fault. But not in a way that meant he was sorry. More like: *So live with it. So fuck you.*

And still my skin was hot, tight, sore, and on top of that it had the audacity just now to start itching. I went into the bathroom and cranked the hot tap. Once steam started to appear I dabbed the offending rash, on the back of one hand, into the gush of hot water, scalding it. A cramp seized my belly. Pain overwhelmed itch, at least for a while.

I wanted to cry. Or did I? I didn't know how to cry. There was so much I didn't know how to do.

I sat still, immobile. I listened. A drip from the kitchen tap. The city outside, humming in the ears. It felt oddly close just then. For a moment the night felt intimate, as if there was some unknown support out in the darkness and it might sweep in if only I could let it.

❧

THE BEACH: BY NOW I knew others had been there, too. In Eugene O'Neill's *Long Day's Journey into Night*, for example, I had been astonished to come across this passage:

> Full moon in the Trades. The old hooker driving fourteen knots. I lay on the bowsprit, facing astern, with the water foaming into spume under me, the masts with every sail white in the moonlight, towering high above me. I became drunk with the beauty and singing rhythm of it, and for a moment I lost myself—actually lost my life. I was set free! I dissolved in the sea, became white sails and flying spray, became beauty

and rhythm, became moonlight and the ship and the high dim-starred sky! I belonged, without past or future, within peace and unity and a wild joy, within something greater than my own life, or the life of Man, to Life itself!

It wasn't exactly what I'd experienced on the beach, but it was close.

This speech, from the character Edmund, was based, it turned out, on an entry from O'Neill's own journal, written during his time at sea in his early twenties. It was autobiographical. That was good to know. Thirty years later, when he came to compose his great play, O'Neill was still writing about it. It still tugged at him.

Well, why wouldn't it? What could matter more?

I could still remember the vivid power of that moment. It was like having been given a most vital clue to a puzzle, a hint that would solve the whole thing.

It had been the Rosetta stone. It interpreted all experience, it translated everything. And the philosopher's stone: it turned all to gold. It was the touchstone, the lodestone; it was compass and ocean, it was course as well as rolling sea. It was the end of everything. And the source of everything. It fulfilled the one thing we lived to fulfill. The end is the beginning. That's what I discovered on the beach. And the beginning is the end. Somewhere, somehow, that moment was surely still alive. Not only could it not be forgotten—it must not be. Life must be organized so as to recover, reclaim, and live it. Nothing else mattered.

At the time it happened to O'Neill, once his ship docked he went straight to the nearest dive and drank himself nearly to death. The experience had not delivered him from despair. Like me, he had had no way to deepen or stabilize it or make it intelligible, or link it to his life. For me, too, it had been a random windfall, a sudden, marvelous rend in the fabric of life. Then it blew on and left the tear behind, flapping in the breeze.

SOMETIMES AN ANSWER COALESCED AROUND one thing: *Get away.*

The maddening thing was that I had the means with me: the wilting manuscript I had written long ago with energy and hope, and which had drooped in my hands when I returned home like a magic weed that couldn't survive the English climate. If I could just revive it, it might prove the ticket out one day.

Prior to that magical day, I did what I could. One summer I stuffed a knapsack with a sleeping bag, a plastic sheet, and a compass and hurriedly—before I could change my mind, in the sandals I was standing up in—walked out the back door of my mother's house in the valley north of Oxford. *West,* I thought. To Wales, a hundred miles off. It was midsummer and the harvest had started. What it was to be crossing a dry field, the ground firm underfoot, and at the far side of it a shadow of deep woodland waiting: the allure, the glamour of woods, and the fear too, as you trod out of the sunlight into the trees' dark world. Only the odd twinkle of sun to guide you. I remembered what it was like to figure out where a stream was, and to find it after pushing through dark undergrowth—a babble of clear light in the gloom of bushes. Days turned into weeks, following the footpaths, pounding out twenty-five-mile days that had me laying my exhausted limbs on the hard ground each night. I kept going, and picked up the Pembrokeshire Coast Path. Poems started to creep up from the ground, and a flicker of life rekindled somewhere near the heart. I remembered what Speedy had said about "old roads" you couldn't see but which were there, spanning great distances across the land, and now and then I wondered if I wasn't catching a glimpse of one.

But before I could be sure, it was back to London, to life in the weatherless city.

During another college vacation I thought, *Fuck it, I've got to live*—and convinced a newspaper editor to send me down to the Sahara. A contact in the anthropology department had a project going on in refugee camps in southwestern Algeria and, knowing that I was trying to write things other than my PhD, she kindly arranged for me to visit the camps.

A long-forgotten war, refugee camps run by women, though they were Islamic: it was just interesting enough for an editor to take a chance on. But it had to begin with the doctor.

He looked at me suspiciously. I explained that, with the risk of infection from open sores in Africa, I needed a steroid cream. He couldn't see a way to refuse me, and reluctantly wrote the prescription.

After a week in the refugee camps, then another driving around in the back of a stripped-down Land Rover with a squad of guerrillas, sleeping under the stars, spying on enemy positions with binoculars, drinking tiny glasses of strong tea, smoking fierce tobacco out of small bronze pipes, eating strange stews cooked over open fires, and coming under occasional artillery fire—we'd hear a pair of thuds somewhere in the distance, followed a few seconds later by two crashes or booms, depending on how far away the shells landed—I came back to life. I liked the danger, and sleeping rough, and living under open sky day and night. I made a sudden decision to hitchhike south across the desert.

The cream ran out in the course of a fiery eruption. But I was a young man. After years eczema-bound in libraries, I just had to have another taste of the globe and its star. I put up with the sores. I learned to let the hungry desert flies feast on them. I became inured to the horror of my skin. I was a traveler again, briefly, and wouldn't let my skin stop me. This was adventure, this was life, and it was all happening in the sunshine.

Along the way I heard about the old monk Père Charles de Foucauld, a former French army officer and Parisian bon vivant who was transformed by the desert into a seeker of solitude and silence. My journey turned into a half-baked pilgrimage as I took in the remote desert towns where a hundred years before Foucauld had built his hermitages. I tasted the silence in his old stone chambers and saw the bullet holes in the mortar from the shots that had killed him. He had befriended the "blue men" of the French Sahara, the Tuareg, and left behind a small contemplative order in the desert, the Little Brothers and Sisters of Jesus. It made unexpected sense: to forgo ordinary Western ways, to stake your life on the magnitude of the desert, on God's garden, as the Tuareg called it. The bare fact of life and death was somehow closer here. They said God kept the desert empty so there would be one place left on earth for him alone.

To live here felt like a kind of existential solution. I picked up Carlo Carretto's *Letters from the Desert*. He had been a party-going city dweller until one day the emptiness of his life overwhelmed him and he gave up everything to come to the desert, where he joined Foucauld's order.

I Sought and I Found, another of his books was called: his whole biography was there, in the title. Something about it kept calling to me, even after I traipsed back home to the mountainous thesis and my semi-functional half-life in the London rain.

"When a man is tired of London, he is tired of life," Dr. Johnson famously said 250 years ago. He was right, and soon, once again, I was both.

But help is always at hand. We just may not know where to look for it.

Stillness

FLORA LIVED IN A SMALL studio in an assisted-living complex on Primrose Hill. An old friend of my mum's, an elder from her Cambridge days, Flora had grown up in the Transylvanian mountains of Romania. In her early eighties now, she knew witchcraft and how to tell fortunes, and she had read all the Greek philosophers. Formerly married to a brilliant Athenian who had been a Cambridge philosophy professor, she had known many gifted people. She had suffered her share of catastrophe and come through. She was tough and tender both.

She understood me better than I did myself. She would listen to me, then pass down firm judgments, critical but accurate. She could see the past clearly, but also the future. She gave hope and stricture in equal measure, like the perfect teacher.

She was the first person to whom I told the whole story of the moment on the beach. When I did, her eyes lit up.

All she said was "Ah." But the air in the room changed. She

understood. She knew that what I described was real, and I could feel it. Then she asked me why I didn't start meditating.

I couldn't imagine how she had found her way to meditation. No one meditated in our world. But it had saved her life, she said. When, after many years, her husband left her for a young student, she had been utterly lost, alternately homicidal and suicidal at the betrayal by her great love. Somehow she found that to sit still each day, as Socrates had done, and Heraclitus and Pythagoras, offered a way to *be*, in the face of psychic and domestic disaster. Although you didn't move, it was a kind of path, and took you in a good direction. It could take you, in fact, on the journey of a lifetime, she said.

I trusted her but was dubious. But my old friend Peter meditated, too.

After Cambridge, Peter had traveled to the other side of the world to work in the music department of a university in Tonga. Three years later, back under the low English sky, he was now struggling to create a freelance life as a musician and composer, trying to get his musical projects off the ground. But instead of slouching disconsolately from library to library in search of a safety net, or from church to church in search of an intangible redemption, or berating his dad, Peter was vivacious and happy. Peter meditated.

He showed me a newspaper article on TM, Transcendental Meditation. The article described the state of crystal-clear wakefulness the writer had reached, in which the London streets had appeared as if dew-rinsed and freshly risen into existence. He'd felt decades of dust slough off his soul, and ordinary, everyday things appeared radiant.

Between that article and Peter and Flora—and the fact that

the TM people were offering a 90 percent discount for graduate students on the steep cost of the introductory course, and that they described meditation as a life tool for the busy, something that would help you in your career, not take you away from it, and that a famous Harvard professor had praised it to the skies—I decided I had little to lose. The Beatles had done it, after all, and look at their careers.

A TIDY MAN IN A gray suit was talking to a group of us in an upstairs room in an ordinary house in Marylebone. There were bankers, marketing and retail people, a lawyer, a graphic designer—regular, respectable people—listening rapt in the room. Not a bunch of flakes. People with real jobs and lives.

The benefits of meditation are clear now, in the early twenty-first century. MRI and EEG scans, blood tests, ECGs and EKGs, and decades of fast-growing neurological research have put it beyond question: pursued diligently, meditation can make us calmer, more attentive, happier, and kinder. Simply to sit still for forty minutes each day—it helps. And there's science to prove it.

But back in 1987 people were suspicious. Was it a cult? Was it dangerous? It was impressive that the TM crew had filled a room with people who looked much more like they had their lives together than I did.

We all showed up for ninety minutes each evening for a week. Gradually, through the week, we were introduced to the practice of sitting still. On the last evening, one by one we filed into a private room where we made an offering of fruit to an altar and were each given our own private mantra—a "sacred syllable" to repeat to ourselves as we meditated.

If I had had any idea what a can of worms I was opening up, what a long road I was setting out on—I guess I would have proceeded anyway.

London rain pinged on the black windowpane behind the altar, and the windows of the houses across the street glowed yellow in the night, and the Euston Road roared quietly in the distance while the trainer and I, two Englishmen, sat on chairs whispering a Sanskrit word to each other, quieter and quieter, until it was a barely audible whisper. Then finally it became silent, a thought, a murmur within my own mind. Never again would I say it out loud. That was the rule. It seemed almost childish, but your mantra was for you alone, and its magic properties were sealed by your silence.

THE INSTRUCTOR HAD MADE ONE thing clear: for TM to work, it had to be done for twenty minutes twice a day, morning and evening. You had to agree to that or you might as well not bother. Sometimes it would be blissful and calm, other times it would be hard not to keep checking the clock. But you would do it regardless.

I agreed. I would do as he said. And I did.

I had anticipated dismal struggles with myself, but right away something else happened. As soon as I started doing it daily, I slept like never before.

The first night, after the evening meditation, I slept twelve hours straight. I woke in the morning disoriented, confused. I did my morning sit, brewed coffee, ate toast, packed books into my bag, and walked downstairs to make my way to the Tube and college. No sooner had I opened the front door than a wave of exhaustion hit me. I slumped against the doorframe. For a second I actually fell asleep on my feet, right there in the hall, leaning against the doorpost.

Something wasn't right. Maybe I was coming down with the flu. I went back upstairs and sat on the sofa to try to figure out what was up, if it was anything serious, what it might be. Next thing I knew it was noon. I had fallen asleep right where I was for four hours.

My head was heavy and my bones ached. I had to be getting a cold. I lay on the couch, staring at the ceiling, and discovered that I was hungry. I went into the kitchen and made myself a sandwich and a cup of tea. My bones eased as I ate and drank. By now it was past one o'clock, but there were still some solid hours left in the day, so I put my bag over my shoulder and went down to the front door to try going to college again.

This time I had gone a few steps down the street when the same thing happened. A dizzying, momentous tide of fatigue slapped me in the face. I could barely walk. I staggered to the nearest tree and leaned against it, afraid I might fall over.

There had been press recently about TM helping with ME, or chronic fatigue syndrome, the so-called yuppie disease. It had been all over the newspapers. Meditation was curing ME all over London. But for a terrified moment I wondered if the meditation had some strange connection to the affliction and might actually be *giving* me ME.

Whatever the case, there was no way I was getting to the Tube station like this. I turned around and staggered back to the flat. It was all I could do to get the key in the lock and clamber upstairs. I collapsed on the sofa again, hoping to get my bearings.

Next thing I knew it was dark outside. Night. I had slept right through the afternoon.

Peter came round and we did a meditation together, then ate some supper, and I told him about my strange day of sleepiness.

"Don't worry," he said. "If you're tired, you're tired. What else can you do? Rest. You're probably just paying off a sleep debt."

The TM teacher had mentioned this possibility. Many of us were carrying around "sleep debts," he said, from years of under-sleeping, and he warned that we might find ourselves needing extra sleep the first few days.

In my case, I spent most of that first week flat on my back, averaging twenty hours a night.

It made a kind of sense. Human skin is thin: we're anxious, reactive mammals. But eczematous skin offers even less protection and is itself a problem. My nervous system had probably been in a stress response for years. At last, in the embrace of stillness and the balm of the mantra, it could unwind as the meditation engaged the "relaxation response," and body and mind could start to restore themselves.

The strange thing wasn't just that the sleep debt came in with such force, but that it cleared just as suddenly. On the seventh morning, I woke up, made breakfast, and had coffee, fully expecting to need to stagger straight back to bed, but instead I felt clear, luminous, refreshed in a way I couldn't remember feeling since being a boy—actually, since I couldn't remember when.

I got dressed and went outside. A soft rain was falling in the street. It was beautiful. I remembered how I had loved the rain as a boy—rain was tender, soulful, and could make a day soft and beautiful, a time for reflection, for deep conversation over coffee. Today the city streets had a somber gleam to them, and the trees dripped darkly, and the mood was wonderful and rich, as if the whole city were somehow made of tin and had some hidden inner energy of its own that expressed itself in the beauty of the houses, trees, and people, hunched under scarves and umbrellas, and the scooters and cars that hissed and purred past. What a place to live. For a moment it seemed magical just to be alive.

THE OLD BOOK DIDN'T NEED to take years to finish. I could see that now. I decided I would roll up my sleeves and tackle it head-on. When the term ended I took a train down to the Pyrenees and hiked to a village just over the Spanish border where you could stay in a farmhouse for five pounds a night, including breakfast and dinner. I smoked up a fog of Ducados in my room and vowed that I would not walk down the track out of the village until the pack on my back contained the completed manuscript. After years of dithering, I couldn't carry it around unfinished any longer.

Each evening I walked around the ramparts of the old walled village, watching swallows skimming the stone walls, the young couples canoodling, the elderly couples strolling arm in arm, and two weeks later it was done.

Back in London, Flora insisted that I go ahead at once and send chapters out to literary agents from the *Writers' and Artists' Yearbook*. She said she wouldn't speak to me until I had. With trepidation I followed her orders, and two of the agencies got back in touch. I settled with one, gave them the rest of the book, and assumed it would be music from here on. But to my surprise, several publishers took the trouble to read the book and turn it down.

That threw me. I was twenty-five. I'd never thought I'd reach that age like this: I'd either be dead or published, I had fondly imagined, and instead was neither.

MR. MORBID AND MR. FUN—in the stillness of meditation, they started to meet. It was some kind of alchemy too deep for my understanding, but a more real me began to crystallize in the solution of deep quiet. Now and then, anyway.

Meditation helped with patience. The atlas of the eczematic life has not the smallest shire called Patience. Yet once I started meditating, weirdly, I found I could sit still. Itches would dissolve. I knew how to sit on my rear. It was amazing.

I went on a TM retreat, held in a rambling country house in Surrey. Mostly we stayed in our rooms, doing "rounds" of yoga and meditation, and slept a lot, meeting for meals and a class each evening, where a solemn man explained the various levels of "cosmic consciousness" on a whiteboard. Most of us yawned and dozed through it. We were more interested in the sleep.

Often while meditating, after a few minutes of restlessness a sense of soothing would come on, as if I were being salved inside and out. In neurophysiological terms, this was the parasympathetic nervous system engaging, turning down the dial on the stress response. I had lived with a dysregulated nervous system for so long that I hadn't considered the possibility that maybe the anxiety I ordinarily felt wasn't 100 percent necessary.

TM was called "transcendental" because every so often you'd find yourself in a strange peace where everything went quiet. There was a clarity, a humming stillness, as if all the clocks had stopped and there was nothing going on in the mind except a calm and minute awareness. You were "transcending," they said: a state of rest deeper than sleep, yet where consciousness remained.

It felt a bit like the old "cloud of unknowing" that I had tasted at night as a boy, and it happened more regularly over time. It provided a relief against which to view the dramas of life, an alternative against which to measure things, and offered the nervous system yet deeper rest.

✿

I WAS DILIGENT WITH THE daily meditation. One thing TM taught was a little self-discipline. Often I sat with a heavy ache in the chest, but I sat.

I went for one of the free consultations the TM center offered and asked the instructor about that ache I had been experiencing. He suggested we meditate together and initiated a session in the small, quiet room where we were talking. As soon as I started to feel it, I should tell him.

I did.

"But we've barely begun," he said.

"Well, I can feel it," I said.

"What's it like?"

"It's like an iron bar in my chest," I said.

He told me to drop the mantra and just let myself feel the sensation. When it eased, I should pick up the mantra again.

For much of the next few months I found myself sitting with the chest pain, waiting for it to clear. Sometimes it would, and I'd get to the mantra, and sometimes it wouldn't. It wasn't easy, but at times I could just let it be.

At some point, an odd thought occurred to me. Was it possible this strange pain was an emotion, that I was having a feeling and didn't even know it?

SOMETIMES FLORA WOULD MENTION PSYCHOTHERAPY, and tell me how certain friends of hers had been helped by it. Perhaps she was sowing a seed.

One day I was walking in the park with a friend, a beautiful, solemn flautist who happened to be in therapy. She said, "You're a talker, Henry. But you don't really talk. You use talk to hide."

I was silently outraged and hurt, because I fancied her.

I asked her what she meant.

"The mind is complicated," she said. "We don't know what's happening in our psyches, none of us do. It's called the unconscious, and it can make us unhappy. But there's hope. We just need to talk to someone."

"Talk, like how?"

"I don't know—talk."

"You mean—to a shrink?"

She drew in a breath.

"A psychologist, yes."

My heart sank, but not as deeply as it once might have. Meditation was mellowing me. I could hear talk of a cure for the wounded mind without said wounded mind reacting against it. For one thing, it might improve my chances with her.

A few days later, I called to ask for her therapist's number.

HARVEY HAD BEEN A TV sex therapist in California before he got struck off the state register and relocated to London. California hadn't been ready for the radicalism of his message, we groupies whispered to one another.

There was a group of us, lost twenty-somethings, who met in his basement office in Royal Oak every Saturday morning. "We're helping you give yourself the parenting you never got as a child," Harvey used to tell us. In the roundabout ways he prescribed, we were all trying to do that.

Along with the expected sofas and armchairs, his office had two large-screen TVs, several VCRs, and a wall of pornographic videos. Anger and sex, Harvey used to say: they were the tools of the trade. Two real things you could work with.

Harvey had been on TV in England too. Channel 4 had made a show about a young Scottish racing driver in therapy with him. The racer had this problem. He drove in Formula 4000, and most of the races he'd be out in front. Then, time after time, he'd mess up in the final lap and end up not placing. He sabotaged himself: that was the diagnosis. Deep down he felt he didn't deserve to win.

There is a legendary moment in the show. During a therapy session, the racer, quietly goaded by Harvey, leaps off the couch, flies across the room, and pulls Harvey to the floor. The producer jumps into the frame and tugs him off, you can hear the cameraman shouting in the background, and the sound guy leaps in, too, and it was all on film.

That was the turning point in the young man's therapy. The moment he let his rage out, he could no longer deny his pain. On-screen he collapsed, sobbing, while Harvey straightened his glasses and put his hand on the client's shaking back. The driver went on to become British GT champion.

One day I tore Harvey's door off its hinges. Instead of trying to stop me, he sat and watched. He was very pleased.

He had been goading me. "You're basically a piece of shit," he kept murmuring in his mellow Californian tones. He was one-eighth Menominee and had a soft Native timbre to his voice.

I had been holding a beanbag at the time, tossing it back and forth from hand to hand ever more vigorously, slumping deeper and deeper in my chair as I listened to him. Then, before I knew what I was doing, I was on my feet, staggering to the door. Everything was bright. I stumbled up and grabbed the handle, tugging on it futilely, then pounding it with my fists.

A door. Why a door?

I was white-hot inside. I could barely walk. I was a two-year-old. I pushed against the door, I hit it, pummeled it, then fell, got up again, shaky on my legs, and beat harder, rattled the handle, tugged it, fell again. Then up and at it, then down on the floor in a raging, hopeless heap.

This went on for a while. Harvey said nothing. He wanted to see what would happen. In the end I pulled the door down, then tore it to pieces.

"Good therapy," Harvey said, and he got out his Polaroid camera to commemorate the two of us standing on top of the heap, me holding the remains of the door handle like a trophy.

ECZEMA CAN MAKE YOU STRANGE. You can't help being a bit odd. You're not fully socialized.

The incident with the door became my doorway. I could no longer pretend. Whatever my parents had done or not done, it had hurt. Dad was an amazing man, but not an amazing dad. He was half right about being a bastard. He hadn't provided all a boy needed by way of love. Mum had done her best, but her own early history cast its shadow, and the marital circumstances had been so hard.

That afternoon, after clearing the rubble into trash bags and vacuuming the carpet and figuring out a payment plan for a new door, I strode off down Queensway with my blood pumping like it hadn't in years. The world fell back into its proper place. Streets, buildings, cars, even people—they were not menacing any longer, not a threat. They were neutral. They were not at war with me. Until that moment, I hadn't realized for how long I'd thought they were.

Why so much rage at a door? Had something happened to me as a toddler? Had my parents shut me in a room, unable to bear the itching and scratching that kept me awake? Aged two, three, four, I'd hurled myself at the door hoping to be released?

I remembered that state I used to go into. Nights on the slab of pruritus, I'd scratch myself to distraction. Having opened the shawl of skin, I'd drift off into the cloud of unknowing. Had that been some kind of post-fury daze?

Somewhere in the drama of the therapy, I noticed that the iron bar in my chest had dissolved.

Years later, I found some lines of the Buddha. He probably wasn't talking about the same iron bar I had known, but still:

Even those with a dart stuck in the breast
Piercing their heart moment by moment—
Even these here, stricken, get to sleep;
So why should I not get to sleep
When my dart has been drawn out?

ॐ

UNDER PETER'S URGING, I HAD been playing music again. He had formed a world music band and needed musicians. The band got busy and started touring. I also started playing with a calypso band, Homer's Odyssey, who performed weekly at the Kensal Rise Calypso Tent, in West London.

The "Tent" was an informal nightclub that took over a working men's club every Friday night during the weeks before the Notting Hill Carnival. Homer's Odyssey was the house band. They were named after the bandleader, Len Homer. They played for the West Indian community, people who felt homesick for their island music, and lit up their evenings with old Caribbean rhythms. I was one of the few white people in the calypso scene, and they welcomed me in. We were sloppy and under-rehearsed, but the irresistible beat of the percussion section kept us on track, and Homer was happy to have recruited a white boy. It happened from time to time. "Spice it up a bit," he said.

We horn men played at the back of the stage while a series of men and women dressed in glitter and sequins trooped on, one by one, to perform their current hit.

Golden Cockerel, who wore a golden suit, had a serious song about world peace, with a haunting melody and scansion that worked ingeniously.

> Let me tell you, girl,
> in this whole crazy world
> I will not find rest
> until there is forgiveness.

It went on to take that year's Carnival Crown.

Cockerel worked as a bus driver and told me he had bought the song for £250.

"Bought it?"

"Man, you think they give it away?"

"Who?"

"Them writers, man. They need their money, too."

People would sit in rows discreetly sipping rum and Coke from plastic cups. They were a well-behaved audience, uproarious when called to be, stomping, clapping, and laughing as appropriate, but orderly.

After the show one night, Len Homer handed me a guitar. "Know any songs?"

I knew some Cat Stevens and Leonard Cohen. We were sitting round a table in the empty hall—a couple of band members, a singer or two, and Len. I started in on a lugubrious Cohen number, and in the half dark, without looking, I felt the light withdraw from the faces at the table.

"Hold on." I stopped myself. "I've got another." And I began an old calypso, "Big Bamboo," which I had taught myself from a record.

I strummed away, fast and furious, and sang in a high-pitched imitation of the recording I had at home. They smiled, especially at the song's chorus, full of double entendres about bamboos and bananas.

"Yes man!" someone cried.

"Yeah!" they laughed.

When I got to the end, Len looked at me. "Where you learn that?"

"From a record."

"We get you up on that stage, man. You ready? If you ready, we get the band ready. A white boy singing calypso? We call you Mighty English."

Once or twice over the coming weeks I was pulled from my place at the back and marched up to the front to sing. The crowd chuckled at the right moments, but it wasn't the hit Homer had imagined. Still, those brief appearances led to something.

Without my knowledge, Homer had been in touch with a friend in Trinidad who managed a band, and they had offered me a spot during the following year's Carnival season. I couldn't go—it was out of the question—but what a thought.

I WAS WRESTLING WITH THE doctoral thesis, still trying to get work as a journalist.

I had been working on an article about a record company in Wales, and met with the company's directors a few times to interview them. They offered me a job. I hadn't wanted to admit it to myself, still less to my supervisor, but the more notes I amassed for the thesis, the more confused I got. I could see now that the PhD was likely forever beyond me, and it was time to give it up.

I arrived at the company's headquarters in Wales so febrile with itches that they put me to bed in one of their cottages for a week, until the attack died down and I was able to present myself in the office.

I had been working there a few months when the old literary agent tracked me down. A new editor at one of the publishers to whom she had sent my manuscript had found it in a cupboard and wanted to meet. A few phone calls later, it was settled. Not only would they buy the book, but they also wanted a second, unwritten one, sight unseen. A two-book deal. A grand old American publisher was chipping in, too. I just had to come up with an idea for the next one.

It was obvious; Len Homer's idea: playing in a band in Trinidad. I could busk my way round the Caribbean, do a modern-day version of what Laurie Lee had done in Spain.

I HAD A VIVID DAYDREAM: an angel reached into my chest and pulled out a scowling homunculus, and carried off the little demon as it screamed in frustration. Exorcised at last. I had a dream: I was up in a declivity on the Welsh moors with a phosphorescent ball floating just over my head. "You can touch it," an old man told me. I reached out and held the ball in my hands, and he said, "That's the moon, you know."

The change of location, the new job, the therapy, the publishers, quitting the PhD: they had all happened once I took up meditation. Was it possible that just sitting still twice a day could bring order to a disordered psychophysiology, and regulate a dysregulated life? On top of that, in fits and starts, my skin was getting better.

Not that it was a magical cure. The same way sight can evolve only in a world with light, so eczema had coevolved in a favorable psychic climate, one rich in despair and anguish. Skin and mind had co-created their own ecosystem: itch and pain in the dermis, frustration and misery in the psyche. As the emotions began to reckon with themselves in meditation, and to clear, so, too, the eczema—even though it might have been in part an armor-plated defense against those very feelings—began to discover it needed them in order to exist. Without them, it became less intense, less necessary. It had less ground to stand on, less atmosphere to breathe. And as it showed signs of giving up its old outposts and fastnesses, the duress on the psyche, the skin-created stress on the nervous system, also eased. It was a two-way street. Back and forth the positive ricochet went, skin to mind and back.

At least maybe that's how it worked. I'm trying to explain something no doctor has yet adequately accounted for. Just as eczema has a "multifactorial etiology," it also has multifactorial cures. Yet surely, among the factors, getting a little happier had a part to play. And daily stillness was the crucible where the culture of well-being grew stronger.

A YEAR ON AND WE had made up, Dad and I. We simply never talked about the difficult evening. It disappeared under the waves.

Every so often I had lunch with him at college.

I'd try to talk about meditation. He'd ask. As a forward-thinking academic, he had a penchant for things American, and meditation was popular over there. He was by no means out of date or out of touch. I thought he'd approve of it.

"So, boychick, tell us a bit about it. I mean, what *is* meditation? Of course I've heard of it, we all have, but what *is* it?"

I'd begin with the solid stuff. "You have to sit still twice a day," I told him, "morning and evening. You have a—" I was about to say the word "mantra" but thought better of it. "Basically you quiet your mind," I said.

"Quiet your mind? That sounds nice. How do you do that?"

I felt my face heat up, and a strange coolness in my chest.

"Well," I tried. "You pay attention to things."

"Things? What things?"

"Like your breath, for example."

"Ah, I see," he said, nodding as if interested, then yawning. And his eyes, large, lucent behind their lenses, were already glazing over.

"The Beatles did it?" I tried, hoping to stir some residue of his Beatnik days, when he'd played jazz trumpet in a Soho club and smoked Turkish cigarettes. Surely he knew about the Beatles meditating.

"Yes, I remember vaguely. It was all the rage for a while. Some Indian bloke with a private plane, wasn't it? Went right over my head, I'm afraid."

And with that, we'd make our way over to the dining hall.

Around Dad, it wasn't just that I couldn't explain meditation; I felt I could no longer understand it myself. His world was one where you didn't need such devices, where you were already okay.

❧

HARVEY USED TO CHIDE ME for having written a travel book. "That's just a holiday," he'd say. "When are you going to do the real work and write your novel?"

I knew he was right. Years earlier I had dashed off three entire novels, while living leprously in London, and had settled on a big one, a multigenerational chronicle of the braiding of two families—one of Jewish immigrants, one of British professionals. Along the way it would open up our own family closet and shake out some old bones.

Mostly it would be about them, the parents. They were interesting. Dad's life was an immigrant folktale: a legendary childhood in a Soho tenement teeming with tailors, amid the clatter of Singers and Frister & Rossmanns. He gets away, to the dreaming spires of a fabled university. Mum's story was another kind of fairy tale: sad orphan, abandoned on an airfield by her aviatrix mother, scooped up by the starched sleeve of the nanny, passed among relatives.

If I plunged into the sea of ancestral legacies, perhaps I'd find a magic key and pull it, shining, from the waters, and unlock all our well-being, even my own. Unjustified, crossbred, experiment gone wrong, I would trace things back to the wrongness at the root, and put them right.

And there was the Cold War. It was a kind of family joke. Not only had Dad been a spy, but so had our mum. She had been trained even more deeply in spycraft—how to tail someone, how to lose a tail, plan a drop—and it had been *she* who recruited *him*, and he never even knew. Now *there* was a book. Why hadn't Dad written *that* for his bestseller? Come to think of it, why didn't I?

It was still the tail end of the age of the novel, when a novel was a life's defining act. Tolstoy, Eliot, Austen, Lawrence, Conrad, Dostoyevsky, Maugham—wherever you turned, there the writers were, defining their times with their novels. Proust, Rushdie, Naipaul, with their single great works, and Fielding, Woolf, James, Melville, Hardy, Bellow. If you were a young man with a head full of literature, there was nothing better you could do with your time than write a novel.

TRAVEL. PUBLICATION. NEW FRIENDS. NEW projects. It was exhilarating. And Harvey had moved me into a new phase of "cognitive restructuring," where I had to unearth negative thought patterns and challenge them.

I had a diagnosis now: dysthymia. Persistent, low-grade,

shame-based depression. It was tricky, because one of its symptoms was a denial of symptoms prompted by shame at the
symptoms—the shame itself being one of the symptoms. Clev-
erly circular. But the new cognitive-behavioral approach was actually helping. I never knew what diabolical habits of mind I'd
had. It turned out that as long as I could remember, I'd been
thinking myself into misery. I beat myself up, put myself down,
*should*ed myself to death, catastrophized and awfulized. I was
an inveterate *must*urbator: *I must do this, that must work out,* et
cetera. As I exposed and gave up these habitual cognitions, to be
alive became stranger and more interesting.

One day as I was leaving the flat, I caught sight of my face
in the mirror by the door, and it was as if I'd never seen myself
before. Who was this person? It reminded me of Derek Walcott's
poem where he meets himself in the mirror:

> You will greet yourself arriving
> at your own door, in your own mirror
> and each will smile at the other's welcome ...
> You will love again the stranger who was your self.

I took a stroll round the neighborhood. It was a sunny day,
and I felt I was getting a true grasp on life. I was wearing my
headphones, listening to a Peter Tosh song. "Here though I trod
through this valley I will fear no evil ... 'Cause I know Jah guide,
Jah guide I through this valley." I didn't believe in Jah, or God,
but what I heard in Tosh's voice was not disembodied faith; it
was hope—hope not about specific things. Hope itself.

Up the street a big puddle had flooded a gutter. The sun was
out and shone on the dull water with a brilliance that pierced

my heart. Out of nowhere I remembered the old moment on the beach, when all existence had appeared as one single great venture.

Just as I neared the little flood, a taxi swerved to avoid a cyclist, its wheels plunging into the puddle. Before I realized what was happening, a dazzling fan of water smacked me in the chest, snapping me out of the reverie. For a moment I felt a heat of anger rise as the taxi growled away. But then I thought, *Big deal*, and turned to go back to the flat to change.

A week later, having spent several years trying to come home, I left England.

Part Two

The Ox and the Mosquito

Lawrence Land

I'M IN NEW MEXICO. IN my late twenties, peripatetic, no longer living from flat to flat but from country to country, I have a
life, kind of, as a travel writer. The eczema can be touchy about
new climates, but on the whole the meditation keeps me ahead
of the old fumaroles, and I seldom need the powerful Dermovate
cream I like to keep in my bag.

I haven't hit it big, but it's the early nineties and travel writing is popular. Some books sell phenomenally well, and the publishers are ready to sign off on generous advances for anything
they think might capture a piece of the market. I'm living off
their optimism.

I like to think this isn't so strange. Isherwood, Maugham,
Conrad, D. H. Lawrence, T. E. Lawrence, Huxley—you could
go on and on with the list of English writer/drifters who lived
abroad. Plus I'm Jewish, sort of. The Jew wanders. And this is
my economic reality: sizable checks arrive from time to time,

and to keep them coming I have to go places. And I have friends who live like this: Nick Danziger, a tireless adventurer, and Pico Iyer, who also dabbles in meditation and chronicles brilliantly his hopscotch life around the globe.

After leaving London, I spent a year in Trinidad and Colombia, playing with bands in Port of Spain and Cali. I came to know a different Caribbean from the one people imagine—of mildewed cement and hot apartments, of cheap diners and factory lots that stage massive outdoor parties, or fetes, of dingy basement nightclubs, of hardworking musicians driving worn-down Mazdas and wishing sometimes they could get to bed before four in the morning.

The eczema has continued to ease up. I still can't definitively say how or why, but, like some poison-soaked mantle in a fairy tale that had been draped on my shoulders long ago by a wicked witch, it has lifted. For sure, the load on the nervous system is less these days, and is different. I've left home, for one thing. And meditation continues to calm the nervous system, to the point where, with old cycles of pain and itch interrupted, I can be consistently busy with other things: something like that. And maybe those brutal cures over the years actually worked, and did clear some malignancy. And the skin likes the freedom—from office work, family, duty. It likes bright and allergy-free climates, though it can also be touchy about foreign suns. Sometimes it rebels at a new place, and after a day or two of loitering with my notebook, the knuckles on my fingers roughen and stiffen, the bubble wrap appears on my wrists, and my flanks turn into sandpaper. When really bad, the sandpaper wraps the whole body, and it all starts to shine like a burgundy varnish.

But even when the eczema is active, if I'm out in the world I mind less, as in those old times as a kid when friends and I slept by the river and meandered through thickets and woods with packs on our backs, sleeping out under the stars like tramps, as we liked to think. And it clears up soon enough anyway. The norm is health now.

Travel, books, articles: I've gone from being a leprous loner to acceptable. Editors routinely turn my ideas down, but not always. For the next several years I wouldn't have a home and wouldn't mind. My skin wouldn't, either. I was fortunate, in work, travel, pen, skin.

I'M IN NEW MEXICO NOW to write about D. H. Lawrence. New Mexico was the only place Lawrence ever owned a home, and he said that nowhere else "changed him from the outside"—a confusing statement, given his childhood on the farmland near Nottingham, and the landscapes of Sardinia, the Tyrol, Australia, and Mexico, all of which he wrote about in ways that showed they affected him deeply. He was sensitive to place. His best work, I thought, was precisely his writing about place. His life had been a litany of places that changed him. In fact, the reason I was a travel writer myself was that I had read Lawrence in my teens, and his writing about place had burned a hole in my imagination. When I went abroad at eighteen, it was his writing that inspired me to try my hand at it.

He lit up when he wrote about New Mexico, summoning its land with vivid sentences whose ink would be forever wet, which conjured the blood-red mountains with an energy that made you feel you were discovering them yourself, firsthand.

I was supposed to be writing about vestiges of Lawrence's time in New Mexico. It was quickly clear that there were just three vestiges, all well known: his old ranch in the mountains above Taos, his oil paintings kept in a dilapidated *fonda* on Taos Plaza, and the rambling adobe home of his patroness, Mabel Dodge Luhan, where he and his wife, Frieda, put up for several months. It didn't add up to a book. So I started driving around the state, visiting Indian pueblos, tribal dances, meeting people.

ALONG THE WAY I MET Natalie Goldberg, a writer who hailed from Long Island, Jewish, with a biography full of Zen meditation and a roster of bestselling books. She liked that I was a writer from England, and half Jewish. To her a half Jew was a Jew. We hit it off. She rented me the basement of her house in Santa Fe, and we'd meet for meals upstairs in her kitchen.

Natalie specialized in writing about writing. She wrote about it in a way that made it inviting, challenging, and thoroughly worthwhile regardless of results. It was liberating, and her books were popular, inspiring thousands of Americans to try their hand at it. She was credited with starting a national craze for filling notebooks in coffee shops, and had catalyzed a number of significant literary careers. And she herself wrote with a lucidity and beauty that was captivating.

Her approach came from Zen. She called it "writing practice." Zen was popular in American letters. Allen Ginsberg, Jack Kerouac, Gary Snyder, Peter Matthiessen—many writers made no secret of their affiliation with Zen. Natalie was another. "First thought, best thought" was the maxim. Get the page covered, outrun the internal censor.

There was something about her—a stillness, a quiet radiance. I'd never known anything exactly like it. As if some kind of jewel shone inside her. She was a devoted Zen student, and I suspected it had something to do with that. She talked openly about "enlightenment." Growing up in England in the 1970s, I'd occasionally heard the word cross people's lips, but rarely since then.

I'd seen something like that inner light in Gustavo, the Colombian priest who visited us when I was a child. It shone in him. He said the poor had a joy the rich never knew, and I thought about the ease I had sensed in people in the Andes.

Years later, far away in New Mexico, I had now met someone else who, like him, believed in enlightenment. Where I came from, there was hope of making things less awful, but that there might be a fundamental resolution to human existence? That had been off the cards since 1969, since Altamont, since "Get Back," since the Beatles broke up, if not since the birth of Newton's mechanical universe, or since back in the Garden of Eden. There was something called the human condition, after all, the fall of man. It meant you couldn't be happy. Not really. We were stuck with ourselves, our mortality, our original sin.

I remembered listening to my brother's rock albums in my early teens: shaggy figures in bell-bottoms singing about the road to freedom; Van Morrison praising the moon and Rembrandt, and some place called San Anselmo. Music in those days came from a land of liberation. No one knew where it was, but perhaps it still existed, maybe even in New Mexico.

ONE DAY NATALIE AND I were sitting on the porch overlooking her small lawn, enclosed by an adobe wall that was just beginning to glow as the New Mexico afternoon thickened toward evening. Cottonwood trees with long silvery leaves overhung the neighborhood like willows, silent in the late air. A cat sprang onto the broad, rounded top of the wall and sat down to lick its paws.

I watched the cat. The trees, the shadows, the waning light, the quiet sounds of a neighborhood concluding its day, and the cat fluffing itself up and resting—all caught me with their beauty. Things seemed to go slower when you were around Natalie. They took the time to show themselves to you. It reminded me of how in my teen years, as an aspiring poet, I'd learned to see beauty in ordinary things. A white cat sheltering from rain under a dark bush. A streetlamp illuminating stucco at night. The hiss of traffic on a wet street heard from a second-floor window.

Natalie opened up a book on Zen and read aloud from it. It was a passage by Dogen Zenji, a Japanese Zen master from the thirteenth century.* In her slow, Jewish New Yorkese (a "Lorne Guyland" accent, as Martin Amis called it), she read:

> Mountains do not lack the qualities of mountains. Therefore they always abide in ease and always walk. You should examine in detail this quality of the mountains walking. Mountains' walking is just like human walking. Accordingly, do not doubt mountains' walking even though it does not look the same as human walking.

She put the book down and looked around, a little dazed, and said, "Wow," shaking her head. "Isn't he mind-blowing?"

I hummed noncommittally. I couldn't make head or tail of

---

* Dogen (pronounced with a hard *g*; 1200–1253) founded the Soto school in Japan, the largest Zen sect.

what I'd just heard. Was it supposed to be nonsense, like Edward
Lear or something? *Mountains walking?*

I asked her for the book and took a look myself. The chapter was called "The Mountains and Rivers Sutra." Whatever that
meant. I reread the paragraph to myself. Then she asked me to
read it out loud, so I did.

I couldn't understand it at all, and said so. She said she
couldn't, either, but loved it anyway.

So it was nonsense. And why did one "mountains walking"
have no apostrophe, while the others did? Was it a misprint? Or
deliberate? But that passage lodged in my mind like a burr. It
was nonsense you couldn't quite shake off. At least I couldn't.
All that evening it vaguely disturbed me, and the next day. How
could someone say something like that? But also, why couldn't I
forget about it?

I was making a cup of tea in the kitchen a few days later
when suddenly I had a thought: What if the monk Dogen had
been talking about what I had seen on the beach years earlier?
What if that moment and his strange paragraph were connected?

As soon as I thought of it, I felt it had to be right. What
else could make sense of Dogen's apparent nonsense? But the
beach moment would make complete sense of it. Not that I could
exactly explain why. But everything had been there, all at once,
in the empty fire I had seen, that single seething, ghostly reality
in which all time and space were present. Anything was possible there—*everything* was possible. How could it not be, if the
universe were one single fabric and one was made of that fabric
oneself?

I felt dizzy and mildly disoriented. Was I starting to understand something at last? My heart was beating hard, my

blood was up. The beach, the sunlight on the ocean, the sand, the joy, the fire, the love I'd felt then—all re-coalesced in sense memory. I remembered the feeling of life being fulfilled, how afterwards I had been ready to die.

Could it be that that revelation was a key to this strange man Dogen? And if so, and if Dogen had been a Zen master, then what did it have to do with Zen? It hit me: Zen and that moment were connected! That was what Zen specialized in.

Was that really possible?

I told Natalie I wanted to know more about Zen.

"So why don't you just do it?" she asked. "Zen isn't a matter of knowing. It's a practice, it's something you do."

I was okay with that. "So how do I do it?"

I HAD BOUGHT AN OLD bicycle, and the next day I rode up a long dirt road on the east side of town to a small square building beside a little arroyo, a dry streambed. The building was a zendo. A man, a friend of Natalie's, was waiting outside.

He was called Robert Winson and was a Zen priest: crop-headed but otherwise normal-looking, no robes, vestments, or paraphernalia. Just an ordinary guy. A few years later, still in his forties, he would die, leaving behind a young widow and a daughter. It was a strange death, in that a few months before it he had complained of not being able to sit in Zen meditation anymore. He had given his adult life to Zen and suddenly he could no longer do it, though apparently in good health. Then his intestines started to bleed and he rapidly declined.

"Natalie says you want to learn zazen," he said.

"Zen," I corrected him.

"Well, Zen is zazen. *Za-zen* means 'sitting Zen.' It's what we do."

I felt uneasy. Was this the right thing to be doing after all? What about my TM? Was I abandoning TM if I tried Zen? I hadn't even thought about that until now. Could I somehow do both? Did it matter if I stopped TM, if I was taking up another kind of meditation?

He unlocked a door and we crossed a flagstone courtyard with a Tibetan stone stupa in the middle and entered a dark room at the back.

It was a nice room. It hit you immediately: a peace about it. It was pretty much square, made out of thick adobe, like most of Santa Fe, and was cool and quiet. There was no furniture, the whole space bare except for a row of black mats lined up around the walls, about a dozen of them, each with a small black cushion in the middle.

The room ought to have felt spartan. Instead it felt thick with peace, with restfulness.

A small Buddha made of wood sat on an altar with a candle. As Robert lit the candle and made a bow to the altar, I noticed a shaving nick on the back of his scalp. Then he pulled out two of the black cushions.

There wasn't much to zazen. He showed me different possible positions for the legs, and I settled on what he called "quarter lotus." He taught me the correct alignment of the spine, and the way to hold my hands in my lap, and told me to start counting my breaths in sequences of ten. And that was it.

"Nothing else?" I asked.

"Not really," he said. "That's about it."

We did it for fifteen minutes.

It was strange: it wasn't that it was a marvelous thing to be doing. Yet it was enjoyable. Though also scary, as if you didn't know what might come at you next. I was still a moody guy, and sitting there like that, with nothing to do but watch my breathing, I felt exposed. A mood might come swinging in anytime. Yet there was something unusual about sitting that way: it was almost as though you were doing something, like driving a boat, perhaps. There wasn't quite nothing to do. Yet you also weren't *quite* doing anything. So you weren't quite doing something, yet you weren't quite doing nothing.

As soon as we walked out of the little temple afterwards, into the peaceful sunlight of the New Mexico morning, I knew it was what I had to do.

There was fear, and longing, and hope, and a vague promise, all while sitting. But those are abstract words. As I walked away down the path into the trees and down a drop into the little gulch of the stream along which ran the track where I had left my bike, it came to me that what I had just tasted was the reality of being alive. It was frightening, as it should be. Normally, I realized, I pulled away from the bare fact of being alive. I didn't know how not to. But now I did. It was zazen. Meditation in the Zen style. It somehow was no surprise that the other form of meditation I had been doing did not offer this kind of taste. The TM was restorative, ameliorative, medicinal almost. It helped you relax and sleep and restore. But this zazen—it didn't seem to be interested in those things. Instead, without any deliberation on its part, it simply let you know what it was to be alive. Yet at the same time, you could tell that you had barely touched the surface of what it had to offer. It was as if a great ball of energy were spinning just under the surface, and it had let you graze its surface with the tip of the nail of your little finger. There was more, much more.

✿

THAT WAS MY START IN Zen. Had I not met Natalie, had I not heard the passage of Dogen, had the door to an intimate sense of being alive not happened to open just then, I might never have left the quiet balm of TM.

I began to do zazen daily. Over the weeks I grew to love it: a sense of clarity, a watery quality to everything, would come on. Zen was done with the eyes open, which made one's sense of the world while meditating more vivid. I'd feel a warmth, a pressure in my chest. Sometimes, for no reason, I'd start crying. Sometimes a strange wind seemed to riffle through me and through the surroundings as I sat, reminding me of Sappho's famous line about love shaking her the way the wind shakes the oak trees on the mountainside. It was as if being in New Mexico, and sitting like this every day, were allowing some ancient sorrow to surface. There was a sweetness in the sorrow. Sorrow wasn't bad after all, if you just let it come.

I fell in love with the hills around Santa Fe, hills of chunky red earth, fragrant with small pines and juniper. I fell in love with the town too, its ocher mud buildings sitting squat and hunched under the sky, fragrant with the woodsmoke that began to be burned as autumn rolled in, overseen every day by sunsets that were apocalyptic, with pillars of cloud smoking over the city, and late sunlight flooding the streets. Thick as concentrated orange juice, it was light you could have scooped up in your fingers. It was palpable, you could feel it in your chest, it enveloped you.

Eventually I fell in love for real, with a woman from Wisconsin, a singer-songwriter recovering from the recent cancer deaths of both her parents. She was the kind of woman I could never have imagined being with, a sensitive, wheat-haired, long-limbed goddess from the album covers of my youth, when American country rock took over the English airwaves for a few summers in the mid-seventies. Andi was a little older than me. It was a relief. She had been through more, she was ahead of me in care of the soul. I trusted her. I didn't have to prove anything. She showed me it was okay to be open to one's wounds. One didn't constantly have to be outrunning them.

There's a kind of hothouse-grown, sensitive young man who does better with a more mature partner. I guess I was one of them. And she was looking for truth, for love, liberation, healing, for spiritual answers. She was a seeker. Somehow, here in Santa Fe, it was okay to be a seeker. They even used the word: *seeker.* Back in the England I had known, there was no such word. There was no seeking, there was no mystery left. Life was as Newton had said. The Bible was a fairy tale written long ago by men who knew less than we did. Nothing had replaced it; nothing needed to. The answers were known, and there was nothing left to find out except a few details. The scientific view had succeeded. It had done what it set out to do: explain more or less everything.

I didn't think I minded. I was basically an atheist, and that wasn't about to change. All I had wanted for years was to know what had hit me on the beach when I was nineteen. I craved a clear, nontheistic, as it were scientific explanation for that. And not just an explanation, but a directive for revisiting it. And finally, just possibly, I was beginning to find it—just by sitting still every day and letting my heart unburden itself.

But how was that even possible? How could it be that zazen—just sitting and watching one's breath—allowed all these old feelings to come up and work themselves out? Was it possible that all the human heart really needed was time? Give it time and it would sort itself out? You just had to be patient, allow it its period of grace each day.

Somewhere in the depths of Zen I even started to feel a strange congruence between Zen's raw energy and the wild, immemorial soreness of eczema, which, like Zen, was open to the world, to rage and urgency, to seismic forces so deep in the psyche they seemed to connect us not just to the earth but to the forces that made the earth. Even eczema had not been all bad, I began to think.

ONE DAY IN A CAFÉ, I got into a discussion with a tall Soviet émigré, an artist who had lived in New Mexico for twenty years. I showed off that I could still quote a little Pushkin in Russian from my schooldays, and our conversation warmed up. We went and ordered more coffee and sat in the café garden, smoking and talking as the afternoon grew long. He told me about the discipline of living as an artist, the need to practice your art every day without fail, how you should get up early each morning to work before you did anything else. You needed to trust your instincts and cultivate wonder.

He was a little severe, elegant in a stern kind of way, but the advice was sound, and good to hear from an elder. He reminded me of Flora, our old Transylvanian friend back in London—here was another Eastern European who had a wider, deeper view than I did and who was willing to share it with me. I remembered how, in Flora's apartment in Primrose Hill, she had encouraged me as I labored through my first book and had steered me into meditation. The sense of support she had given me came on so strong just then, there in the café, that I had a strange thought: perhaps Flora had somehow sent this man.

Back in my studio, there was a message on the phone. I punched in the code and heard my mother's voice, and right away I knew why she was calling: to tell me Flora had died.

I didn't believe in telepathy or that kind of thing. But it turned out I had been right.

Is it possible a person can send out a surge of goodwill at the moment of death, and someone five thousand miles away can receive it? Who knows. But death unites us, love unites us, and grief unites us.

NATALIE SUGGESTED I VISIT A palm reader. On the principle that I never knew what might offer material for the book I was supposed to be writing, I was up for anything, and I went.

"You're in your Saturn Return," the "palmist" told me. "You're twenty-nine. Saturn returns to where it was in your chart when you were born. You come back to your life's purpose."

I quickly computed that she wasn't only a palmist but an astrologer too. *Oh boy*, I thought to myself, but gritted my teeth and stayed.

She started with the backs of my hands, scarred and parched by long-term dermatitis. I saw her frowning at them.

"You have to slow down. You're always in a rush? Often anxious?"

I wasn't sure. "Maybe."

"It's okay to take care of yourself, you know."

Frankly, I didn't. I lived in fear of being self-indulgent, and was confused about where to draw the line between that and self-care.

She turned my hands over and studied the palms.

"Hmm," she said. "Well, you're going to have some kind of breakdown."

"No," I corrected her. "I already did. Back when I was nineteen."

I was impressed nonetheless that she'd even spotted it.

"Maybe that was just a warm-up? This one—after it, you'll either kill yourself or become a Zen master."

She frowned at my hands, head turned a little sideways. "Yes, you might become a Zen master."

Where did that come from? I ignored it, because it was obviously ludicrous and because I was much more concerned with this second putative breakdown. Not again, surely. Hadn't I worked long and hard to get over the first, with some results at last?

I was in a honeymoon period. With New Mexico, with my girlfriend, with life itself: I had broken free of the long shadow of childhood. I was entering life willingly. I had work, I had love, I was coming home to myself, I was approaching thirty, and now I had Zen. I *wanted* to join the human race, be the human being I was. I ignored the palmist.

THE NATURAL NEXT STEP WAS a *sesshin*: an authentic, week-long Zen retreat. One day Natalie mentioned that she would soon be heading up to an old ranch in the mountains north of Santa Fe to do one. A guest teacher was flying in from Boston to lead it. He was great, she said, and the location stunning—aspens, Douglas firs, elk, wild sheep—and the food excellent. It was advertised as a retreat for "burned-out environmentalists," but anyone could come.

I imagined some kind of inner luxury—a *retreat*, a chance to relax and recharge.

I had heard that *sesshin* retreats were the heart of Zen training. The word—*ses-shin*—literally meant "encountering or touching the heart."

Natalie explained that in Japanese the word *shin* meant both "heart" and "mind." That right there was the difference between East and West, she said. We cut off the heart from the mind. Not so the East. And according to Zen, our true *heart-mind* was infinite, knowing no bounds or limits, and included everything.

She lost me with the last part, but it didn't deter me. It was scary, it was a step into the unknown, but I had a queasy apprehension it was the right thing to do.

Reluctant Mystic

I T WAS THE GAS THAT really got me. All I was doing was sitting still on a cushion. But every time I took my place in the makeshift zendo up at the ranch where the retreat was being held, and heard the bell signal the start of a new meditation period—the beginning of total stillness, no fidgeting allowed—the first thing that happened, before the pain in my knees woke up, before the troupe of demons in my cranium put out their cigarettes in the wings and stumbled onto the stage of what I had previously thought of as my own mind, before the choo-choo trains of dark, difficult thoughts began to clunk out of the railway sidings where they had been temporarily parked, the first thing I would become aware of, deep in my innards, was my intestines tying themselves in fresh knots.

What was going on in there? The retreat was at nine thousand feet, and gases expand at altitude, but still. It was driving me mad. Like some half-wrecked machine finally come to rest,

I was off-gassing horribly. Sitting still all day was a public exorcism, with legions of fuliginous demons being chased out of hiding.

I found myself thinking back over the past year or two. Vague images surfaced, of bands I had played with in the West Indies, of pockmarked rooms where I had stayed and huge tropical leaves glistening in sunlight. And stage lights and ominous towers of black speakers. Then how, back in England before coming out to New Mexico, I had leapt into an unseemly round of promotion laid on by the publishers for my book about the Caribbean music scene. I had feasted on the publicity wagon, whoring out the pen at every opportunity, guzzling wine at junkets, soaking up the attention. In retrospect, I had been disgraceful.

Now here I was, stuck on a mountainside in New Mexico, not allowed to move—not just from this room but from the one square yard of my *zabuton*, my sitting mat. I was trapped not just on the cushion but in my skin. It felt like the last place I wanted to be. What had I been *thinking*? Like all people I was broadly speaking trying to get happier. But like *this*? A whole week of *immobility*? Who ever got happy doing nothing?

What would my dad say, if he knew? Actually, I knew what he would say, because he'd said it.

Boychick, life is about doing. Like Freud said, love your work and work at your loving.

Here I was on my first real Zen retreat, and in spite of the beloved moments I'd had in my new meditation practice over the previous months, I was having an awful time: sitting in rigid stillness hour after hour, longing for the sound of the two bells that signaled the end of each period. Sometimes there was an agony of waiting after the first of the bells, while the timekeeper lingered, just to see how much anguish he or she could generate in the room, before teasingly tapping the bell a second time—the signal that allowed us to uncreak our sparking knees, unfold our dead feet, and get up.

But even then we couldn't actually go anywhere, not until everyone was standing, and we'd all made a little bow together, and the wooden clappers had sounded for the start of walking meditation. Only then were we allowed to move. Sometimes someone would delay incomprehensibly, slowly lifting themselves from their mat, turning back at the last moment to straighten their cushion, before joining us all for that final bow, the one that would spring us. And even then there might be a pause. Why? Who knew?

I would be seething, gritting my teeth, and the instant the clappers finally clacked, as everyone gently, quietly turned to begin the walking meditation, I would step over my mat, which you weren't supposed to do, and make directly for the door out onto the porch.

From being a novice in love with Zen, I had transformed into a jaded cynic who had had more than enough of it, thank you.

What on earth was I doing here? And what *was* Zen, anyway?

I HAD BEEN READING ABOUT Zen the past few months. "What is Zen?" was a question that Zen itself had been wrestling with for fifteen hundred years. But that was less because it didn't know than because it didn't know how to say it. It was about something, but that "something" wasn't exactly a something, though nor was it nothing. At least that's what I'd gathered.

Zen had been enthusiastically welcomed into mid-twentieth-century America, through the efforts above all of

D. T. Suzuki and Alan Watts, neither of whom was actually a Zen teacher. The first, a onetime monk, moved from Japan to the United States and became a writer and speaker who promoted Zen as an ideal form of spirituality for modern times, free of encumbering beliefs and creeds. The other was an English minister who didn't practice Zen but was inspired by it, and spoke brilliantly on it.

It was mostly books that had made it popular: *The Three Pillars of Zen, Zen in the Art of Archery, Zen and the Art of Motorcycle Maintenance.* But you could read a lot about it and still be in the dark.

Some things were clear enough: Zen was a form of Buddhism influenced by Chinese Taoism wherein the main activity, rather than forms of worship or scriptural study, was meditation. The Japanese word *zen* derived from the Chinese *ch'an,* which in turn came from the Sanskrit *dhyana* and meant "meditative absorption." But unlike other kinds of meditation, it was short on detailed instructions. The advice Robert the Zen priest had first given me—to count breaths in sets of ten—was about as elaborate as it got.

Zen had "lineages" of masters who had "confirmed" one another down through the ages. What they had confirmed was that the student had had the same insights into the nature of consciousness or reality that the master had, and had learned to live by them in daily life.

It was weird: it was about some kind of radical experience that shifted one's view of things, yet it was also about absolute ordinariness. If you saw reality more clearly, ordinary things became miraculous.

I liked that idea. It was consistent with the power of poetry to transform the everyday. It wasn't that you had to transport yourself to other realms. You just had to puncture a conditioned view of reality that had been filtering your experience. It all rang vaguely true.

THERE WAS A WOODEN BENCH on the porch just outside the door. It had armrests at either end and wasn't long enough for a lie-down, but while they all did walking meditation indoors, I would curl up on my side on its slats, close my eyes, and try to catch a ten-minute nap.

Yet it wasn't sleep I really wanted. I wanted relief from the torment, physical and mental. Here I was, giving myself this precious opportunity to "touch my true heart," and I was hating it.

I had done some half days, even whole days, of Zen. I had done an introductory weekend. I had been sitting zazen daily for several months by now, on the back of several years of twice-daily Transcendental Meditation, yet none of it had prepared me for this.

Each time we sat on our cushions, I immediately felt an ache deep in my sacroiliac, and my knees would start to shriek. And my shoulders and lower back seized in aches and random stabs, or cool sheets of cramp that made me sweat. At the same time, it was only the pains that kept me awake. New reservoirs of exhaustion had been unearthed. Gales of sleepiness flapped through me. Again and again I'd nod off, only to jolt awake to the hell of immobility. At least I never fell over.

And there were my insides, where a little magician was busy tying and untying the long balloon animals that were my guts. But all that was nothing beside the mental anguish.

The retreat had billed itself as a recharge for burned-out environmentalists. But it was a real *sesshin*, as became clear the evening before we started, when the teacher explained what we'd be doing for the next seven days: sitting on a cushion from 5 a.m. until 9 p.m. Yes, we would also walk, eat, rest a little. But there would be nothing else. No reading, no writing, no talking, no nothing. Just sitting.

My knees were right: What *was* I doing? What had got into me? I had thrown away my sanity and joined some piece of late-millennium folly to feed my self-importance. *You, too, can be a mystic. Come on up. Enlightenment is only one check away.* I knew better than this, surely. I came from generations of British lawyers and businessmen and from impoverished, intelligent Jewish tailors who were rationalists, realists. I had grown up with a head full of Homer and Cicero. I knew what argument was, I breathed the humanism of the West. What had I to do with Asian mysticism? Or the mountains of New Mexico, for that matter? How had I fallen for this?

It was Natalie's fault, obviously. It had been her idea. She was sitting in the room, too, on the other side of the fireplace. But such was the depth of my torment that she might as well not have been here. I couldn't summon any animosity toward her for having dragged me here. She hadn't; I had.

Yes, I had signed a contract with my publisher to produce a narrative about searching for D. H. Lawrence's footsteps in New Mexico, and I was getting late with the delivery and needed things to write about, and I'd hoped this retreat could somehow be one of them, but here I was in the very country Lawrence had loved, had called his one true home, and I was staring at a wall all day. Just what kind of research did I think I was doing?

THE MAN SHARING MY CANVAS tent had come for the kind of recharging I had fondly imagined. He was a genuine burned-out environmentalist, and after the first morning he made a quick, healthy decision at lunch: this was not what he had signed up for. He asked for his money back, packed his bag, and drove away, ten miles down the long, rutted, muddy track, back to the world.

I envied him. By now he would be in his home city, among cafés, cars, buildings, with sidewalks to walk down, people to watch, horns to hear, and blessed bustle all around. He had had enough self-knowledge to stand up and say, *This is not for me.* Why couldn't I? I blew about like a leaf in the wind. A friend says, "Hey, Henry, how about a Zen retreat?" like it was an ice cream. Next thing, I'm giving up a week of my life.

That was another thing: I had work to do, and more work to drum up. I was in the middle of some back-and-forth with a magazine editor I'd never written for, and badly wanted to.

Worse, I'd received a phone call the day before the retreat started from two English friends who happened to be visiting New Mexico. I would miss them! I couldn't believe it. What a special experience it would have been to meet up with them out here in the desert. That wouldn't happen now because I was too busy staring at a wall.

On top of all that, after two days my digestion seized in dismay. That was bad news. Somewhere I'd picked up the notion that eczema's eruptions indicated that toxins weren't getting released the proper way. "How's your digestion?" one alternative practitioner used to ask me every time I saw her. Lawrence himself had said that sleep had an "evacuative function." Hence the morning bowel movement. Sleep, shit, skin: in my mind they'd become an unholy triad.

The first three days of that *sesshin* were the hardest I've ever known on a meditation cushion (so far).

ZEN IS NOT EASY. ZEN is baffling. Zen is impossible to pin down. On the one hand, it's easy to pin down: it's about sitting on a cushion every day. You try to be aware of what is going on. Breathing, mostly, and thoughts that come and, you hope, go. It's nice when they go. You can find yourself in a state of exhilarating peace.

Zen is a journey back to radical simplicity. No mantras, no "sacred syllables," no sacred anything.

I liked that. It was refreshing. Zen was easy to like. It didn't claim to know anything. No rebirths, no deities, no special states. Just sit down. See what's going on. Nothing special. Nothing that isn't self-evident.

But I didn't like *this*. You could have too much even of the plainest things, evidently.

THE TEACHER, GEORGE BOWMAN, GAVE a talk every morning. We'd turn our cushions to face the center of the room and he'd speak for forty minutes. One morning he talked about Bodhidharma, one of the grandfathers of Zen, an Indian monk said to have brought Zen from India to China in 527 c.e.

Soon after Bodhidharma reached China, an emperor summoned him for an audience. This emperor was interested in Buddhism and had been building monasteries, sponsoring monks, financing the translation of Sanskrit texts into Chinese. When the genuine living article, an actual Buddhist master, reached his shores, he invited him to his court right away.

There was a view that charitable acts could earn one "merit" toward a better rebirth next time around. The emperor asked Bodhidharma how much merit he had acquired through his support for Buddhism.

Bodhidharma said, "No merit whatsoever."

Not a reply the emperor had been expecting. According to George, Zen didn't believe in reincarnation, let alone a cosmic moral bank account.

Then he asked the holy man to expound his highest, holiest teaching.

Bodhidharma answered, "No holiness. Vast and void."

In Zen there was no such thing as holy. It didn't separate sacred and profane at all.

This was more like it. I found myself starting to like Zen again, and Bodhidharma.

In frustration, the emperor then asked Bodhidharma who on earth he was, this man standing before him.

To which Bodhidharma answered, "I don't know."

Zen refused to let us settle into any known, durable sense of identity, George explained.

You couldn't help admiring Bodhidharma's chutzpah, his refusal to allow for inflated ideas of the practice.

As George told the story, there were knowing chuckles around the room. The others seemed to be enjoying it all, with knowledgeable smiles, chortles, and so on, while I was basically sitting in hell. But the story also stirred a vague sediment of recognition in me, a dim echo of sense. Yet I didn't like that either. I liked sense that could be explicated, replicated, and used to help orient one in life. I couldn't see how this kind of talk, whether or not in some distant, remote, half-unknowable way it was "true," could possibly help.

After dispensing the above inscrutable teachings to the emperor, Bodhidharma promptly crossed the Yangtze River on a single blade of grass and went to sit in a cave in Shaolin for nine years.

Nine years. Staring at the wall of a cave. It was because of him that Zen continued the tradition of facing the wall during meditation.

Here I was, in a warm room on a cushion and mat, worrying about one *week* of sitting. Yet the thought of his nine years, while putting our ordeal in perspective, brought neither inspiration nor comfort, just a sense of utter inadequacy for this practice.

What an impossible example to set for others. Not only that, but Bodhidharma cut off his eyelids to make sure he wouldn't fall asleep. No sleep. Nine years. (What would my skin do with that?) He threw his eyelids on the ground, and where they fell, tea bushes sprouted. Thus did tea come to China. So at least there was acknowledgment of the story's legendary nature. And at least China got tea out of it.

ZEN CALLED ITSELF THE "SUDDEN school," George explained. You didn't have to go through a gradual process, through stages of practice. Instead, in one sudden leap, you could find all you were looking for. Bodhidharma said the practice wasn't based on scripture or words, but rather "directly pointed to the human mind."

"Sudden teaching." You didn't have to travel by stages. Somehow, in spite of the torment, I recognized that too. The answer to life was right here already. Maybe that connected with why I had had a hard time trusting the doctors and quacks back in the days of the worst eczema: it had been able to clear itself up miraculously in South America, without stages of improvement.

"What does 'Buddha' mean?" George asked rhetorically. It meant to wake up to the fact that our true consciousness was shared with all things. It was vastly broader than it seemed.

Much as I was hating the retreat, something in me couldn't help but perk up when I heard this.

"Immediate" might have been as good a name for Zen, too, he said: both in the sense that its teaching happened at once, immediately, and in that there was nothing in between. You and your experience were one. Nothing mediated subject and object.

In other words, George told us: Sit down, be quiet, find out that the relationship between you and everything else is not what you thought.

All of this ought to have been a breath of fresh air. No veering away from reality. No hovering above it. A chance to get down and investigate experience closely. But instead it was riling me. I didn't want to hear it. I didn't like the idea that the kind of experience it was pointing to could be cultivated at will. Such a thing should surely be a gift, a grace, if it happened at all. It was almost avaricious to seek it.

I HAD EVERYTHING I WANTED. I was twenty-nine years old and I had already published two books and had contracts for a third, from fine transatlantic publishers. I was overpaid, I was free, and I had created the life of a wandering writer-poet I'd dreamt of as a teenager. I was doing it. I had escaped the drizzling, eczematous sump of my youth. Meanwhile my skin was supple and smooth, acquiring a milky coffee hue as the New Mexico sun coaxed forth Sephardic pigments from deep in the genes. Much of the time I was free of the psychic crevasses into which I used to fall. I had a girlfriend. I had what people called a life.

Not only that, but I'd come to a place I always wanted to get to. I could still remember the night long ago, as a student at university, rain pinging on the panes, an essay long overdue, when I pulled a book from the shelves of my rented digs and opened it randomly. The prose I landed on lit up my imagination and transfigured the night: Lawrence, writing about his little ranch in New Mexico, high above the magical, lonely town of Taos, with its formidable, sacred mountain, its Pueblo Indians who danced and drummed to keep the sun moving.

And I should light my little stove in the bedroom, and let it roar a bit, sucking the wind. Then dart to bed, with all the ghosts of the ranch cosily round me, and sleep till the very coldness of my emerged nose wakes me. Waking, I shall look at once through the glass panels of the bedroom door, and see the trunk of the great pine tree, like a person on guard, and a low star just coming over the mountain, very brilliant, like someone swinging an electric lantern.

The ink rose an inch off the page. I was transported. I was reading the life I wanted. *If I could just be there*, I thought. What a life Lawrence had led, inscribing the globe with his wanderings.

Now here I was doing it, too. Making my living by writing. Not only that, but I was actually doing a bona fide Zen retreat, under a real live Zen master. It was awesome. What had happened to my life defied understanding.

So why wasn't I happy? What more did I think I needed? Dysthymia. Dogged, determined, unflagging. It won't let you go. It may hibernate for a season, go underground, stay low, but get left behind? No way.

In the silence and stillness of the retreat it concentrated, amplified, intensified. There was no way of dodging it even for a moment. It got thicker and thicker, like one of the London fogs I thought I was so lucky to have escaped.

I DISCOVERED A POND ON the ranch not far from the lodge where we were meditating.

The main house, built of logs, dated from the 1920s, when it had served as a hunting lodge for wealthy East Coasters. Our zendo had been set up in the lounge, with the furniture cleared out and the fifteen cushions arranged on its thick, dark rug in two rows. But the ranch had other buildings and facilities, such as the pond.

If I ran from the zendo the instant the wood clappers sounded, pulling off my shirt as I went, I found I could get to the pond, on the far side of a meadow, whip down my trousers, dive into the limpid brown water, swim six strokes, grab one of the towels spread in the sun on the wooden dock, dry off cursorily, dress, and run back to the zendo just as the ten minutes of walking meditation was coming to an end. I'd be on my seat in time for the next period.

It helped. I liked the run, I liked the chilly water and the sunshine, the trees, the bright green meadow with its long grass, and the sense of doing something to help myself. I would settle in my place with a flush to my skin, and find it easier to concentrate.

After the first couple of days, during which George wanted us to keep our minds on our breathing—the expanding and emptying of the lungs—he suggested that if we felt like it, we could also "float" a little question on the breath: *Who am I?*

I found myself falling into occasional periods of quiet when thoughts were not storming through my mind, when my torso felt like a big, dark cave, gently filling with air and emptying. The peace wouldn't last—the distracting pain in the knees would start up again, or some regret, or horror at the length of the retreat—but it made a difference to taste any peace at all.

EVERY DAY WE WENT UPSTAIRS one by one for a private interview with George. I used these sessions not only to stretch my legs but to harangue him for leading us through this pointless torture. Between sits, when not lurching to the lake, I scribbled down notes to bring to him at the next opportunity.

During my interview on the third day, after delivering a paragraph of invective, suddenly I felt unsure of my remaining points. I stopped midsentence. A pregnant pause opened. Something popped out of my mouth, unbidden. "I suppose one day I might look back on this meditation as the best way I ever spent my time," I heard myself say.

The prediction came out before I knew what I was saying, and it brought an unfamiliar tenderness to my chest. Then, immediately after, as I plodded back downstairs to the zendo, I remembered the long hours of sitting that lay ahead, and the warmth in my heart vanished.

SOMETHING ELSE OCCURRED TO ME. The TV show *Alias Smith and Jones*, about two maverick cowboys, which I'd watched religiously every Monday night as a child, was set in these same southwestern mountains: the same dry tracks, ziggurat-like cliffs, and pine trees. They had been my escape. There was *Kung Fu* too, set in the same lands. I'd loved that show, but rather than the feats of martial arts, what really got me was the meditation: all those guys sitting for hours and hours in the temple, not moving an inch. How did they do that? Didn't they itch, get fidgety, want to blow their noses? I had loved the sense that through their sitting they could change, become different.

THE FOURTH DAY WAS WARM, and in the afternoon George decided to have us sit outside in the long grass.

"Let the wind give us a dharma talk," he said.

Typically, during the morning talks about Zen training, Zen wisdom, Zen history, I would listen with bitter recriminations composing themselves in my mind—toward the other sitters as well as myself—for allowing ourselves to be duped into wasting a whole God-given week. Perhaps, in this deeper pool of Zen time, greater torments than I had touched before were being released and finding their way to the surface. In the deep quiet of the retreat, I was at their mercy. I had no perspective on what was going on; I just felt frustration, pain, regret, and longing—to be anywhere but where I was. It was all somehow reminiscent of eczema, with its longing for the skin to be different. If it had mostly healed, perhaps it had left a long shadow, which was now finding a way to clear.

Or was that quack talk?

On the other hand, a principle of Zen, George had told us, was the discovery that we had been wrong about everything. There was great relief in that, he assured us.

I wondered if perhaps Zen had seemed to suit me, when I first found it, because my body had in its own way been wrong for a long time. It had been mistaken about the environment—what it ate, breathed, touched. Allergies, after all, were the immune system believing it was doing a bang-up job as guard but turning its vigilance into self-attack. The sinuses went into hypertrophy because a mote gusted up the nasal duct, the skin raged against a little dairy milk or a brush with grass seed. Allergies were a mighty exaggeration.

According to George, Zen's view was that we were busy being wrong all the time in ways we didn't realize. "Awakening" was nothing other than to see this.

On that fourth day, as we all sat outside on the grass in a rolling meadow, listening to the wind, I suddenly felt good. My habitual thought patterns went quiet. I noticed the sound of the wind in the firs across the field, plunging through the boughs. It was fascinating. The breeze roared like a jet engine. Then hissed like surf withdrawing from a beach. It was nice to hear, and reminded me of happy moments in childhood.

Then, on the uneven ground of the field, my knees began to hurt like never before. If two red-hot pokers had been stabbed straight into them, it surely couldn't have hurt more.

What was I going to do? We were virtually forbidden to move during meditation. And anyway, I'd found that slight adjustments only made the pain worse. It was better to tough it out. Yet this time it was as if scalding oil were being intravenously injected into the joints. Surely I was damaging myself.

In desperation, I remembered the question George had posed and poured myself into it, heart and soul: Who am I? Who *really* am I?

It worked. A little. It temporarily distracted me from the knee pain.

Then another deep gust traveled slowly through the pines across the meadow. It caught my attention. It was fascinating. And suddenly something happened.

The knee pain was still there, the sound of the wind was still there, but there was no one experiencing them. It was the strangest thing. There was no me. The very center of my being, the core of my life, vanished. *I* vanished. Where had I gone? What had happened to me? Where I used to be, there was just a broad openness. All things were happening just as before, nothing had really changed, yet everything had changed, because there was no *me* to whom everything was happening.

It was as if a flashbulb had gone off in my skull, and that's what it suddenly illuminated: *no me.* The idea of "me" had been just that—an idea. Now it had burst like a bubble.

The relief was indescribable. All the worrying, all the fretting—and all along there had been no one home. Life was a ship, and I had assumed it had a captain. But the ship *had* no captain. There was no one on board.

I had found the answer to the teacher's question. Who was I? I was no one. I had made myself up.

There was a bursting in of joy. It was glorious to be seated outside on the grass now, to be hearing the wind and experiencing the sensation in the knees, which a moment ago had seemed unbearable but now was just an interesting tingle, one of many stimuli and impulses that arose in a limitless field of awareness.

It was suddenly clear that all my life I had been assuming these many stimuli happened to a being called *me.* They were connected to one another by virtue of happening to *me.* But there *was* no thread connecting them. Each arose independently. They were free.

Not only that, but without me, there was no past or future. Every phenomenon that arose was happening for the first and only time, and filled all awareness entirely. That made it an absolute treasure.

The rest of that day I was in bliss. Peace suffused everything. A love burned in my chest like a watch fire. I could hear the grass growing, a faint high singing sound, like the sibilance of a new snowfall coming down. I remembered the Jewish saying: "No blade of grass but has an angel bending over it, whispering, 'Grow, grow.'" Every blade of grass deserved that. Each blade *was* an angel. I cried. My heart was mush. Somehow it felt as though the grass were growing in my own chest. Every object contained an inner lamp, and now I could see it.

When we queued for meals, I no longer felt impatient, eager to fill my plate, eager for the meal prayer to be over so I could fall upon the food and bury myself in the distraction of eating. Every moment was joy. To walk was to wade through glory.

THE NEXT TIME I WENT upstairs for a private interview with George, as soon as I sat down in front of him, all I could do was let out a long sigh of relief.

To my surprise, as soon as I did so, he let out exactly the same sigh, just like a mirror.

I was going to try to explain what had happened, but I didn't need to; George already knew. He smiled. He understood. He could tell.

We laughed and laughed. Deep belly laughs. The powerful relief that I felt, he felt too.

THE REVELATION, ALTHOUGH IT HAD happened in a flash, lingered with a gorgeous afterglow. The last two days of the retreat, I walked on air. The ground itself was air. I no longer skipped any of the walking meditations. My physical ailments—the pain, the sleepiness, the indigestion—all evaporated. The sitting was exactly what I wanted, the walking likewise. I ate lightly, patiently. An agony was over.

Now I knew why was I here. It was perfectly obvious: because of what had happened on the beach ten years before. The inexplicable *thing* I couldn't communicate to anyone, that had changed my life, that most impossible of grails, an *answer*, which fell by itself into the life of an angst-ridden, eczematous teenager. It had opened like a "portal" between worlds in young adult fiction. One minute it was the earth you knew, the next you stepped into a different world, where all trouble was healed. It was almost like dying, so far was it from the life you knew. Yet you hadn't died. Then it was over and you were back in your old life. It was all just the same except for the fact that something extraordinary had been revealed.

Now, a decade later, having given up hope of recovering it, here I was, doing the one thing that might help. *That* was why I was sitting on a Zen cushion halfway to the sky on a New Mexico mountain. That was why I had found myself telling George that perhaps the sitting was the best use of my time.

This new discovery was different from the one on the beach, yet also the same. It, too, struck out of nowhere, with a sense of complete resolution. Part of its nature was that it could never be different, and when you saw it you knew it had been with you all along. Yet it could never be the same.

I WROTE A POEM FOR George, folded it in half, and pinned it to the noticeboard where we could leave messages, with his name on it.

> The river runs through me.
> Dayflowers hover in my chest,
> risen like radiant thoughts
> from my belly.
> My heart is overgrown with grasses.
> I am a house with no roof,
> no door, no windows, no walls.
> Wind plunges into the trees.
> Cool tickle of a fly on someone's arm.
> Here, I cannot even remember
> what freedom means.
> I am nowhere.

The next time I saw him, he gave it back to me and said, "Thank you. So it was worth it after all."

I smiled, and we didn't talk about either the poem or what had happened.

ON THE LAST NIGHT, AFTER the retreat was over, after supper, as we all lazed around the room where we had been sitting for the week—now restored to a sitting room with sofas and bookcases—I picked out an old copy of the Buddhist magazine

Tricycle from a shelf and read an interview with the writer and Zen teacher Peter Matthiessen. He spoke of "openings" in Zen training and said it wasn't always an advantage to have an "early opening."

I wondered if that was what had just happened to me—an "opening." If so, then I must have had an opening ten years earlier, too, before any formal training, on the beach. Perhaps I was an early opener.

At one point I worried a little about returning to normal life, but then I remembered: Whose worry was it? I knew the answer now. It was no one's. This Zen thing, I thought: I had it licked.

A LITTLE ZEN CAN BE a dangerous thing. Some learn fast but open slow. Some open fast but learn slow.

Was Peter Matthiessen an early opener? Is that why he'd said early openings weren't necessarily a help? He knew?

At the end of the retreat I tried to talk to George about what had happened, but he cut me off, saying he was all talked out. He wanted to chop firewood. I was welcome to join him, but he didn't want to talk.

As we stood near each other in the warm sunlight, he swinging a sledge down onto a wedge to split drums of pine, I hefting an ax into the half drums, a mild despondency crept over me: I wasn't going to get the talk I needed. Was there some next step? That was all I wanted to know. And if so, what was it? But when I tried to ask him, George would only say, "Keep your attention on what you're doing."

But now that I'd seen through the cherished *me*, I couldn't help doing just that anyway. It wasn't even a matter of attention. My old mind seemed to have dissipated like a cloud. All there *was* was eating, walking, listening, seeing, and so on. It was "very heaven"—everything radiant, singing with life.

So what next?

George wouldn't say.

Maybe it was some Zen thing. Thwart the customer; the customer is always wrong.

I was finding it hard to say nothing, and told him I was a little afraid I might start to feel sad and troubled again. He said, "Trust the sadness. It knows how to unwrap you."

Which was an interesting suggestion, but it didn't help with the main point. Something unprecedented had just opened up, and the teacher says, "Go back to the next breath, attend to what's happening now." But I wanted to know what had happened. It had huge implications, after all, to find that the very self one had believed oneself to be was a mirage.

At the time, I was mostly so blissed out that George could have told me to bury myself in manure and I'd have done it. All was well, because I had seen that I didn't really exist. Instead, a marvelous process was going on, of things freely arising in some deep yet depthless space, like electrical impulses, or like the colorful lumps rising from the bottom of a lava lamp. Therefore, because all things happened freely, without *me*, all was well.

So in a way the teacher was right: it was fine to just come back to the next breath, to whatever was happening now . . . now . . . now.

But over the weeks and months ahead, the advice would become problematic. I did need to talk with *someone*. The world had turned upside down; I had been gutted. Yet if even a Zen teacher, and even the very teacher under whose nose it had happened, wouldn't talk about it, who would?

It's a strange business. Zen as a whole is quite divided on the issue of "awakening experiences." Zen calls them *kensho*: seeing reality, or seeing one's "original nature." But one great tranche of Zen, the Soto school, prefers not to talk about *kensho* at all. Apparently Soto's followers used to, but in the nineteenth century they dropped it for historical institutional reasons. The other, smaller branch of Zen, Rinzai, has a training system that does and must acknowledge *kensho*, because you can't proceed in its methodology, known as koan training, unless *kensho* has happened. *Kensho* is the "gateless gate," the "great barrier of the Zen sect," as the thirteenth-century master Mumon* called it.

There's doubtless something to be said for the silent approach. The less said, the better; don't turn an experience into *something*; just stay present. But the fact is, I couldn't. The implications of the experience were too radical. The idea of forgetting it—even if I'd wanted to, I couldn't. And I didn't want to. And that, too, would become a problem.

✢

BACK IN MY LITTLE RENTAL in Santa Fe, things at first fell easily into place. My second book was out, a third under contract and coming along, and I was making progress on a fourth. The continued back-and-forth with magazine editors resulted in new assignments. Through Zen I seemed to be developing a bit more ease in my work. Assignments scared me less—I wrote them on time, found them fulfilling, and was being reasonably well paid for them. Meanwhile the meditation in my room each day was

---

* Chinese: Wumen, 1183–1260.

like an immersion in a bath of effervescent water, in which all concerns dissolved.

I loved Santa Fe. It reminded me of Oxford. Like that other ancient city, it was surrounded by higher ground—the Sangre de Cristo Mountains to the east, the Sandia and Jemez ranges to south and west, which I could see along the skyline from my latest home, a one-room studio on a low hill above downtown. They were beautiful. And Santa Fe was an old cultural center too, like Oxford, much older than most American cities, with an artistic and literary life far in excess of its size. And its streets were shaded by trees.

Other parts of New Mexico felt oddly like home, too. The tussocky fields around Taos, lined with cottonwoods that resembled elms, looked like England, but with some oppressive element drained out. My old land love woke up for the first time in ages.

Maybe my biography would turn out to be no more than a footnote in a greater project, I mused—finding a home for the intense, studious, neurasthenic Jew. Honed by generations of prayer and study, of debate over fine points of scripture, he could think you under the table—but where could you put him? The banished tribes, trying out New York, Hollywood, London, Paris, the Rhineland, Granada, Israel, the campuses of New England—they try New Mexico too, far-flung colony of New Spain. There had been crypto-Jews here for generations, Spaniards who didn't know why they lit Hanukkah lamps each December, and since the last century, thousands of Jewish artists, intellectuals, and social experimenters from the East and West Coasts had come. Where to install the thinkers of the earth, the procrastinators and ruminators? (And was it possible my unwanted mystic proclivities came not from my mother, as I'd always assumed, but from my pragmatic father's forebears, the ecstatic Hasidim behind him?)

Andi and I explored the hills, deserts, and mountains, stopping off at wild hot springs, camping, pulling in at lonely grocery stores for supplies. New Mexico was still wild. Away from the atmosphere of its few cities, it felt remote. Then we'd return to Santa Fe, to the small kiva fireplace in my rental, resiny with piñon and cedar smoke.

ZEN WAS GOOD FOR WRITING. It liked the concrete. It relished details and particulars. Zen had a long literary tradition of its own, and I had unwittingly been inspired by it at a young age. One of my favorite books as a teen, *Imagist Poetry*, featured a clutch of London poets from the 1910s who had been influenced by Chinese poetry of the Tang dynasty. These Imagists appreciated the way the old Chinese poets built their verses out of concrete images. The Tang had been the golden age of Zen, when government ministers would withdraw to the mountains to meditate and to consort with Zen masters in monasteries and hermitages high on cliffs. It was an enlightened era, when the examinations to enter the civil service required the penning of poetry. You could fail if your poetry wasn't up to it.

With my poetry-loving friends I had devoured the works of the young Ezra Pound, Richard Aldington, T. E. Hulme, Hilda Doolittle—Imagists who in their turn had plundered the works of Li Po and Tu Fu.

I hadn't made the connection with Zen until now. Once again, Zen was teaching me to write: less padding, more concrete.

But more than that, New Mexico's mountains, plains, hills, its cliffs and mesas, were themselves like artistic expressions, to be matched or emulated. They showed the way. This, too, was in line with the old Zen poets, who sought to lose themselves in landscape so their poems could arise out of the same creative potential from which the mountains, rivers, and clouds—indeed all phenomena—arose.

Zen monks were called *unsui*—"cloud-waters." They drifted among mountains like clouds, they flowed like streams and rivers where the valleys took them. I wanted to be like that: meditating, wandering, writing, and now in some ways I was.

I JOINED NATALIE FOR A "Day of Mindfulness" at another Zen center, in the hills on the edge of town. It was a quiet place, built out of adobe, set in a sequestered valley of its own. It had no regular practice going on, no one lived or worked there, and Natalie's little group rented it for one day every month.

We sat in the old mud zendo on a kind of platform known as a *tan* and did a mixture of sitting, walking outside on the dry, warm ground among juniper and piñon trees, and writing in our notebooks. After a snack lunch we had some time to wander around on our own. I threaded through chamisa bushes into a long arroyo with a sandy bed that ran beneath tall pines. Up into the hillsides wound small side canyons, with miniature landscapes of boulders overshadowed by twisted junipers. Here and there, subterranean ridges of gritty red granite broke the surface, with trees clinging to them by tough roots. Up above, I could look back and see the zendo itself through the trees, a hall of earth-hued adobe, with carved beams projecting from the roofs.

It was a magical place, but somehow desolate, as if deserted or abandoned.

That was my first glimpse of Mountain Cloud Zen Center.

ANDI GOT BOOKED AS A vocalist and keyboard player for studio work in New York City. Santa Fe had brought us together, but as long as the rent wasn't too pricey, perhaps it didn't matter too much where we lived. This was America, a fluid working population. I was an itinerant writer, so I went, too.

We found a small sublet on East Thirteenth Street, with a strip of a view down the street, where I meditated each day to the sound of church bells. The sitting often felt transparent, clear as a mountain lake. I'd start on a quarter hour, chimed by the nearby bells, slip into the lake, and next thing I knew I'd be hearing the chime for the next quarter hour, and the next. Time vanished, swallowed by that lake.

By day I went down to the Cooper Square Diner or up to the Public Library to work, and by night I joined her at the studio. It was a period of grace. Fees coming in, and a love that required no censoring of the personality. I was on good terms with my parents, too, albeit from afar. Work and love. After all the trouble of growing up, the world had finally slowed down.

And did you get what
you wanted from this life, even so?

asked Raymond Carver in his "Late Fragment."

I did.
And what did you want?

To call myself beloved, to feel myself
beloved on the earth.

I ran into an old friend I'd been with in South America long ago, now working as an architect in Brooklyn. Reviving that friendship in this new location seemed like a confirmation that I had picked up the thread of my life.

Yet with the exception of the daily meditation, the irons were all still set in the forge of the world. What about enlightenment? It wasn't just about momentary flashes, surely, nor about getting a semi-regular life together. So what was it?

Monastery

SOMETIMES I'D JOIN ANDI AT a recording studio in
Woodstock, in upstate New York. We rented a room in a
clapboard house on the edge of town from a kindhearted
local baker known as Disco Linda, because she moonlighted as
a DJ. Even though I got up early, she would already have left for
work. Andi would still be sleeping upstairs. I'd make a cup of tea
and sit on the porch overlooking the road. In the early light, with
clouds massed over the wooded hills above the little town, the
asphalt gleamed like a silver river in the trees. There might be a
bird calling, a gust shaking a handful of drops from a branch. I'd
sip tea and settle on the porch for meditation.

Somewhere in the peace of meditation there was a burr of
unease. Sitting itself was well and good, but another step was
needed. How did one *live* in the world of Zen? In some sense I
knew we already were. But I also wasn't.

A few miles up the road, there happened to be a Zen monastery. It was a large, forbidding place, an old Norwegian church camp that had gone bust and been taken over by a Zen group. The main building was a behemoth of stone and wood with a huge roof that came low to the ground. Lofty trees surrounded it, hissing gently all day long.

The Zen master, a onetime industrial chemist with an anchor tattooed on his arm, legacy of his days in the merchant marine, ran the place like a navy ship. The shaven-headed senior monks were apt to shout if you so much as wiped your nose in the zendo. "Let it run!" you'd hear them bark down the hall at some poor sniveler.

Something had given way in me. If my legs were sore in the sitting, I just kept going, solid as a rock. Snot would dangle from my nose, threads that eventually reached my hands in my lap, where I'd feel the cool as they made contact, and the long strands would sway less. Tears of unknown origin would wet my face, and I would sit entranced by nothing in particular, just by the fact of sitting among a group of intent meditators. I didn't flinch.

I WENT ON AN INTRODUCTORY retreat at the monastery. I got myself properly schooled in the protocols of Zen.

The master was strange and impressive, a figure from a world of oceans and of adepts with towering wisdom commensurate with the cloud-wrapped mountains where they lived. He himself lived in a low cabin hidden by foliage, and he would arrive at the zendo in the dark before dawn in his jeep. You'd see him step from the vehicle in his robes, a cigarette between his lips—he was a regular smoker. In his strange white footwear, neither sock nor slipper, and his Japanese vestments, he might have been about to perform in *The Mikado*, I couldn't help thinking when I saw him.

He'd let his butt fall like a red star, crunch it into the gravel, and, with a senatorial swirl of his robes, vanish up the stone steps into the hall, leaving behind a whiff of tobacco on the early air. It may not have been Gilbert and Sullivan, but to my sour, skeptical mind it was impressive theater nonetheless.

The first time I had *dokusan* (an interview) with him, the monk training our little group of recruits had told us, "The space between the student and the master is the center of the universe. Bear that in mind when you speak."

I made my deep bows, one at the threshold of the little interview room and one in front of the teacher, receiving an impression of a dimly lit room as I did: tatami floor, wooden walls, all in a cramped space like a cupboard under the stairs. Dark wood panels behind the master. A candle on a low altar, a fine line of smoke from an incense stick. And his bare scalp catching a wood-like gleam.

When I sat before him, the air between us seemed charged with voltage. I wanted to say what was most needed, since I was speaking to the center of the universe, but I wasn't sure what it was.

After an awkward silence, out of nowhere something bubbled up: "Thank you."

It came from the bottom of my heart.

Instead of answering me, he put his hands together and made a deep bow, so that I was left staring at the top of his skull, burnished like oak.

It happened so quickly. Why was he bowing to me?

When he rose back up, his lambent eyes gazed into mine, and he asked whether I'd ever had a master.

It might have all gone like clockwork. The seeker finds his

master. The path is clear. The master asks a question that slides through the student like a hot blade through butter, opening the student up. But in my case, the butter had been in the fridge too long. The butter had impurities in it. The knife got stuck halfway down; the right answer would not come. Had I had a master? Of course not. But I lost my footing. I began to think.

"Well," I began. "I'm not quite sure. A friend got me started in Zen. I've done a *sesshin*. A Zen priest trained me."

He averted his eyes, said, "Ah," and rang his little bell to signal the end of the interview. I bowed and withdrew.

I CAME BACK TO DO a weeklong *sesshin* at the monastery. On the first morning I woke at 4:00 a.m. on my bunk in the dorm as everyone was getting up. The first meditation began at 4:30, but they asked you to be in your place by 4:25. I'd heard that rule in other zendos—to arrive five minutes early—and thought I had noticed that people tended not to be too strict about it.

Having made it through the line to a sink in the bathroom, to wash my face and brush my teeth, I returned my washbag to the dorm, passing a couple of guys doing yoga out in the hallway, and fussed around with my bag before making my way downstairs.

At the back of the zendo there was a corridor from which two entrances led into the main hall. Just as I was stepping through one, I noticed a party of three men in robes, wearing white booties, entering by the other. As I took my first step onto the old floorboards, a monk sitting just inside the entrance spun round and barred my way. He was on his feet in a flash, silently pointing me back outside, motioning me to sit on a cushion out in the corridor.

He was one of the monitors, and I did as he indicated. Then he clipped back into the zendo, leaving me out in the hall.

It had cost me a bit of struggle to come and do this retreat. It was a big deal. I was in the middle of some intense writing, working once again on the old family novel, excavating a seam of material I had long hoped to uncover. There it was: true ore glinting in the sun. I had thought that if I broke off the writing now to do the retreat, the ore might disappear. But on the other hand, it was possible a retreat might generate still more clarity, as well as give me a chance to reapproach the question of finding a Zen teacher. It had all stirred up some uncomfortable indecisiveness. Finally I had made up my mind and come, but now here I was, being kicked out of the zendo and missing part of the very first day.

The first period hadn't yet started, though. The bells hadn't sounded. Had that monitor monk made a mistake? Or was there some rule about not entering at the same time as the crew in white socks? Might it be okay to enter now, since they were already inside? My assigned spot in the zendo was just a few feet from the door, and I knew the abbot would soon be performing an early-morning ritual in which he paraded round the room, acknowledging every meditator as he passed. We were supposed to lift our hands to prayer position as he went by. I wanted to be part of it.

I decided to get up and stand in the doorway and see what happened. The officious monk didn't seem to mind. Just two or three steps and I'd be on my cushion. How bad could it be? I gave it a try.

But once again, as soon as I stepped forward, the monk was onto me: up went his arm, and he leapt silently to his feet, pointing me back outside.

It stung, like being a child all over again, banished from the classroom. Even though I had mixed feelings about being here at all, facing seventeen-hour days of meditation, nevertheless, now that I was, I didn't want to be excluded. And I was having to sit still out in the corridor anyway. I heard the bells for the start of the period, then the soft susurrus and quiet adjustments of the floorboards as the abbot perambulated the hall in his robes. I hated to think of him noticing the one empty spot, mine.

When the first period ended I got to my feet, thinking that surely now I would be allowed in. But no. I had to stay out for the whole first block, two hours long.

I later learned what my infraction had been: you had to be seated before the guys in white booties set foot in the zendo. That was the rule. After that, the portcullis came down and you were barred till the next sitting block, after breakfast.

But the treatment here was lenient compared with how it was at traditional monasteries in Japan. There, novices weren't even allowed through the monastery gate for days on end. They had to prove their resolve by not getting up from the doorstep for as long as the senior monks deemed necessary. Then, once they were allowed into the compound, there followed customary abuse, physical as well as verbal, before they were allowed anywhere near the zendo itself. It all helped to beat down their pride and willfulness. And my tiny, negligible taste of this process had been enough to bring up a storm of hurt, shame, pride, and scorn. Clearly there was work to do.

THE PERIODS HERE WERE THIRTY-FIVE minutes long, with five minutes of slow walking in between. There would usually be three periods to a block. During the walking meditation you'd pass the occasional person still sitting in their place, doing heroic back-to-back periods.

After just one round, my legs would either be aching or sparking with pain, or else asleep. I couldn't imagine how anyone managed such marathons. Yet in time, as I attended more retreats, I would actually find myself settled enough to start doing it myself now and then.

DURING MORNING WORK PERIODS AT the monastery, everyone was assigned a task. It might be preparing food in the kitchen or hoeing in the garden. Once I'd been on a crew that maneuvered heavy boulders around the bed of the creek that plunged through the monastery grounds, seeking to reduce the effects of erosion with the rocks. Another time I had to "smoosh" canned tomatoes with my bare hands, as the head cook put it, for the lunchtime pasta sauce.

One time I was assigned the task of "cleaning dirt." After cleaning it, I was supposed to spread it out in depressions in the lawns. The idea was to level the dips and declivities in the turf, and the monks would then throw grass seed on the new patches of earth to make the whole lawn smooth and even.

The dirt I had to work with was a mess: a heap of soil full of stones, pieces of bark, stalks, wood chips. The monitor told me to "clean it up." After wondering how to approach the job, I spent a long time sifting it through my fingers, picking out everything that was not soil for safekeeping in a separate bucket. Then the resulting pure loam I crumbled in my fingers until it was fine, brown, and uniform. By the end, it actually did look clean. I heaved wheelbarrows of it up to the lawn and spent the work periods shoveling it into the dips, stamping it down to get it as level as possible. It looked nice: swaths of even brown soil spread across the turf. It reminded me of camouflage I had painted on the wings of World War II model planes I'd made as a boy.

Apparently the master noticed my good work with the dirt. I knew this because two different senior monks pulled me aside to say, with a significant stare, "Your good work on the lawn has not gone unnoticed." I guessed that was code for the master himself having noticed. Who else could merit such deep stares?

ONE NIGHT, SOMETHING WEIRD HAPPENED.

I hit some kind of groove where sitting was preternaturally easy. My mind was silent, the breath silky and evanescent. If I'd asked myself who it was breathing, I probably couldn't have answered. *Why stop?* I thought. I was totally at peace, clearheaded, freehearted, without a trace of sleepiness. So when the zendo emptied at ten that night, I kept my place.

One candle was burning on the altar. Maybe one monk was still sitting somewhere up at the front, far from my place at the back.

I reentered the place of silken ease. I sat and sat. The sense of the world around me faded, until there seemed to be nothing else but the quiet. Time dissolved.

I had no idea how long I had been sitting there when a weird kind of vision started. Skulls were flying around the zendo, a long train of them. They didn't seem particularly intent on me, but it was spooky nonetheless. I watched and waited, and they vanished. Sitting again became warm, deep, smooth. Then, again, somewhere in the middle of the night, the skulls were back.

Feeling a little shaky, I decided to leave them to it and went upstairs to my bunk. I slept for maybe an hour before the wake-up bell rang for the predawn sitting. This time, I was one of the first to be seated in their place.

IN SPITE OF COMING REPEATEDLY, there was one step I couldn't find it in myself to take: formally joining the monastery and becoming a novice here.

I'd had *dokusan* with the abbot a number of times by now. They didn't last long: one or two minutes generally. He would gaze out of the mists of Zen history with his doe-like eyes, brown pate catching a somber gleam in the candlelight, while I fumbled to explain myself.

One time, during a chat at a picnic table outside under the big trees, I managed to blurt out something about the "experience" I'd had up the mountain in New Mexico. I nervously said I had seen that I didn't really exist, and I didn't know what to do about it.

"Tell me more," he said.

I described it.

"Congratulations," he said. "You should be happy. You've had an important insight."

There was relief in having him acknowledge it. So it had been valid, somehow true, as I'd felt.

"But I'm not sure what to do next," I said.

He gazed at me.

"What do I do next?" I almost wailed.

"You might consider some residential time," he said.

He meant at the monastery.

In other words, the solution was to move in. Nonresidents like me slept in dormitories in the main building. Residents shared cabins up among the trees.

The practice was good. The abbot was articulate and inspiring in his Zen talks, and had a gentle, deep gaze that was slightly at odds with the steel hand of his rule. But could I come and live here? I had a girlfriend, I had work, a life. Even had I not, would I want to? He ruled the place like the headmaster of a boarding school at which I'd briefly sojourned as a young teen. You could feel a weight of power hanging under every ceiling. The caustic lieutenants who had the authority to bark orders would stare at you with icy, distant eyes as they told you off. It wasn't a cult—it was easy to come and go—but there was a subservience, a disempowerment among the resident body nevertheless.

But maybe that was necessary in Zen, in any spiritual training.

I heard a story about how once, during a night off, while the staff were discussing what video to watch, one had quipped, "*Absolute Power?*" and the others looked away in uneasy silence.

And they all smoked, scurrying out of the zendo on breaks to spark up hurriedly. I didn't mind—I smoked now and then, too—but I couldn't help wondering if they smoked because *he* smoked.

ONCE, WHILE ANDI WAS TOURING, I stayed for longer than just a week's retreat and was granted temporary resident status, which meant a bunk, hard up against a plywood wall, in a cabin in the woods. On the other side of the wall, two senior students shared a room. They were a couple, senior enough to enjoy the privilege of sleeping together. We could hear them after lights-out, their headboard banging against the wall. A quiet wail would begin, and rise in pitch until it reached a climax, after which the banging would wind down and, with a creak and a groan, the whole cabin would fall silent.

Hey, it's Zen. Anything goes, right?

But hearing the senior monastics hard at it felt vaguely abusive of us underlings, perched on our bunks, awake in the dark. And weren't they *monks*? But in Zen, monastics don't have to be celibate.

I wanted the training, I admired the abbot, but moving in was out of the question. Quite apart from how I felt about it, I still had a life. Maybe I also had pride, self-importance, fear, consternation, wrath—a number of things that might one day have to be worn down. But whatever the case, moving in wasn't happening.

MEANWHILE I WAS GETTING OVERBOOKED with work, and so was Andi. Having struggled to get assignments for years, this didn't look like a problem. But my commissions all involved traveling, and they started to take me away so much I no longer felt allied to our beloved little sublet in New York. And she was often away, too, recording in studios, performing in clubs. We began to drift apart.

That threw me. We had always been so close, so able to communicate freely.

And the Zen was somehow still a problem: What to do next? If what I'd seen in New Mexico was true—that there was a gaping hole in the middle of me, that there *was* no me—then how on earth did you follow up on that?

Perhaps ambition and hard work could offer a way of avoiding that bizarre discovery. If I could just be busy enough, worldly enough, perhaps I could forget all about it.

Although I carried on sitting, I also embarked on an attempted antidote to Zen. I threw myself more than ever into work. I gorged on work and its rewards. That gaping hole—viewed the wrong way, it was a maw aching to be stuffed with distraction.

I STILL HAD SOME NOTION deep inside that the purpose of activities was to do them to the point where you no longer needed them. Perhaps it came from the early imprint of my parents' divorce, or the misguided longing to split up my father and stepmother so I could restore our family. Part of me still viewed a relationship as a training whose goal was to no longer need it. Somewhere in the maelstrom of work and travel, Andi and I broke up.

Thereafter I often woke in the middle of the night. I'd smoke cigarette after cigarette by the window of whatever hotel I was staying in, in whatever city or backwater I was traveling through, as I hopscotched Latin America on writing assignments with a fat wallet of flight coupons, and more money pouring through my bank account than ever, chomping my way through paragraphs and dinners and debaucheries, like a voracious sea lion desperate to find the one tasty morsel it still hankers after. I had an on-and-off love affair with alcohol and could get lit up at night. I had a touch of hypomania in me, especially while in the midst of a creative project, which I almost always was.

But I was doing the same thing with Zen. I thought the point was to get cooked by it so you no longer needed it. The plan was to do it, "get" it, and discard it. I had trouble getting my head around the maintenance model: that you might keep doing things for their own sake. Maybe the blind spot also came from writing books, where you threw yourself into a project until you gratefully finished it and got on with a new one. Or from eczema: itching and sores—how to get over them, be done with them.

I wanted the result, not the process. Was it just me, or was the Western spiritual way, with its emphasis on redemption, more inclined to results? The Day of Judgment, the end of days: one day, everything will count for something, every last deed and smallest act. But what if the day when things counted was not far off, but here, now, and the closest we would get to a result was what we were seeing before us. *This* was the result. Perhaps in a sense there *were* no results—this whole universe was just doing what it did. It wasn't interested in results, only process.

LOVE HAD FALLEN INTO TATTERS. I remember sitting on a beach on the small, unvisited island of Providencia, off the coast of Colombia, where I was writing a story about conch divers. For a few dollars a local fisherman had sold me a bag of cocaine that he said had washed up with the tide. I didn't know how much was in it—five or ten grams—but it was pure, he said, *perfectamente puro*. With me was a woman from New York, a writer, TV producer, sometime actress—an accomplished woman.

Why was she willing to be here with me? Because I had money coming in, I was on the masthead of a glossy magazine, I was single. Because the island was exotic, and a trip down sounded like an adventure. Why had I asked her? Because we both had a twinkle in the eye for each other, and I was no longer with the woman I had loved. And because sex was one activity that could temporarily assuage the hole in the middle.

We took turns snorting the powder from the back of a CD, sipping ice-cold bottles of Colombian beer beaded with dew, while the sun lowered a dazzling path onto the water. This could have been another magic moment on a beach. But I wasn't available for any magic. I had tried, I thought—with love, therapy, writing, Zen—and what had it all come to? Here I was in proverbial paradise, lost.

BACK IN THE CITY I started visiting the Friday Night Workshops of Dr. Albert Ellis, a notorious psychologist. He lambasted Freudian analysis while promoting his own approach, Rational Emotive Behavior Therapy, which involved the use of classical Stoic philosophy. In time it became the basis for cognitive behavioral therapy.

Friday evenings at his Institute he would invite unwitting subjects onto a small stage, and proceed to expose and ridicule their implicit belief system. At the end, far from feeling humiliated, these victims would rise from the stage feeling supported and freed from long tyrannies of self-wrought misery.

He was also a pioneer of affordable therapy, and offered low-cost half-hour sessions in which he would power through his ingenious methods, culled from Epictetus and Marcus Aurelius, for eliciting and disputing the hidden beliefs that caused emotional disturbance. I discovered that it was he who had coined some of the terms Harvey had taught me, such as "catastrophizing" and "must-urbating." I was evidently still wrestling with these demons of the mind, and did a series of sessions with him. It turned out to be just what I needed, dotting the *i*'s on Harvey's

work, and gave me tools for managing my errant psyche for decades ahead.

IT ALL ENABLED A SUNBEAM of sanity to reach me. When it
came to Zen, I realized, the cure had to be homeopathic. Only
like could cure like. I needed more Zen, not less. I had to find a
guide.

Teacher, Teacher

A FRIEND TOOK ME TO HEAR a Tibetan lama give a talk. He sat on a cushioned throne, carefully working his way through an arcane text, sweeping sections of parchment flat with the back of his forearm, which protruded, bare, from his burgundy robes. As he expounded on the ancient scripture, a long-legged blonde at his side translated for him. Every so often they broke off to whisper to each other and exchange furtive smiles, her beautiful face tipped toward his.

In the course of his long exegesis he paused to tell us what a rare, special teaching we were receiving, such that if we were to hear it and question it or be skeptical, it would not be good for us. I was wondering what he meant by that, when finally he divulged that such was this teaching's profundity that any non-Buddhist who heard it and did not then and there "take refuge" and become a Buddhist would be risking "a bad rebirth."

In other words, by stumbling into that room that afternoon,

we had inadvertently put ourselves in a most perilous situation: either we believed the teaching, to the extent that we at once became students of the master, or we faced rebirth as an earthworm, at one stroke invalidating the rest of our lives, condemning ourselves to incalculably more lifetimes merely to regain the level we were currently on—a level fortunate enough to allow us to encounter these very teachings.

It was brilliantly circular. In fact, it was similar to the churchmen of my youth, who had told us we must believe them or else burn eternally. By comparison, Zen seemed a meadow of reasonableness.

I TRIED A SESSHIN AT the Zen Studies Society, an august old center in New York where D. T. Suzuki had taught, enticing J. D. Salinger and other New York luminaries to try the practice. (Salinger had used a Zen koan as the epigraph to his *Nine Stories*.)

At the New York center, the busy Manhattanites bustled down a long corridor lined with cupboards, where they shucked off their suits and work clothes and donned Japanese monks' robes, then clipped about self-consciously in zoris, which they slipped off at the door to the zendo.

It was all a bit strange. During the chanting in the zendo, for example, they swayed in unison, reciting the verses at an ever more frenzied pace, until they were screaming their heads off. Then a peal of bells rang out and everyone stopped, and a fizzing silence filled the room.

They were good at it. They'd practiced together a lot. You could feel a satisfied glow in the room afterwards.

The sitting periods were unpredictable. The teacher didn't like to be tied down to certain lengths of time. If he felt the meditation was getting deep, he would have a period go on and on. Which was all very well for whoever was finding it deep, but for any poor souls who might be having a shallow, challenging time, it could be hard. Whatever normal lifeline you could throw yourself, along the lines of *It's only half an hour, how bad can it be*, was gone. You had no idea how long you were stuck there.

The first time *dokusan* was announced, they all grabbed their cushions, leapt to their feet, and careened down the hall, like kids racing for a treat.

I was sitting in an annex to the main zendo. The second time the opportunity for *dokusan* came around, I thought to myself, *Well, why not?* I picked up my cushion and nipped out the door into the corridor. I was expecting to see a throng of eager students already on their way to the line where you waited for interviews, but to my surprise, there was no one in the hallway. I briskly trotted down to the far end, just in time to meet the stampede emerging from the main zendo. Thus I found myself near the front of the line.

When I met with the master, a small, hefty Japanese man called Eido Shimano Roshi, he simply told me to sit some more so that we could "start." I didn't know what he meant, but humbled my way back to the zendo to do what he said.

During the next break, one of the zendo monitors, a tall guy, lean and scarecrow-like under his billowing robes, took me aside and scolded me for jumping the line. I should not have made my way up the back corridor. Instead I should have passed through the main zendo. That way, I would not have had such an advantage in the *dokusan* line. That was evidently part of the reason unseasoned newcomers like me had been placed way back in the annex. The corridor was to be used only for purposes *other* than *dokusan*.

Oy vey.

AT THE LUNCH PARTY AT the end of the retreat, a pair of beautiful young women who looked like they might have been models or actresses floated about the old patriarch in his robes, waiting on him hand and foot while he sat cross-legged at the end of a low table, his minions around him.

A plump old guy, he had a flinty gleam in his eye. The young women were students of his, they had been on the retreat, and now they kept bending over him to help with the dishes on the low table. No one else seemed to think this odd, yet I thought I could sense an uncomfortable air in the room.

Meanwhile his Japanese wife rushed about, bossing people, making them do chores, telling them off for not doing them well enough, me included.

The people here seemed cowed, as if they either had some secret to protect or else some sense of not living up to an ideal they ought to. It was hard to put a finger on, but there was something oppressive in the air.

When I tried to chat with one of the beautiful women, she glanced in the master's direction and then looked away, reluctant to talk to me. This surprised me, because she had given me the odd encouraging glance during the retreat, when we'd passed each other in the corridor, and across the room during meal times. I had begun to make a little story out of it. How cool it would be to have a girlfriend who did Zen. We could encourage each other in our practice and go to retreats together. And it didn't seem that the fantasy was entirely groundless. Once, when we brushed past each other in the corridor, she had flashed me a tiny but unmistakable smile.

But now, during the post-retreat lunch, she quickly turned away, ignoring me, and returned to her geisha duties. Just as she did so, I caught the old master glancing at us from his low table.

After my failure with her, I sat down on a couch with my plate of food and tried to make small talk with the older man beside me, who wore an odd little four-cornered beret.

I asked whether he had done many of these *sesshins*, or if this was his first. His response was to send me a brief scowl and get up, leaving me alone.

Later, when the lunch party was breaking up, I noticed the old master pull precisely the same kind of hat onto his head. Was it some insignia of office? Had that man been an assistant master, veteran of a thousand retreats, too enlightened to talk to a novice like me, who anyway was too deluded to recognize his enlightened stature? I never found out.

But later on, I did read about the master when *The New York Times* ran an exposé on his long history of alleged abuse of female students. Some said he ought to be in jail. He would offer "special teachings" to certain honored students, inviting them up to his private chambers, only to force himself on them.

Sex had messed up my childhood family. Dad used to say, "You have to *organize* your sex life, boychick." But he organized his in such a way that it led to disarray in the wider family, misery in the closer.

In the Zen world, some people said this particular scandal in New York was complex. The master's teaching was remarkable, and you had to put up with the less desirable aspects. But according to the book *The Zen Predator of the Upper East Side*, the master was simply a serial abuser.

Zen could be tough. Some old masters used to make their monks sit naked on a rock all night in summer, enduring the mosquitoes without flinching. It was mind over matter, as in the TV show *Kung Fu*. Nevertheless I didn't believe it was right to have to push through a barricade of wrongdoing to find authentic teaching.

WHEN WORK TOOK ME TO Europe, I used a few days off to explore the peaceful, tender teachings of the beloved Vietnamese Zen master Thich Nhat Hanh. His base of operations was Plum Village, in the wine country of Bordeaux, France.

Here, on every quarter hour, when the clocks around the property chimed like electronic Big Bens, everyone would freeze. You were supposed to pull your face into a half smile and breathe gently while the bells sounded. It helped us stay mindful, conscious of what we were doing.

I couldn't help remembering a *Doctor Who* episode I'd seen as a child in which the members of a cult did the same thing. Having been conditioned like Pavlov's dogs, at the sound of a bell they would stand still and await their great leader's orders.

I liked the place, though. It was a large complex, spread out over dozens of acres. There was a men's village, a women's village, and a family village. "Thay" ("Teacher"), as everyone called him, would sometimes stay in a modest wooden hut in a dell, down amid a stand of fruit trees.

It was a quiet time of year, with no big retreat going on. Thay invited all the Western students to join him in the hermitage for tea one afternoon. Some fifteen of us gathered in a circle on the floor to talk about emotions and practice. He said a few words, then, as we all slurped from our hot little cups of tea, we were invited to go round the circle, offering our thoughts. He might or might not comment when someone had finished. Then he would say the next person's name, inviting them to speak.

It was a good way to have a discussion. At first, listening, I was hoping for some kind of exploration that would lead to a conclusion. Instead it seemed to be more about allowing a spaciousness in which people could have their say. It was more like airing a topic and trusting that that in itself would allow it to work its way into people's lives.

I knew that Thay was virtually a business unto himself. He'd put out a great number of books, which had sold prodigiously in multiple languages, such that the organization had its own publishing imprint. He traveled the world lecturing to large audiences, leading huge retreats. Yet he seemed quite at home here in this one-room hut. I gathered that he used it for small meetings rather than living in it. But a short clothes rack stood in an alcove, with six wooden coat hangers, five of them holding simple robes and jackets and the sixth empty, presumably the home of the robe he was wearing now. There was a humility and simplicity about the hut that suited him.

Plum Village was home to a lot of non-Westerners. In fact, the project seemed to be as much about establishing a place for Vietnamese to come and live in the West as about bringing Zen to Westerners. Cohorts of vibrant nuns from his home country ran the place, preparing delicious and exotic food, having us clean and sweep the various buildings of the center with foreign brooms and mops. It was like being at some kind of summer camp. It seemed to have a demographic and sociological function as well as a spiritual one, and it was built to accommodate a lot of people.

Meanwhile the more senior Western members spoke of their leader in tones of awe and adulation that managed to convey, all at once, that a mere visitor would naturally have the same feelings about the great man that they did yet wouldn't be so privileged as to know, as they did, just how far he exceeded all other human beings, though even a mere visitor would sense his exalted status.

I found it a bit nauseating. Apparently I was still just too full of myself to surrender to the kind of help the place had to offer.

But I made friends with an interesting man from Korea, a former motorbike champion who had suffered two catastrophic crashes on the racetrack. The first led to six months in hospital, after which he resumed racing. Then the second had him hospitalized for eighteen months, and he gave up racing for good.

"I just couldn't think what else to do," he told me in his excellent English. "I missed racing so much. Then I knew there was only one thing—I had no choice. I had to become a Zen monk."

He said he had never imagined how happy he could be without racing.

I MIGHT GRUMBLE ABOUT THESE centers, yet every time I went to one, there was always a sweetness, a sense of justified indolence, of coming closer to life, to a more authentic self. They weren't holy places resting on holy laurels. They had a practice, a way of helping ordinary people that was itself ordinary. It didn't rely on magic or the supernatural. It just asked human beings to shelve their usual busyness and look deeper into their own experience, their very consciousness, and offered a means for doing so.

In the stillness of retreats, new ideas would surface, new poems, stories, book plans. I wrote more deeply, more naturally, afterwards. They brought me closer to material I wanted to work with: stories of troubled men and families, poems of appreciation for the things of the world. The meditation practice reawakened my love for land—for fields and woods, for the look of hills in rain, of trees tossing in wind. I wrote poems about them and remembered how I had loved the land around our home back in my teen years—the hedgerows and woods and river.

After any retreat, there was always a sense of having been cleansed, absolved even, and of returning to the world with new eyes.

YET YOU HAD TO BE careful. Once, in London, I saw a plaque on a house near where I was staying: WEST LONDON BUDDHIST CENTRE. *How lucky*, I thought, and went in to find out more.

Some people were milling around the ground floor. Two of them disappeared behind a door as I entered, another went downstairs to a basement, and a fourth, a guy in a woolen hat pulled low, walked past me, hands in his pockets. None of them said hello, and I found myself standing alone in the hallway.

With the doors closed, it was dark. *What should I do?* There was no obvious reception area. I had the distinct sensation I'd arrived in time to witness the end of an argument.

The guy in the hat reappeared. *Great*, I thought.

But he brushed past me again and vanished through a door at the end of the hall.

A moment later he reemerged, peered at me through the gloom, and asked, "Can I help you?"

"I was just wondering—" I began. "I was walking by and saw the sign, and wondered if you had meditation times."

"What's that?" he asked. "Meditation?"

"Yes."

"We don't do much of that. That comes later," he said.

"Oh," I said, starting to feel uncomfortable. Whatever this place was, it wasn't like any Buddhist center I'd been to before.

"I can show you something to read, if you want to know about Buddhism." He opened a door off the corridor, into a narrow, bright room with tall windows down one wall and bookshelves lining the others.

It was either a bookshop or a library. But as I started to browse the shelves I saw not one Buddhist book that I recognized. Instead, it dawned on me that every single spine had the same name on it. Every book in the place had the same author: someone called Sangharakshita.

"Who is Sangharakshita?" I asked.

He let out a laugh of scorn. "Are you serious? He's only the one truly enlightened master in the West."

I was taken aback. He probably didn't mean it, but he seemed to be suggesting that all the other teachers currently active, some of whom I had visited, many of some renown, were unqualified, in spite of having followings who clearly felt otherwise. In one casual, caustic phrase he had dismissed them all—in favor of the mysterious Sangharakshita.

I left.

Later I discovered that I had stumbled into an outpost of the formidable empire of an Englishman who had gone to India as a military recruit in the late 1940s and come back "an enlightened master." He soon attracted twelve disciples in Bayswater and proceeded to build a powerful organization, with an awesome portfolio of properties, and centers up and down the land, presenting themselves as orthodox Buddhist centers even though the teaching was a mix of Theosophy, Rosicrucianism, and Buddhism. Some said they were a dangerous cult, and not long after I encountered them, *The Guardian* ran a front-page story with a photo of the leader under the headline IS THIS MAN EVIL? In a tide of negative publicity, the group changed its name to the Triratna Buddhist Order and, after some institutional soul-searching, carried on.

NOW THAT I HAD FINALLY concluded I needed a teacher, I had underestimated what was involved in finding one. I was my own man, authority-free. I didn't like teachers. They scared me. They were like my dad when I was a teenager: they found me lacking, distasteful. They made me feel ashamed. My response had been to do without them. I hadn't drifted into an independent profession, answerable to no one, by chance.

One exception had been my old trombone teacher, Jack Pinches, a remarkable man from the North of England. His father, a coal miner, had locked him in his room with a trombone from the age of six, forcing him to learn to play. By fourteen Jack had a spot in the fabled Black Dyke Mills Band, and by sixteen he was its principal trombone, in which office he traveled to the Royal Albert Hall, in London, to play a solo under the baton of Sir Thomas Beecham, broadcast live on BBC Radio. Next morning he received a telegram inviting him to join the BBC Symphony Orchestra. He moved to London and never looked back.

Jack was a good teacher and taught me how to be a student.

I knew what he expected of me, and when I let him down, I didn't like it. Under his guidance I rapidly improved. He was pleased, and I liked pleasing him. By the time I was sixteen he was booking me for semi-professional concerts, insisting to the organizers that I be paid like any other musician. I'd come home with checks for then-staggering sums like thirty or forty pounds.

But aside from Jack's tutelage, I didn't like men telling me what to do. I thought our task as a new generation was to overthrow the status quo. The men I idolized were Che Guevara, a few rock stars, some poets, and Gustavo, the Colombian priest who had visited Oxford.

I TRIED ANOTHER ZEN CENTER, a train ride away in Northumberland. It was the kind of place a monastery belonged: a stone house with a chapel-like zendo high on the gray moors, a place fit for the old Celtic saints, where the wind ruled and the rain lashed through in showers that soaked you in a moment. In winter, thin snow lay on the ground and yellow light filtered over the dark hills.

I went a number of times. The monks were given the title "reverend," followed by an old Saxon, Celtic, or biblical name: Rev. Ethelred, Rev. Ishmael, Rev. Frideswide. There were "very reverends" and "right reverends" too, like in the Church of England. They wore habits reminiscent of those of Christian monks and moved with stooped, medieval-looking shoulders, seeming to enjoy the old-fashioned costumes. There was a touch of the Sealed Knot about it. The Buddhist sutras, normally chanted in a deep monotone, here were set to Anglican plainsong, accompanied by psalm-like chords on an electric organ. I found it a little strange, yet very warmhearted.

The whole place had been set up by an imposing Englishwoman, the Reverend Master Jiyu-Kennett Roshi, who in the 1950s went to Japan as a piano teacher and underwent a series of turns by which she left Japan "an enlightened master." She had written two volumes about her life. They were autohagiography, a genre I'd never read before, full of wonders that had befallen her on the path—a far cry from the literalist versions of Zen I had come to know in America. There were beautiful moments in them—the descriptions of sitting at dawn in the old wooden zendo, of wise old monks who helped her, and wicked ones who tried to block the foreign woman's progress, and timely interventions by the holy abbot that helped her training to its early conclusion—but it was a bit like reading the life of a saint written by said saint.

It was also hard to understand just what exactly had happened to her at the monastery in Japan. Something had, and whatever it had been, the abbot had taken it as a sign that she must "inherit his Dharma," and teach Zen. She left for Northern California, where she set up her own monastic order and a thriving monastery, of which this Northumbrian center was an outpost.

Portraits of her hung around the abbey, icon-like images with fans of light beaming from her generous frame.

The reverends at Throssel Hole were gentle souls. They were in the Soto lineage of Zen, and their practice was neither following the breath nor pondering a koan, but "just sitting." When they gave instruction to newcomers, the body posture was set up as I was used to, but when it came to what to do once meditation started, the bright-faced, dark-robed monk teaching us simply said, "So that's it. Just sit."

I couldn't believe it. "What should we *do*?" I asked. "No breath counting, no breath watching?"

"Sometimes there's a kind of bright feeling" was all he said.

The people were friendly. There was a lot of sitting around drinking cups of milky English tea. There were several daily services—matins, lauds, and vespers, the round of an old English monastery but carried into a Zen context. The Buddha was called Lord Buddha (as opposed to Lord Jesus) and there were Buddhist festivals, in which they paraded around the zendo tossing handfuls of colorful confetti into the air. Dragons were painted on the ceilings among clouds, and they followed a traditional calendar of "fourth" and "ninth" days that cut across the Western weeks and months.

I signed up for "spiritual counsel" and was assigned to a sweet Swiss monk working as the monastery cook. He had no particular advice about my now weary "insights" and "experiences," but he told me the story of how he'd given up life as a banker in Zurich to become a Zen monk.

He'd had a good job and a nice apartment and liked to ride his BMW motorbike fast on the weekends.

"I used to tear off into the Alps when work got too much. I'd tell myself, *Just wait for the weekend*," he said. "Then it stopped working. One weekend I emptied the tank three times, and inside I was still burning. I left the bike in a forest and walked into the trees, not caring where I went. I didn't know what I was looking for, but something boiled up in me and I knew I'd been living wrong. I'd heard about this monastery in England and knew I had to come. I sold everything and handed in my notice at work."

Was that what I would have to do? All I wanted was a doctor

to set my broken limbs, but here it was again: the residential way. You had to move into the hospital.

ONCE, WHILE I WAS ON retreat there, the monks held a festival in which they paraded around while chanting a psalm-like sutra, until the abbot settled on a throne under a canopy. They were each allowed to come up and ask him a public question.

One young monk about my age approached the throne and quietly said, "I don't know why I'm here. I'm not sure it's right."

He spoke with downcast eyes, clearly in some inner torment.

I held my breath for the abbot's answer. After a long pause he pronounced, "It doesn't matter."

And that was it.

The monk bowed and thanked him, as protocol required.

I felt shocked. It hit home, what this monk had done: given up his life. Pubs, friends, girlfriend perhaps, job, career, home, car, Mum, Dad, siblings, all of it. There were people who did that. And now he was regretting it. The trail of hope that had brought him to it had vanished. And all the abbot had to say was that it didn't matter.

Later, with the abbot's retort still rankling, it occurred to me: What if there was some wisdom to his response nonetheless? I was familiar through my own practice with how overwhelming thoughts could be, yet when you recognized that they were just thoughts, their power could evaporate, and you found yourself back in the here and now, where all was easier, where you could experience things without judgment, without reactivity. Still, I was glad I wasn't in that monk's position.

I wanted a dharma practice compatible with Western life: no zoris, no robes, shaved skulls, or chopsticks, no power vortex within an enclosed chamber. The insights that I'd stumbled upon had been indiscriminate, and though there was surely more to Zen than random revelations, nevertheless the world Zen spoke of was the one they had revealed. I didn't see why it couldn't be practiced with Western manners and ways, without donning costumes, without entering an authoritarian force field.

Nor did I believe there was anything intrinsically wrong with Western cultural trappings; or at least there was nothing necessarily better about Eastern ones. To adopt a culture not one's own was affectation or contrivance. At least it would have been for me. English poetry, for example—the best of it was as good as anything on earth. I didn't want the foreign culture. I just wanted the insight into existence—the one place Western culture dared not go.

I went several times nonetheless, and up on the moors I learned more about getting by in a Zen monastery. You were assigned a locker in the zendo for your bag, bedding, and mattress, to be unrolled on the floor each night. I learned how to scrub grout in a shower stall with a toothbrush and bleach. I got used to the vaguely unnerving smell of a monastery bathroom. It helped break down some of my pampered squeamishness.

Yet if I were to have to make a commitment like that monk, and change my life, where would I do it? And what about work? What about finding a partner? What about friends? It seemed an awful choice to face. I was no longer a youth; I had a career that had taken years to get off the ground and required constant effort to maintain. Could I do it?

I GOT BUSY WITH ANOTHER round of publicity for a book, into which I plunged again with undignified enthusiasm, vainly trundling around the country on a promotional tour.

Meanwhile I had found a little Zen group in Bristol, not too far from the rented cottage near Stroud where I was temporarily living. The group met weekly, and I started driving down to join them when I could. They had no teacher but were very formal: you had to pull on a robe from a rack by the door when you walked in, and sit in a precise posture, and when it came to walking meditation, the forearms had to be held just so, each breath released in time with each step. They'd correct you if they weren't satisfied with your style.

It didn't feel like home, but I didn't mind. It was Zen. The group was part of the International Zen Association, a movement founded in France by a monk called Taisen Deshimaru. He was famous for a hagiographic incident during the Second World War, in which he had been on a cargo vessel with a holdful of dynamite when the ship hit rough weather. The crew panicked, fearing the explosives would be set off in the rough seas, but Deshimaru calmly sat himself down on top of the volatile cargo and meditated, keeping it quiet through the storm. So his devotees whispered.

He found his way to France, where his Zen spread like wildfire. Zen had become so popular there, largely thanks to him, that the word had entered the language as a synonym for *calme, tranquille, cool.*

This Bristol zendo, just up the street from the VIP Massage Parlour, was an outpost of his empire. It received an occasional visit from a Belgian monk but, as sometimes happens with Zen groups, was currently in a teacherless lull.

There were different styles of Zen, but it was possible to find the same warm heart in all of them. This was the point, I thought: Zen looked formal from the outside, but its heart was warm. Yet it was a secret—you had to find that warmth yourself. No one could direct you to it.

It always felt good to be traveling toward a Zen center, no matter what kind of journey: grinding up a freeway on a Greyhound bus, taking a train north through the rain, sitting in traffic on the M5. Journeys toward the dharma—the teachings of Zen—had a way of trumping other concerns.

THE EIGHTH-CENTURY MASTER YAKUSAN* SAID that during his Zen training he had felt like a mosquito hovering around an iron ox, trying to find a way to penetrate it. Then he met his master, Sekito Kisen,† had his awakening, and "gained entry."

I could relate to the early Yakusan. Sometimes I felt as if I was buzzing around like a mosquito, trying this center and that, this teacher and that, unable to find an entry and not even knowing what I was trying to enter.

I still wasn't living anywhere permanently. I put up in sublets and rented rooms and kept the leases monthly. I wrote books and wrote for magazines, had novels and short stories taking shape, and now and then a clutch of poems. I bounced where the assignments took me: I never had to deal with much except writing; I was always out the door. There was always another assignment. I could justify any restlessness: moving was work. Along the way I threaded in Zen as best I could. I sat every day without fail. I did retreats when there was a center nearby, or when a goad of guilt or promise

---

* Chinese: Yaoshan, 745–828.

† Chinese: Shitou Xiquan, 700–790.

pricked me. I tried other places. I didn't stop. But I gave up
on finding a teacher.

I KEPT IN TOUCH WITH writer friends in New Mexico, and
when a teaching assistantship opened up at a college out there, I
applied for it and went for a semester, and then longer, living in
a quiet house in a suburban neighborhood of Las Cruces, in the
southern desert, under cottonwood trees. Each morning before
dawn I drank pints of weak American coffee and read poetry,
devouring work I'd ignored for years, then went in to class to
teach composition.

Meanwhile I had reconnected with a childhood poet friend,
Sam Willetts, and in some unanticipated throwback to our teen
years, we started sharing poems again, faxing them back and forth.

The meditation helped the poetry, and the poetry helped
foster a meditative life. There was a kind of indolence that was
essential for poetry, which was kin to Zen. And teaching writing
was a reminder of something beyond sales and promotion that a
writer could be concerned with. It was like taking off a cagoule
of angst and receiving a little sunshine on the skin. Some things
could only be done in their own time, and that didn't make them
less worthwhile. Teaching, poetry, and Zen were among them.

I began to learn from other writers at the college. I had been so
much my own man, I hadn't realized there were people willing to
help. Perhaps the wisdom of Zen was creeping in bit by bit, touching the way I lived, not guarded but ready to give and receive help.
One could feel goodwill toward just about everybody if one wanted.

THERE WAS NO ZEN CENTER in Las Cruces, but two hours
away, out in the desert, in a stony valley where no river ran, stood

a small Vipassana center. I used to growl up there in my beaten-up car some weekends for their practice days.

Vipassana was another form of Buddhist practice. A friendly, handsome man ran the center, and a little group of us would lounge around the walls of the meditation room, sitting in whatever position we liked, with blankets and a variety of cushions piled around and beneath us, enduring painfully long sitting periods—so long that even the props would stop helping. Then there'd be equally long periods of slow walking meditation, done alone in the yard outside. One weekend I helped them build some new walls, fueled by slices of home-baked bread spread thickly with peanut butter, tahini, and honey and mugs of coffee.

The feel was different from Zen, even though the practice was similar: Watch the breath, watch body sensations, watch thoughts, and so on. It was less crisp, less concerned somehow with the fundamentals of raw experience. Even though Vipassana was already starting to burgeon nationally, it attracted me less. After Zen, it seemed a little murky. But it was a stopgap, and the people were kind.

I also drove up to Santa Fe now and then, four hours away, to visit Upaya Zen Center, led by the charismatic former anthropologist Joan Halifax. The beautiful center had grown up around the very temple where I had first been taught zazen. Joan was a powerful intellectual, versed in psychology and sociology, and a powerful teacher. Committed to her work helping the poor in the Himalayas, she was famous. I'd first heard of her while studying for my PhD, in London, when a tutor of Greek religion, a troubled, brilliant man, gave me a book by her on Amazonian shamanism. It was exciting to meet her, shaven-headed and robed in black now, with bright blue eyes that you felt could pierce any artifice.

I started going up for as long as I could, and in time started to study more formally with Roshi Joan. During breaks I would stay in Santa Fe, walking over to the center before dawn each morning for the early sitting, followed by a short, formal "service" and sometimes a bowl of hot cereal afterwards.

⚱

LIFE SPED UP. A BEAUTIFUL English photo researcher came and visited me in the desert. She was also a part-time printmaker, a tender, clear-sighted woman. We fell in love. A little younger than I was, she was wiser, with her feet on the ground.

I sometimes wondered if it was the renewed commitment to poetry, my first creative love, or the support of the small group of devoted writers I had fallen in with, or having recently read *War and Peace* and seeing in the narrative a reflection of my own vagrant search, and realizing under Tolstoy's scrutiny that it might all have been preparatory, a prologue to something larger, more important. Or maybe it was just turning thirty-three. Or maybe it was the practice bearing more fruit. But suddenly the relationship was serious.

In fact, I sometimes wondered if I'd known from the start that it would be. When Clare and I first sat down together the day we met, right away as we began talking I had a strange sense of there being a new kind of earth under me, a ground that extended I didn't know how far, but that could be trusted, on which I belonged, and perhaps so did she. Her being beautiful, well-read, and reared on a farm in a village not far from the valley where I had roamed as a boy all helped, but they weren't the reason. It was that ground itself.

She had grown up in south Warwickshire, then studied medieval history at college before working for several years in a medical history library on the Euston Road in London. She was everything I was not: not only cultured, but graceful, witty, and grounded, never having strayed too far from the soil that bore her. I fell in love quickly, but she made us take it slowly. If this was going to last, better to let it grow roots and not shoot up like a young bamboo, she thought.

In time she joined me in Las Cruces, where the college had extended my assistantship, and she enrolled in the art department. We decided this was it, and pledged ourselves down in Juárez, just over the border in Mexico, in a fabled bar called the Kentucky Club, sealing it with the tang of salty, tart margaritas.

She was part of a new well-being, and so were my colleagues at the college, and so was poetry, and so, too, the modest, steady paychecks that represented a departure from the lone-wolf freelance life. When I was offered a poetry fellowship back in England at Oxford Brookes University, she was already pregnant and wanted to be closer to home, and we moved again, back to Oxford.

Because of the coming child, and because of her sober influence, I found the self-discipline to start sending out more of the poems and stories I had been compulsively reworking over the years, and over time some of them won prizes, and a collection of poems followed, and, hesitantly, I let the draft of a first novel out the door, then another, and entered into another kind of literary life, one I'd been batting against the windows of for years, joining the reading circuits of literary England. Meanwhile our first son arrived, then a second. It all happened in a rush. Husband, poet, fiction writer, father.

I HAD A DREAM ONE night that Doctor Who's Tardis had dropped into our garden. It was good news. All I had to do was enter it. But I didn't know how to open the door.

With no particular hope, I started going to the little local Zen center in Oxford. The master here was a stately, brisk Canadian nun. She had done her training in Japan, and when she gave dharma talks, once again I'd feel a start of recognition at the world she talked about: unlike this one in every regard, except absolutely the same.

The glimpses of Zen's world had become albatrosses rotting round my neck. I had given up hope of either getting rid of them or knowing what to do about them. I knew what I had seen; I knew Zen dealt in what I had seen; yet I still couldn't seem to get the two to connect.

When I met with the teacher, I tried to explain how, in spite of my efforts, I couldn't seem to get my life and practice to align, and now my wife and I had kids, and parenthood wasn't making it easier to practice. She told me that if life was not supporting my practice, then I had better drop it.

Perhaps it's supposed to be like this. The Zen postulants used to sit outside the monastery gates for days on end. Maybe the dharma was far from satisfied with the spirit I had shown—too prone to vacillation, too attached to my precious identities as writer, partner, father. The monks left me outside the gate, and when they came back and opened up again, I had gone off and got married, got lost in publication.

Yet at the same time the dharma is infinitely patient. And also won't be rushed.

I KEPT GOING TO THE Oxford center once a week anyway. I'd sit in my place and stew quietly, letting the forces in my psyche exhaust themselves.

This is part of Zen training. There is the sudden side—the unbidden revelation of the nature of self and world—and the gradual: the soil prepared through long cultivation.

One night the teacher gave a talk about Master Kyogen.* Kyogen had been a clever young man, she said. He went to see Master Isan,† a great figure of classical Chinese Zen, with a battery of scriptural knowledge at his back. Isan, who led a large monastery, asked the brilliant young Kyogen a question: "What was your original face before your parents were born?"

This is a famous "barrier" koan in Zen, the teacher explained: a question given to novices that may help precipitate a breakthrough. Kyogen took the question to his scriptures and commentaries and searched for a quote to bring back to Master Isan by way of an answer. All night long he pored over his texts and searched through his papers, but he found nothing. Crestfallen, in the morning he went to the master to confess his failure.

Isan said, "I could answer the question for you, but you wouldn't thank me later."

---

* Chinese: Xiangyan, d. 898.

† Pronounced "Iss-an." Chinese: Guishan, 771–853.

Kyogen was despondent. Here he was, a gifted young man, at an impasse. He did what many of us might do—packed his bags and left.

Convinced he was unworthy of being a monk, he wandered the countryside as an itinerant laborer. Years passed, and he found himself working as the caretaker of a rustic shrine. One morning as he was out sweeping the yard, a piece of broken tile got caught in his broom and flew against a bamboo stalk, where it struck with a hollow knock.

Tock. The teacher tapped her lectern to illustrate it.

When Kyogen heard that sound, something unexpected happened. He and the sound became one. The whole world was swallowed up in the knock. He was ready. The soil had been tilled.

He wrote a verse afterwards:

"One knock, and I have forgotten everything I ever knew."

She repeated that line. "He means everything is forgotten. But *everything.*"

I didn't think I had heard the story before, but something about it resonated.

Apparently Kyogen then bathed, changed his clothes, lit incense, and bowed in the direction of Master Isan's temple, saying, "Thank you, Master, for not having told me the answer before. Your kindness was greater than that of my own parents."

A YEAR LATER. A SUNNY April day in Oxford. A sense of well-being, solidity; another book of fiction being published soon; an ongoing fellowship. What more did I want? I couldn't say. Except—something.

With the same kind of motivation with which some might

go to yoga, in hopes of a little self-improvement, I was still drag-
ging myself now and then to the Zen center. It had a new teacher
these days, a lawyer who'd taken early retirement, an Englishman. As luck would have it—almost like in a fairy tale—I was
about to find my first real teacher, right in my old hometown.

Sweet Obedience

FROM THE OUTSIDE, YOU'D NEVER have known that the modest house in an ordinary suburb was the Oxford Zen Centre. Two rooms had been knocked through to make a zendo from front to back. A sheet of board closed off the fireplace, which backed up against the hearth of the house next door. If you were sitting in the right place at the right time, you could hear the evening news, quietly but clearly, broadcast from the neighbors' TV.

I liked the center. I would slip in at the back and settle on the nearest cushion before anybody could ask any questions. The customary black mats here were made of foam rather than the usual kapok, softer on the knees, and the small, stiff cushions gave good support. The room was kept in twilight—the shades drawn in daytime, the lamps low at night. The twilight sometimes felt to me as I imagined the Dead Sea would, supporting us as we floated on our cushions.

I began to sense something new here: I might have had some tastes of Zen's reality, but this teacher was seeing it *now*. That was different. Something woke up in me and knew it had learning to do. Perhaps I was reconstituted enough now, after the New Mexico mountain vacuity, after years of fast-forward careerism, after the flurry of activity around marriage and childbirth, to go further down the path.

The group had been sitting for twenty years, meeting every Thursday evening, and although people came and went, there was a core of seasoned meditators, and I was starting to realize what a difference that made. And they not only sat together but also ran the Prison Phoenix Trust, an organization that brought yoga and meditation into prisons around the country. One of them was a national leader in restorative justice. They were doing their part to make a fairer society.

I'd sit through the rounds, listen to the teacher's talk, and always slip out at the end. An urgent need to get away would come over me, fearful lest anything at all deter me from practice.

But one afternoon I came early, and while getting a drink of water I happened to run into the teacher in the corridor, and he invited me to join him for tea. We sat at a table by the window in the upstairs kitchen, blowing on our hot mugs. It was sunny outside, and our tea steam lit up in the sunshine from the street.

We talked about how long the group had been going, when they'd bought the center, the work they did in prisons.

I quickly found that John Gaynor was a nice man to be around. Whatever I might have thought a Zen teacher should look like, he didn't. A pair of glasses, a handsome, kind face, a mop of mousy English hair: he had been a lawyer most of his career and now ran two charities for the disabled, and still looked like a regular Englishman.

He asked why I'd been coming, what my interest was in Zen. No teacher had directly asked me that before.

I tried to explain about the retreat I'd done in New Mexico years ago but got muddled. I mentioned some of the centers where I had sat, but that didn't go right, either. I wondered suddenly if I had any idea why I had turned to Zen. Then I remembered the beach.

"I guess it dates back to something that happened many years ago," I said.

Just then the refrigerator clicked and started to hum.

In his stride John said, "The fridge seems to agree with you," and only then did I realize I had even heard the fridge.

"So what happened?" he asked.

JOHN AND I SETTLED ON cushions in the *dokusan* room facing each other. A stick of incense on a simple altar released a straight line of smoke. With the Oxford evening coming on, the light was thick both inside the room and out, over the back gardens of the neighborhood.

I felt good. It was April, spring in the air, and as John and I spoke I felt an unfamiliar sense of possibility. John wanted to know what had happened on the beach, and on the New Mexico mountain. As I talked, those moments became vivid again, as if John felt them, too. I'd never known anything quite like that.

It turned out he, too, had had an "opening" early in life. He also acknowledged what I had long felt: namely, that Zen not only knew about these kinds of experience, but in some sense they were, or could be, central to its training.

John had studied this kind of opening, incorporated it, gone beyond it, forgotten it, and now he was here to help. He knew what to do next. "It's high time you took up the koans," he said.

So there was indeed follow-up. Here it was: John was a traditional koan teacher.

Why it took so long to find a teacher able to see where I was coming from, take me in, and start me on the path of training, when Zen is so clear on this process, still baffles me. But that's how it was. Clearly the student had not been ready, or else the teacher would have appeared.

THE FOLLOWING WEEK, WHEN I met with John, he explained that, of the two major forms of Zen that had survived, Soto and Rinzai, the latter favored koan training as a means of working with "experiences." Koans could help to deepen our awareness of the reality we glimpse, and teach us to embody it in our lives.

Exactly what I'd long been seeking.

John also explained that his teacher, the Canadian nun I'd met previously, had studied in Japan with the abbot of a Zen lineage, a man named Yamada Koun* Roshi. Yamada used to explain the process of training with a metaphor:

Imagine a pane of opaque glass. A hole is driven through it, and suddenly we see that there's a world on the other side of the glass: that's *kensho*. Koan study seeks to enlarge the hole, and create new holes, until over time the whole pane becomes riddled with holes, small and large, loses its structural integrity, and collapses. Then the separation between that world and this world is gone.

---

* Pronounced "ko-un," two syllables.

John gave me my first koan there and then, the original ur-koan described by Zen master Mumon in the thirteenth century as "the Gateless Barrier of the Zen sect":

> A monk asked Joshu* in all earnestness: "Does a dog have Buddha-nature?"
> Joshu answered, "Mu."

I'd heard about this koan in talks given by various teachers in other centers. Literally, *mu* means "not." But the real meaning of the koan is something else, something unspeakable.

In the Rinzai sect, the master gives a student a koan and waits to see what happens. The koans are verbal formulations that the student ponders while meditating, said to be impossible to penetrate with the mind: "dark to the mind, radiant to the heart," they say. The only hope is to give up trying to understand the koan and instead let it reveal itself to us. Whatever that means.

Mu is traditionally the first koan. The student uses *mu* as a kind of mantra. On every out-breath, while sitting, they silently voice the sound *mu*. The student is encouraged not to think about its meaning. The koan has work to do. Its work cannot be done by the conscious mind. Only *mu* itself can work on the practitioner, releasing them from a kind of prison they didn't realize they had been caught in. While the conscious mind is kept busy attending to the sound "mu," the "real" *mu* can slip in unnoticed through the back door.

WE ARE LIVING WITH MY mother in her flat in Oxford, the boys sleeping on airbeds, us on a pair of bunks set side by side,

---

* Chinese: Zhaozhou, 778–897.

while we look for a place of our own. Somehow we all get along well, grandmother at peace with the young family, young mother fulfilled in the company of an older woman. Each morning and evening I meditate out on the fire escape. The boys, a pair of leprechauns, enjoy themselves a lot.

Clare and my mother get along well. They understand each other, and their flourishing friendship makes it easier for my mother and me to get along, too. Somehow, with Clare beside me, I appreciate my mother more. Through some adolescent blindness, I long resisted seeing her for the remarkable woman she is. After her career excavating, translating, and promoting Soviet literary theorists, she became one of the first women ordained into the Church of England. We all thought she was just teaching Russian literature at university, but she was also quietly earning a degree in theology, which led to the title of deaconess, then deacon, then finally the Movement for the Ordination of Women (MOW) won their cause, and our mother became one of the first Anglican women priests.

There was some stress at first, being a woman in a passionately sexist organization, until she was invited to lead a small Russian Orthodox institute for visiting scholars. It suited her better. By temperament she preferred the Eastern Church, for its mysticism and its broader moral view of humanity. She was a lifelong seeker, not too proud to keep on learning and deepening in her own religious experience. Clearly I owe more to her— these days, I think, much more—than I used to be willing to admit. Obsessed with my inner troubles, I was blind to the gift of an impulse to explore life deeply that she bequeathed me.

Mum puts aside her institutional concerns when back in the flat, and devotes her attention to toys and foods and things she knows the boys will like. It's a delight to see the love they develop for her, and back the other way. Sometimes she and I talk about Christian mysticism and its congruences with Zen, and our friendship is growing deeper than ever before.

THEN WE MOVE TO A place down by the canal overlooking a boatyard where narrowboats come in for repair. All day long you can hear tinkering, hammering, scraping, and chitchat. Somewhere in the welter of births and books I picked up another poetry fellowship, and I now have two concurrently, one in Oxford, the other at the Wordsworth Trust, in the Lake District. Every other week I take the train up to Grasmere, where Wordsworth lived.

Married, sort of settled, working with modest results, truly on the path of Zen at last: the weary pilgrim has reached the sanctuary, the "refuge," as Buddhism calls it: the safe harbor of practice under a teacher. From now on it's not so much about an external search as an inward one, and as that search will have an inevitable outcome, the story is starting to be over. The seeker has landed on the right shore. Now it's a matter of a long path up a mountain, then a long path down again. But he has found the mountain.

LIVING IN OXFORD AGAIN, I remembered stray moments from my childhood. How I used to be preoccupied by whether I was really awake or not. I'd be walking down the street to school, kicking a pebble, satchel strap digging into my shoulder, when I'd realize I had no idea how I'd got from one lamppost to the next.

Was I fully awake? How could I know? Who could get inside my head and tell me? But I wanted to know.

I remembered the time my brother drove us up the M1 in our

mum's car for the Lindisfarne reunion concert in Newcastle, and we picked up a hitchhiker at a service station. He had a straggly beard, John Lennon glasses, and a lank ponytail. He looked like the guys in Lindisfarne, in fact, the folk rock band we were on our way to see. He climbed into the car with his army surplus jacket dark from rain, and after he twisted in the front seat to pull it off, I laid it down beside me in the back as we hissed up the motorway through the rain.

Somehow we got onto the subject of meditation. He liked to do it, he said. As we traveled in the car he taught me the secret Tibetan formula, *Om mani padme hum*, and showed me how to sit cross-legged. I was thirteen, and spellbound. We tried it for ten minutes while my brother drove, listening to the traffic and the clunk of the wipers on the windshield.

I liked how it felt: quiet inside, but with all the sounds of the world somehow closer.

He told us how he'd been mugged one night by a gang of "bother boys" and left for dead in a stairwell. A neighbor found him and called an ambulance, and he spent three weeks in hospital. He was lucky to have survived.

"Funny thing is," he said, "I didn't mind. I was there, but I wasn't there. It was like I was watching the whole thing on TV."

He didn't mind? It was the seventies, the decade of skinhead violence, of *Clockwork Orange*, and I lived in mortal terror of bother boys. Trembling with hope, I asked, "Do you think the meditation helped you not mind?"

"No question," he replied.

It filled me with a mix of fear and hope. So there was something that could help one in desperate situations: meditation. But would it work for me?

Now, years later, I began to wonder if I'd been seeking Zen or something like it for far longer than I had realized. Perhaps it was no surprise I'd spent years in distress: I'd been looking for something all my life, without knowing what it was.

I'D BEEN A REBELLIOUS BOY. I resisted mindless authority and hated being told to do anything without a reason, and I didn't mind getting into trouble for it. It was a principle. Authority was a violation in and of itself. So I took it on. I smoked, I drank, I secretly sold hash, and soon enough I got thrown out of one school.

My friends and I were rebels. Our icons were iconoclasts, and our role was to tear down the establishment. The Church was ipso facto disqualified, being a tool of the powerful.

It was the age of the backpack and the Shoestring travel guides. We couldn't wait to get away. We practiced, roaming those valleys north of Oxford with our canvas knapsacks, and eventually we did get away, some of us. While working in South America as a youth, I used to think of the old French poem:

Happy the one who goes off on a great voyage—
like Ulysses, or the hero who captured the fleece—
then returns brimful of experience and wisdom
to live the rest of their days amongst their own.

I had done that: gone on a journey and found the Golden Fleece. I just hadn't managed to bring it home.

By the time I found Zen in New Mexico I was already a wanderer, a black sheep who had half-heartedly tried following the family way into academia but veered off into a peripatetic writing life. Unlike my siblings, who developed solid and admirable careers, I was too busy railing at the page in solitary rooms. I couldn't settle as part of the family, couldn't settle anywhere, at least until I'd found my wife. I had been my own boss, footloose, subject to none.

I hadn't realized it had been a life devoid of trust. All my early attempts to find a Zen teacher had been unconscious attempts to puncture an insulating membrane of distrust.

It's funny how it works. The Zen relationship of teacher and student is concerned with one thing: our very existence. As the relationship develops, as the teacher listens to our reports, as our blind spots get exposed, as we feel more keenly their unconditional support, we come to realize they have no agenda of their own.

That's what I was starting to realize about John. Sometimes he would set aside time to see me in London. We'd meet on a corner near a Tube station and go to a café to discuss some point of practice and its implications, or some new glimmer of understanding that had recently dawned on me.

It's hard to express how helpful this was. I saw that meditation was not just meditation. It was a means, a vessel, a vehicle. Through daily sitting, through going on periodic *sesshins* at Cold Ash, a retreat center on the Berkshire Downs where some three dozen of us would sit with John for a week, it was possible to undergo much more than a calming of the nervous system. In meditation we could pursue the fundamental investigation of a lifetime: the search for our identity.

But a few things had to be in place: a steady daily practice, a life sufficiently in order not to create constant demands on our nerves, a reasonably stable psychology (though the practice itself should help with that), and two final pieces: a community of practitioners and a guide.

I used to think I shouldn't need a teacher. I should be able to handle things myself. Wasn't that the measure of a competent, responsible adult? To the extent you didn't handle it, life would knock you around until you did. It would teach you the lessons you needed to learn. But it was between you and life. It was a long time before it occurred to me that one of the lessons life had been trying to teach me was that sometimes you needed a teacher.

The point of the teacher, and the community too, was none other than to develop trust. Trust in people. Without trust, Zen couldn't really kick in. Somehow we had to relinquish our hold on the self. I didn't know I'd been doing this, but for as long as I could remember I'd been gripping on to "me" as to a piece of wreckage on high seas. And this in spite of having seen through "me." The Zen teacher allows our grasp to loosen, and one by one encourages our fingers to let go.

In the end we may find we hadn't been holding on to anything at all; we just thought we had. When we stop holding, all is fine. And then the community shows us what to do next: direct our concern toward others. But it all takes trust. And trusting the teacher in the limited realm of Zen is a first step.

PROUST CALLED LITERATURE VICARIOUS SPIRITUALITY. It can't come close to direct spiritual experience.

Zen does literature, too, but in a different way.

Zen is a "mind-to-mind transmission," the old ancestor Bodhidharma said. "It doesn't rely on letters or words." It can't be communicated with words, yet it can be conveyed person-to-person. That's why it still exists.

On the other hand, it does deal in narratives of a sort. If a story is fulfilled by a character's encountering an opportunity for growth, as some scholars say, then a Zen koan is a story. It just happens to be the shortest story of all, and its central character is always us. How to compress a radical shift in worldview into a few words? Koans have mastered that.

They are impossible. A monk asks Joshu, "Does a dog have Buddha-nature?" Joshu answers, "Mu." End of story.

Some story.

And the teacher says: "Sit with *mu*. Just that syllable. No meaning. Breathe it out with every breath, give yourself to it."

"How? I don't know how to," you rail.

"No one can find your way but you," says the teacher.

John once explained that sitting with a koan was like a scene from the famous book *Zen in the Art of Archery*, in which the Japanese master archer is blindfolded and led into a barn where the shutters have been closed and the lights extinguished. The assistant leaves him to aim blindly at a target at the far end.

The students wait in the dark. They hear two shots strike the target. The second makes a sound different from the first. They turn on the lights. The first arrow is right in the middle of the bull's-eye, and the second arrow has split the first in two.

Koans are like that but more so: not just "Where is the target?" but *"What* is it?" How are we supposed to aim for something we can't even identify, let alone locate?

They allow only one path: *Be still and give in.*

There's a Native American saying: if you're lost in the forest, the forest knows where you are; be still and wait for it to show you. The koan wants to show itself to us. But it has to be that way round. We can't go to it; it must come to us.

Koans require patience, even a kind of surrender beyond patience. For a restless wanderer, koan study wouldn't seem an obvious fit. Yet it was. Yamada Koun wrote that we are like billiard balls: it doesn't matter what color a ball is—if struck a certain way, it will travel in a certain direction. Like Zen: whether we're rich or poor, young or old, sharp or dull, healthy-minded or sick-souled, put us in certain conditions—namely, on a Zen cushion with a specific koan—and things will happen.

I REMEMBER WALKING INTO THE zendo once during a retreat with John and having it occur to me that my priorities could change. I could make Zen a higher priority. It was nice to consider that. Somehow I had always done it with just a little secret reluctance. I could let that go now.

And Clare was in favor of it. When I went on retreats, three or four times a year, she would take the boys to her parents'. It didn't seem to conflict with the priorities of family and work. At last I was finding the training I'd sought. Zen's demands were few: daily sitting, occasional retreats, being open to what life brought in each moment. It had benefits for others: It made me more attentive, less fretful. It opened up more love, and I'd return from the retreats with vivid eagerness to be with the family.

At the Catholic retreat center where John led his retreats, the nuns had their graveyard in a clearing among hazel trees—a circle of tiny gravestones of the sort you might see used for a beloved pet. You could easily miss them when the grass was long.

I remember one of the early retreats I did. It was late February. The trees were bare, but you could already see new buds forming on their twigs. During some outside walking I wandered into the grove and thought to myself: *In six weeks the buds will have opened and young leaves will emerge. In six months those same leaves will be yellow and wilting, and will fall.* Like these generations of nuns buried here, who had lived, served, and died. How foolish if one leaf started admiring itself, thinking it was special, that it had a destiny unlike the others, was "chosen" for special treatment. No matter what it thought, the frosts would come and it would go the way of all leaves.

How hard it was, then, to realize the same was true of me. Somehow I still held some lurking belief that I was a bit special. But of course the seasons and years would roll around and I would end up like these humble nuns, whom no one outside the order had ever heard of. They had known they were leaves on a tree, and that what made them precious was not some imaginary separateness, but being an essential part of the whole life of the tree.

Something more was starting to shift. Some deeper glacier of isolation and selfishness starting to melt, to slide off the mountain, down a valley toward the sea.

❧

IT'S EVENING. IN THE BOATYARD behind our house the tools are silent, the workers gone home for the day. Canal boats stand at odd angles, propped on cinder blocks, their hulls burnished by grinding tools. There are oil drums, hoses, toolboxes strewn around the yard, and dustbins. Some of the boats have flower boxes on their roofs, like camper vans being serviced while still full of a family's belongings. One has a bike on its roof.

I know this because I've been gazing out the window. Beyond the yard, the late sun pours through a stand of elms in a smoky stream. It's the tail end of summer.

I've been making supper for my wife and myself. The boys ate earlier. I carry two plates of food upstairs. In the little bedroom, Clare lies sprawled on the bed with the boys, watching the movie *Who Framed Roger Rabbit.*

The room is suffused with the last of the sunlight. I bend down to give her a plate, fork balanced on the rim.

"Thank you," she says.

I stand up straight for a moment, my own plate in hand. I'm about to sit down but get arrested by a scene in the movie where Roger Rabbit's tail is singed on a stove, and he proceeds to accelerate faster and faster round a kitchen, trying to outrun his flaming rear, turning the kitchen cabinets into a centrifuge, like a biker on the Wall of Death.

I remember loving this scene years ago when the movie first came out. I start laughing. Something happens. A tingling, a whirring inside me. I notice how malleable the apparently solid surfaces in the cartoon are. The tingle becomes a flywheel in my belly, spinning faster and faster, until it is almost unbearable, a sweet agony. It's in my chest now, and at once my heart just about breaks and the sensation whips itself into a cyclone, a dust devil, a whirlwind, and spins up the throat into the skull.

My head explodes. A thunderbolt hits the room. I black out—except I don't; I'm still standing. Everything else blacks out. All the circuitry that keeps the world going snaps off. A fuse blows. I find I'm not standing on anything. Below, a chasm; above, a void; all around, in every direction, nothing. Dark, radiant nothing.

I let out a whoop and start laughing.

Clare looks up from the bed. "Oh, God," she groans, "it's not that Zen again."

Stevie, five years old, looks up at me, eyes huge, clear, brown, luminous as marbles, and asks, "Daddy, what's 'growing old'?"

I don't know where this question comes from—maybe he heard a line about it in the movie. I stare back into his eyes, which are alive like I've never seen before. Perhaps I'd never noticed. Without thinking I lean down and say, "There is no growing old; there's just being alive."

We stare at each other and his face blossoms into a grin as he says, "*I'm* being alive."

"Yes, you are," I agree, and we both laugh.

I'VE BEEN WORKING WITH THE koan *mu* ever since that first *dokusan* with John several months back. During a recent meeting, he told me, "I want you to start asking yourself, 'What is *mu?*'"

I've been doing this assiduously, while riding my bike up to my office at Brookes University, while walking around town. The question "What is *mu?*" has started to feel like a broader question, as if it's also asking, *What is the street? The house? The bicycle? The rain?*

A few weeks ago, while riding home through the drizzle, I suddenly thought to myself: *Biking through the rain, getting damp: I don't like it. But what if it's okay, fine, it's just what it is? Who is it saying it's not good?* For a moment I sensed that all was perfect just as it was.

And a few days ago I found myself wondering: *What if there's a mind that creates the experience of being alive, and even creates my own mind, the mind with which I apprehend things—the road, the cars, the trees? What if it's all one mind?*

Somehow what's going on right now, with Roger Rabbit and his centrifuge, and the abyss, is connected to that question.

Yet this thunderclap is outside all calculation. There's just empty sky in every direction. "Not one speck of cloud to mar the view," an old Zen saying has it. Not one thought in the whole universe. Nothing exists! All this earnest training of the mind that we did in Zen—or thought we did—and there *was* no mind!

IN THE ROOM, EVERYTHING IS bathed in rich light, a dark, lucent limpidity drenching the bed, the window, the TV, the three other people sprawled on it.

Giddy, dizzy, I totter downstairs with my untouched plate, delirious with joy, feeling like any moment I might topple into the abyss and not caring. How is it even possible to take a step, to be suspended on this imaginary surface called the floor? It's all a dream, a floating illusion, a mirage-like reflection, a ghost of something on nothing.

The food looks magnificent on my plate, like a still life from a seventeenth-century master. I can't imagine what to do except admire it. I can't imagine what to do at all. Everything is one glorious abyss of peace that fizzes with energy.

I pull a cushion off the sofa, fold it in half, and sit down in zazen. I can't think what else to do. At the end of twenty minutes, the carpet, sofa, and cushions are all still alive with energy.

A flicker of alarm: *Am I going mad? Will this never end?*

I let myself out and go for a walk around the dusky neighborhood. Billows of smoky energy seethe everywhere. The houses hang still and quiet in the gray-blue dusk. They, too, are smoky and alive, poised between being there and not being there. The mind is a wisp of smoke, the remains of a blown-out candle. Not just the houses but the seeing of the houses is the same: there and not there. I could go up and knock on their doors, tap on their windows, but "being there" isn't what it seems. The world "out there" is a reflection quivering on nothing, even when you rap on a door.

ONCE AGAIN, EVERYTHING ANSWERED AND fulfilled.

I still can't put into words what it was—indeed, words were one of the principal devices for screening this reality—but when you saw it, when it appeared, it folded up everyday reality like a piece of paper and dropped it in a furnace. *This* reality, unbearably real, loved us fiercely, it loved all things—it was like discovering that the whole world was one heart. Yet at the same time it wasn't anything.

Later I heard John quote an old master, Dahui* ("Da-way"), from twelfth-century China, who said that Zen's reality was a hot stove, and all phenomena were snowflakes that melted when they came near it.

Was that true? Was reality like that? Or was this some kind of madness? Was I being misled by John, and by Zen? But then why was I feeling so redeemed, so all right?

I had no answers. Only what I felt. Which was that, by some miraculous power, I had just been granted a glimpse into reality, into the true fabric of the universe—into its DNA, as it were, and what I had seen there implicated me too, so that it was clear that, like everything else, I was a child of the universe. I wasn't separate from it.

And all without any god. So good was this universe, intrin-

---

* Japanese: Daie Soko, 1089–1163.

sically and unto itself, that no god was needed. Nothing extra at all was needed.

I WAS DYING TO SEE John, and went as soon as he was next available.

I told him what had happened. He diagnosed it as a "clear but not deep" experience. I was delighted. He seemed to understand every last detail of what I described, and I bowed my forehead spontaneously to the floor in a wave of gratitude such as I couldn't remember ever feeling. I never wanted to get up. He knew. He recognized it. He understood. That was all I needed.

Then he started plying me with odd questions about the koan *mu*. They seemed like nonsense, yet I found responses stirring in me, and when I let them out, John would smile at my ridiculousness and agree, and tell me that I had just given one of the traditional answers. I had never known anything like this, in Zen or anywhere else. So the experience had not been random. It actually had something directly to do with *mu*. This was what a koan was for: to bring about a radical shift in experience. The koan could offer access to an incredible new experience of the world, free of all calculation, all understanding. But more than that, I was discovering that the koan could allow you to *meet*: the student could come to the teacher *with* their "experience" and have it met. And they themselves could *be* met, right in the midst of what they had awakened to.

After a number of interviews like this over the following weeks, John gave me a new koan, the famous one: "You know the sound of two hands clapping; what is the sound of one hand?" It was the best thing: a way of not just confirming and growing confident in the experience, but sharing it. It was what I had been crying out for, for decades: to *meet* someone in this reality. This was the magic of the koans. They didn't just open us up; they offered a way to the most intimate kind of meeting.

But it went even further: an authentic koan teacher could lead you *deeper*. Only through the meeting, the sharing, the guidance was there hope of integrating the experience, and living it out in an ordinary life, in kindness, in concern not for self but for others.

THERE'S A *NEW YORKER* CARTOON in which planet Earth is filthy, churning out smoke, fizzing, simmering unhealthily. God and an archangel are bending over the globe, scratching their heads.

The archangel asks God, "Have you tried turning it off, then on again?"

This was like that. The whole world turned off: gone, as in a conjuring trick. One flourish of Zen's robe and it all disappeared. Instead a scintillating darkness, a radiant dark—vast, limitless, totally empty.*

But why should it be such a deeply happy experience for things to disappear?

---

* I had recited the *Heart Sutra* many times over the years. The bodhisattva of compassion, Kanzeon, sees that all existence is empty. The sutra says, "Form is exactly emptiness, emptiness exactly form." The word "emptiness" gets glossed in different ways by commentators. Things have no "self-substance," all is boundless, there are no boundaries between things, and so on. The fundamental reality of "emptiness" is nothing at all. But that nothing is infinitely fecund, and marvelously healing to the human heart.

Perhaps because the "void" is intrinsically marvelous. It has not just marvelous power but all power. Everything is made out of it. Or perhaps because it's the way this reality we know actually *is*, and to be somehow closer to it makes us happier.

So I make an assertion like that, and why should anyone listen? They shouldn't. Instead, you either throw this book across the room or else one day go and find a Zen teacher, learn to meditate, pick up a koan, and see what happens. That's the traditional advice: it's about personal experience. Our own, not anyone else's.

IT'S RELATIVELY EASY TO THINK this through these days, with the most lax, lay knowledge of modern physics: like everything else, we're made of atoms and their constituent parts and energies. It seems a wild claim to suggest that we are capable of experiencing things on that level, yet as many commentators have pointed out, there are striking resemblances between some aspects of modern physics and what Buddhism has been saying for thousands of years: things are "empty," lacking in the solidity so convincing to us; if you really track substance down, you end up with energy and space: that's what the physicists say.

Yet even "space" is open to debate now. Some physicists theorize that this whole universe is a membrane, a two-dimensional screen on which nine-dimensional space and matter are projected as a species of illusion.

FOR THE NEXT FEW WEEKS there was a sublime clarity to things, like on a dewy morning.

As with other moments of revelation, I soon made the mistake of thinking I had seen something quantifiable, knowable, transferable into the memory banks as a property of this universe.

But I was in the right hands now. My teacher wouldn't let me cling to an insight, living, as one Zen master called it, in the "pit of emptiness" or, as another put it, "in a cave of demons on Black Mountain."

Zen never stops. "Someone may have discovered the Buddha-dharma," the early Tang master Sekiso* said, "but it is not yet real. They must step forward from the top of a hundred-foot pole and manifest their whole body throughout the universe."

You might find yourself hanging in a universal abyss, but like a character in a cartoon, you still have to step forward. There's nowhere to go but onward, into life, into service.

THERE WERE SEVERAL "FIRST KOANS" to work through. One of them was about a "distant temple bell." I don't want to give too much away—koan training is an intimate thing, not to be bandied about in loose talk—but I can say a little.

The koan about the distant bell is pivotal, in that it's the first of the major "presentation" koans, meaning a koan where no amount of discussion will help. The student has to come up with a wordless "presentation" of the koan, to show it, embody it, be it. It's no use talking about it. The whole thrust of koan study is away from language into liberation from language. The great silence of all things opens up, where words are just flotsam and jetsam.

I sat with the koan about the bell for quite a few weeks. Already the recent experience was turning itself into a metaphysical understanding in my mind, and that held me up with the new koan. Had John not been there, had he not known so instinc-

---

* Chinese: Shishuang, 807–888.

tively how to work with me, it would probably have gone the way of the other experiences and become a troubling memory. But here he was, and he'd given me the strange koan about the bell.

"Stop the sound of the distant temple bell," it runs. How on earth do you do that? "There's no place for discussion," John kept telling me. "We have to do it. Trust the experience you had. Let it show you how."

After several *dokusan*, with John probing and prodding me, finally one evening in the *dokusan* room, after I thought I'd exhausted every imaginable possibility, an urge came and I randomly trusted it. As soon as I did, I fell into a groove of centuries of practice worn smooth by others. I no longer cared if I was making the "right" presentation. The koan disappeared, a great expansiveness opened up, as I did what I did.

I could see John quietly smiling. This was what koans were for: to allow two people to wake up together into the same reality. Well, I guess John was already awake in it. But now I could briefly join him.

Zen wasn't—had never been—about individual revelation. That was all very well, but the core of Zen was sharing.

As I began to work more consistently with the koans, groping my way through the first collection that John's lineage dealt with, it seemed the most amazing thing, almost as amazing as an experience of Zen's "reality" itself. Knowledge of the unspeakable, all-pervasive fact sometimes known as the "dharma body," or the "Buddha-dharma," had somehow been discovered, preserved, and passed on, in the koans. It was secret yet somehow storable. Through the ages people had known of it and found a way to share it. I was neither mad nor alone.

But the way of sharing was wordless. That's why the koans,

although couched in words, had to be "shown," without words. Koans precisely fulfilled that early description of Zen given by the old ancestor Bodhidharma: "a mind-to-mind transmission outside scripture, not relying on words or letters." It was true. Words could only confuse and obscure them. But when you "showed" a koan, if you'd directly experienced the reality that was its province, then it came alive again through the koan and the teacher.

Not only that, but it was a training, a matter of subjugating oneself to a wisdom inherited over generations. It wasn't a one-off thing. There was a process you could enter, which might not exactly keep the magical doors hooked wide open all the time, yet changed you in a good way, in accordance with the reality beyond those doors. You could enter a lineage of practitioners bound by that reality—at least, with a bit of luck and a lot of training you might.

LINEAGE IS A BIG DEAL in Zen. The authority of the teacher is bestowed not by oneself but by one's teacher, who received it from theirs before them. But it's more than a form of teaching authorization. To enter a lineage is to accept, in a limited way, entry into a kind of shelter. The traditional suffix in a male teacher's name is -ken, which means "eaves"—eaves that offer shelter. Likewise, women teachers have the suffix -an, which means "hermitage"— also a shelter.

From the outside, at the various centers I had visited in the past, I had sensed lineage as a vague menace, a species of coercion or sectarian zeal. But now that I had found a teacher myself; now that I was ready to make the practice a higher priority, to accept it as not just a boost to life—not just an aid to a calmer attitude, better writing, and so on—but as a gateway to a new way of living; now that the practice did not glower with the guilt of a failed commitment but shone with promise, I felt grateful to John and his teacher, and hers before her, who had painstakingly safeguarded the teachings.

It was as if by starting to really follow the Zen path, I was picking out the traces of a true road. Amid all the confusion and welter of my days, there actually was an authentic way to be followed. It was like the old roads Speedy the tramp used to talk about—relic of a deeper life that had left its trace in the land. But it was hidden, disguised within things, waiting just under the surface for when you were ready to discover it.

Black Hole

D AD HAD RETIRED BY NOW. He kept busy with translating and editing jobs, as well as with various pet history projects, but he had a lot of time for talking. That had always been his favorite activity: conversation.

Sometimes we'd go round to their house, the boys, Clare, and I. She and my stepmum got along well, with their shared interest in art and artists, and Dad enjoyed supervising the boys on the swings he had set up in the back garden. While pushing them and fielding their questions, he'd tell me historical snippets he had discovered in his researches. Meanwhile my stepmother was a wonderful grandmother, anticipating the boys' wishes far in advance of the slow reflexes of their own dad. And she took a keen interest in my writing life, following the readings I was giving, catching up on articles I wrote, which left me moved and grateful.

The boys loved them both. She would ply them with questions while scooping out bowls of ice cream. Dad was not just a bright-burning intelligence, as well as a warm and sometimes quite lazy man whose laziness did not trouble him, but he was domestic: he loved being at home. He was solid. A mensch. His priorities were straight. He loved people—people were his great pleasure. He would be fast friends with new people so quickly I used to wonder if he already knew them, and ponder how he possibly could. He carried his home with him like a tortoise does its shell. People felt that and he welcomed them in, and they liked it. The boys would leap onto him on the sofa, and he would coax them into the gentler pastime of conversation and soon have them rapt. It was nice to watch.

Dad and I had had our ups and downs. But one way or another, through therapy and Zen, through being partnered with a clear-eyed woman, things had changed for me. Perhaps I had finally done enough of what Harvey had said: "give yourself the parenting you didn't get as a child." I'd have the odd flare-up of rage or sunburst of shame, but I had learned to meet him as he was, and on those terms we enjoyed ourselves together. After all, we were still two literary-minded Jews who enjoyed a good bit of argumentation and debate together.

DURING THE EVENING SITS IN the zendo, the room soft gray with twilight coming in the windows, a lamp glowing near the altar, John would give a talk about a koan.

The way the talks happened felt good. In fact, everything about the zendo felt good. Perhaps as the teachings moved further away from Japan, there was increasing risk of their ossifying. In other zendos where I had sat, I had sometimes sensed a chilly trace of fear discernible in the room. But in this humble house in Oxford, although the sitting was the deepest and stillest I had yet encountered, I felt a warm responsiveness. The teacher conveyed the teachings in such a human way, not as a cold formality to be enforced but as a way of living to be shared. Yet this was the closest I had got to Japan itself. By some uncanny intuition I had stumbled into a zendo where the master had no need to play, twice removed, at being Japanese. Rather, John continued his own training directly under the Japanese master who was the abbot of the whole lineage, and there was no need for him to mimic a foreign style not his own. He was natural. And kind. And insightful. And English, and okay with it.

Could it be that the nearer the source, the warmer and kinder the teaching, the more natural and easy? This surely went against the stereotypes you heard about in other zendos, of fearsome masters across the Pacific wielding canes over cowed students. But perhaps those stories were part of an older mythology.

The evening would start with a round of sitting. Here the rounds were only twenty-five minutes long, which was kinder on the legs. There might be two dozen people in the room, facing its twilit walls. At the end of the period the bell would peal quietly, there'd be five minutes of slow walking, then we'd all stand waiting for John to come padding in, in his socks. He'd leave a few sheets on his cushion at the front, offer a stick of incense at the altar, then, to the sound of a small handbell, we'd all make three deep bows.

I was familiar with these rituals from other Zen centers. Elsewhere they had tended to incite a faint anxiety, especially when most of the people were clad in robes and comported themselves with priestly dignity. Here, we were all in street clothes, and instead of feeling foreign, it felt natural. Again, the lineage was still actively Japanese, so it had no need to assert its Japaneseness. It had form in its sits rather than formality, and within the basic structure the tone was relaxed and comfortable. We'd all sit down and wait for the talk to begin, amid a hush of anticipation.

John gave wonderful talks. You'd feel his love for the practice, for the old masters he spoke about, mostly from the Tang period of China, and for all of us. He loved the world Zen opened up, and the way that Zen allowed one to love this world. You could feel that he loved what was going on right now, and he'd make us feel that love, too.

I was slowly beginning to understand that Zen wasn't just about meditative absorption and insight, nor was it something done alone. It was about activity, about how you lived and interacted, how you treated others. It wasn't enough to "be enlightened," whatever that might mean; what counted was living it. The interactions with the teacher in the *dokusan* room were a kind of paradigm for how you'd interact out in the world. They were a training in connecting more intimately and helpfully.

ON THE OTHER HAND, IT wasn't all perfect. The next time I saw John, I gave him a copy of my poetry book. He thanked me and said he'd pass it straight on to his wife, who liked to read.

Stung! I wanted *him* to read it. That was who I was—a writer, a poet. My books were the best thing about me. They were the only thing. How could he not be interested? But he wasn't interested, not at all.

That was lesson one.

I was on the brink of saying something, but somehow I knew just enough to thank him and keep quiet.

JOHN WAS A DILIGENT, LOVING teacher. It was unlike any relationship I'd had before. He was unlike anyone I'd known. No sense of being exceptional, no claims to anything remarkable: just an ex-lawyer with a deep devotion to the dharma and a clear conviction that, while it was nothing special, while it was here all the time and was the intrinsic nature of life, Zen was also precious.

He helped by reminding me that there was always further to go. I didn't exactly believe it, yet I trusted him. In time I came to wonder if he wasn't the first person I'd ever fully trusted. As the trust grew, I found I could trust everyone a little more. I was finding a home—not just the "sangha" of fellow sitters, not just John's guidance, but the ordinary life of family and work, subtly transmuted into something more wondrous.

John had worked for years as a financial lawyer, then taken early retirement in order to set up two charities—one for the severely disabled, one offering respite to caregivers. I came to feel that he was the most selfless man I'd ever met. He had no aspirations for himself. His career had by all accounts been successful, but he seemed to have left it with no regrets. It was clear he himself had been deeply changed by the koans, so when he gave a talk on one, it was not just theoretical, but a personal stepping-stone. At the same time, his own history had lost all interest for him. He just sought to assist each of us in finding our own way to the selfless love Zen could open up.

In *dokusan* he'd gently encourage me to release beliefs I didn't realize I still held. One by one I'd bring the next koan into *doku-san*, and he'd gaze at me from his seat opposite, and put questions to me until something melted. My view of things would be stymied, and there'd be no choice but to give up, and a scintillating life without name or form would flow in, borne on a tide of love.

I'd see him every two weeks. It was like power lines by the roadside: the wires rose at each pole and slumped in between. Some part of me rose up each time I saw him, and slowly trailed off in the fortnight between. It was like being fed, watered, and forgiven, and taught to stand up in a new world, again and again. He also taught in London, and when I could, I saw him there as well, to reduce the time between boosts.

KOAN TRAINING IS A LONG process. After an initial breakthrough, a student works through five collections, each with many koans. Often the master isn't satisfied and sends the student back to sit longer with a koan. Patience and constancy are needed, and will duly develop, of necessity. The process thwarts the mind that wants to press on and get ahead. In doing so, it returns us again and again to now, to this moment in its fullness and tenderness.

The zendo in London was a makeshift camp in an octagonal chamber high in the tower of St. James's Church, Piccadilly. The church allowed the Zen group to keep its cushions there, and we'd pull them out on Tuesday evenings and sit beneath the old stone walls and creep up a ladder to a loft for *dokusan*.

It's not like a monastery, this kind of training. Life goes on. You have to keep making sense of the ordinary daily grind. But the training starts to infiltrate normal life, and odd moments of joy and minor revelation fall on us as we push the toddler on the swing, or step off a cold street into a warm shop, or get in the car and listen to the choking of the starter motor. Everyday sights and sounds start to hit us in a more immediate way, and we meet them with appreciation.

I understood more clearly why Zen had its historical affinity for poetry. It accentuated the senses, it opened up a capacity for cherishing the things of the world—a curtain stirring in a breeze, an unpeeled potato waiting patiently on a counter, a bar of soap in a beam of sun. The part of us that loved things Zen revived.

It also helped with our manifest inadequacies. Or mine, anyway. Since Zen accepted everything as it was, it accepted us, too, as we were. Procrastinating, letting the bills pile up, drinking too much coffee, acting selfishly, stubbornly—whatever our shortcomings, Zen liked us just the same, and enabled us not to mind ourselves so much, and because of that, it made it easier to roll up the sleeves and work on what needed working on.

One old master, when asked what Zen really was, thought for a while and said, "Zen is doing what needs to be done."

⁂

A FEW YEARS HAVE PASSED. It's August, the late-summer bank holiday. I've been on a writing assignment in the Hebrides and I'm returning south toward Glasgow at night in a rented car. Every hotel is booked up. I stop at every pub or bed-and-breakfast along the way, hoping to find a room: all full. Finally I pull in to a fancy golf hotel along the shore of Loch Lomond that has one room left, for a preposterous price. I'm on expenses and take it, then eat a meal at the bar and drink two pints.

Next day, a little hungover, dazed, smoking a cigarette, I

continue south. As I'm driving over the Erskine Bridge, high above the River Clyde, sparkling far below, a song from northern Spain starts playing on the radio. It's about the sea: a cappella, a layering of voices, contralto and soprano, all women, all interwoven, singing with passion about the sea that feeds them yet takes away their loved ones.

It gets my attention, becomes vivid, then suddenly . . .

How to introduce epiphany? As matter-of-fact as possible— that's how the great writers like Chekhov and Tolstoy do it. Just tell it like it is . . .

In the sunshine on the bridge high above the Clyde, listening to the song on the radio, the voices in the Cantabrian tune form tangible strands of melody, like laces weaving through one another. Whether it's the lines of melody or the braid of feelings in the song, they activate a weave of emotions in me.

It so happens I am in a complicated tangle: in my early forties, in a textbook midlife crisis. The changes in my career over the past few years have unsettled things. I can't claim to be even an obscure poet, yet the minor recognition, and the prizes, fellowships, readings, as well as advances for the novels, have turned my head, and I've created a painful marital situation. It's entirely my fault, but I can't seem to take the steps to sort it out.

Self-help gurus might say: *Get on with it, do what you want, you don't live forever.* But Zen said: *Wait a minute.* Check out who is calling the shots. Who is the tyrant declaring what must and must not be, what we must and must not do? See the bigger picture: Who else is involved, who has the most at stake, and will this situation lead to more suffering, all told, or less? If actions arise from compassion, from concern for the well-being of others, then maybe—

But that wasn't what I wanted to hear. The dybbuk of lust and risk pricked up his ears.

"Well-being"? "Others"? Fuck that. Don't get sanctimonious on me. This is once in a lifetime. Come on. Just take a look at what I've conjured for you. You only live once. What would Picasso do? Or Liszt, if you prefer? Or David Herbert? Reach out and take it, man.

But again Zen said: *Wait, take a breath, sit down.* Suppose that voice is no more solid than a flash of lightning, suppose all the solid things it wants are also no more solid than that? And yet: all the drama, generation after generation of drama. Can we really exit the stage but without actually dying? How? And what would we do then?

I haven't known what to do.

But right now, in the rental car up on the high bridge, the melodies in the song entwine with the feelings in my chest, moving over one another like a bucket of eels. I'm listening, and feeling it all, when suddenly, in the midst of the noise, an endless peace appears, as if all the turmoil and emotion at the same time contain a hidden silence.

I drive on among the trees of the mainland, and soon I am approaching the edge of Glasgow airport. The road ahead shines, and the steering wheel in my hands becomes black and glossy, weirdly hyper-present. Then the strangest thing: all of a sudden in the middle of me, at the core of my midriff, a black hole opens up, and from this hole the steering wheel is leaping forth like a flash of lightning. Likewise the hands holding it. Likewise the trees, the cars, the tailfins of the planes lined up on the taxiways of the airport, and the terminal buildings, and the clouds, the sky—all are pouring forth, like a river of lightning, out of the infinite black hole in the middle. I, too, my very body and mind, pour out of that infinite point of nothingness. All things are flashing into being. The world is nothing but lightning, empty as the hole from which it leaps.

"Thus should you think of all this fleeting world," says a line in the *Diamond Sutra*: "As a flicker of lightning in a summer cloud."

I knew that quote but had always taken it to mean that we should remember that all things are ephemeral. They pass away. Now I saw that the author meant it literally. All this world was *literally* a flash of lightning.

I pull over, incoherent, sweating, trembling, and park at the roadside and put my head in my hands. My face is wet with tears. Everything is blindingly bright, yet at the same time dark. This whole world seems a construction, a fabrication, a quicksilver mirage. The only thing real is the mysterious hole from which it all springs. But that hole is nothing. Everything pours forth, like the rods of light in the darkness of a cinema, composed of the same nothing. Yet the fact that they pour forth is the greatest marvel of all—all things are infinitely blessed, as old Master Mumon said in the thirteenth century; in fact, they are all one single blessing, because they arise.

After a few wrong turns among the lanes and byways of the airport, I find my way to the rental car drop-off. I check in, walking through the terminal toward my gate, and all the while it's a being made of nothing walking through a world made of nothing. I buy a sandwich and sit at a table, wondering if eating some food might calm things down. Instead, as the food is swallowed, it's emptiness swallowing emptiness. It's all a system made of nothing, a phantom, a dream.

Who am I? What is the world? Master Unmon* said in a koan, "Everyone has their own bright light. But when you try to see it you can't—there's only darkness." One void. Yet it functions: it *does* all this. The twentieth-century master Yamada Koun said that this whole earth is "the acrobatics of emptiness."

I WROTE JOHN AN EMAIL.

> It's like the channel tunnel: like being dug through, from the inside out and the outside in. The two tunnels, from the British and French sides, have linked up now.
> As if every last shred of matter pours from this reverse black hole. It's the birthplace of everything.

He wrote back that this sounded like "good news."

I waited for my plane, I flew home, I took the bus to Oxford; I returned home to our domestic strife. And at the same time, no one went anywhere. In spite of everything that was going on, for a few weeks I moved through a bewilderment of peace.

Gone was the mistrustful, mean person I could be, blindly obsessed with a career, arrogant to boot. He believed he had the capacity to be a good writer, and to his warped way of thinking that meant he already was. The fact that the little taste of success he'd had came only when he was less self-obsessed, more generous toward others, was lost on him. Perhaps there was only so much discouragement a literary writer could meet before, for some, the path forked into despondency or arrogance. But a third

---

* Chinese: Yunmen, 864–949.

way had opened now: to be free of the all-demanding inner tyrant who had been running the show.

BUT I'M A RATIONALIST, NOT a mystic. I'm a writer, poet, ex-scholar; I go no further than the written page. Mystical experience? Leave that to the flakes, the monks, the religious professionals . . . Oh, no . . . surely I'm not becoming one of them.

John's not. He's a lawyer turned charity director. He looks normal. He *is* normal. So does everyone else in the zendo. They're normal: professors, therapists, plumbers, schoolteachers, doctors, nurses, construction workers, business consultants, executives. They just have this *other* thing going on—namely, they have found the dharma, this *other* side to existence, which is no other than *this* very existence, yet if you haven't seen it you haven't seen it, and if you have it's a good idea to study with someone who has integrated it into their life and become ordinary again. Except that "ordinary" may then be a little different from what it used to be.

THE CHRISTMAS BEFORE MY PARENTS broke up, when I was six, my mother took us away for three weeks without a sign of Dad. I wondered why but didn't dare ask. Then we were home again and he was back, too.

A few nights later I saw my mother on the landing, shouting, dancing, crying, stamping her feet, waving her arms, hair flying. The next day we all gathered for our meeting, and Dad left with his navy suitcase in the little Fiat.

Right now, our oldest son was the age I had been when our parents split up. And here I was, dicing with divorce, putting my own pleasure ahead of the well-being of others. We had been on the brink of splitting up. Was there programming in the blood, some early-life encoding, that I must make my son like me, and therefore now was the time to abandon him for the sake of a whirlwind?

The task was to resist the programming so intent on passing down the misery. If we could arrest it in this generation, then we could change the legacy, stanch the flow of suffering down the generations.

There was the zendo. I could go and sit, and let the sitting do what it needed. I could sit still, and wait.

THE EXPERIENCE ON THE BRIDGE shattered me. A goodness beyond anything I knew had been burrowing into me and broke something open, shattering attachments I couldn't otherwise have released.

It was the crux of the crisis. Without Zen, without John's guidance, the story would have been equally predictable, perhaps, but different. And there was Clare, my remarkable wife. We went to therapy, she didn't talk to others, she kept her own counsel. We worked at it. Eventually she led us both back into love.

AS MY TRAINING WENT ON, sometimes I walked about stunned by love. Not the quaking love of romance, though it was every bit as intense, but like it in that it seemed to hover just beyond conditions. It was calm and rich: not the promise of fulfillment, which is an engine of romantic love, but fulfillment itself.

But what *was* the reality of *kensho*? The word literally means "seeing nature" or "seeing reality." It couldn't be God. I didn't believe in God. It seemed diametrically opposed to the God I'd heard about at school. It was not just universal acceptance, not just—somehow—universal love, but the coterminous nature of the self with all creation. It was nondiscriminating. Its boundless generosity meant that everything we ever thought or felt or saw or heard was it. We couldn't lose it. Or be lost. We couldn't strive to find it, either. This was why, if we tried to find it, assuming it was different from the here and now, we wouldn't find it. It was always perfectly apposite. It couldn't do anything but manifest with utter appropriateness. It *was* us. Already. All along.

Except it didn't end there. There was something *beyond* creation, which had no dimension at all yet was undeniably real.

One of the unfortunate attributes of "mystical experience" is that if we hazard an attempt at describing it—or if I do—we can't help but tumble into cliché. Yet the experience itself is the opposite of cliché, definable in part by its infinite invention, its departure from all familiarity.

Which may be a key to its healing power for depressives: depression is the opposite of love. Depression leaves us isolated, bereft of meaning. Love does the opposite. If love heals, universal love heals universally: another cliché.

In *kensho*, consciousness is plunged into a bath of formless, nameless love. That we afterwards fall short of what we "realize" can be an incentive to train with our teachers until we do find durable peace. At least we know that it might be possible now.

Kensho is the inverse of trauma. Here, unlike in trauma, the shock is of love and belonging, not pain and hurt. Researchers in psychology are now finding that a true epiphany can leave a beneficent shadow on the psyche, a positive counterpart to PTSD.

Zen can't avoid paradox. But it's paradox only before we've seen what it's driving at. Once we've tasted it, paradox is gone.

Had my own chronic mild depression been conditional, a response to the problems of life, a defensive measure? Or was it endogenous, with engines of its own that needed no help from outside?

Who knows. Depression is well mapped yet little understood. Why can a mild depression incapacitate one person, as the writer Andrew Solomon has said, while another person bounces back from a major episode? In spite of research into neurotransmitters and brain activity, psychiatrists still don't know. It's as mysterious as inner suffering itself. We may be sitting in torment in the zendo, mired in misery and resentment, for example, and the next moment we're free, fulfilled; yet our circumstances are identical from one moment to the next.

Zen begins with our own suffering, then evolves into concern for the suffering of others. To be free from suffering sounds like a fairy tale from which all my instincts—Jewish, Scottish, Oxford positivist—would recoil. Talk about tempting providence. Yet it's for real, and not magical. If anything it's scientific. Some recent neurological research into meditation suggests that long-term meditation under a guide diminishes neural activity in areas of the brain associated with painful emotions and increases it in areas of compassion and attentiveness.

CLARE AND I HAD BEEN planning a move back to New Mexico, which we had longed to return to for years. The kids were still young. It seemed like it might be our last chance.

Once again there was a book to be written, and we had the means now: fresh publishers' advances and an American editor who secured us visas. Clare was eager to go, and I stacked up a series of assignments with American magazines. One year, we said, two at most. Some friends found us a rental house. It was hard to leave John, but I knew I would be back. And as it happened, there was a Zen teacher from the very same lineage out in New Mexico, with whom he put me in touch so my training could continue. We packed up and went.

Part Three

Calf Born of a Bull

Koan of the Suburbs

THIS CABIN IS FREEZING IN the morning. Breath fogging in front of the face, nose ice-cold, the only warmth found by nestling deeper in the blankets. Eventually I rouse myself and get the kindling going in the stove, then pull on extra layers of clothing, stuff in some thin pine boughs, close the little iron door, and hear the stove begin to rumble, then quietly roar.

I slept in my socks, and now I pull on my boots by the door. Outside, cool pale sky. No cloud. Gaunt bare trees, mostly black. And the snow, with my boot prints from yesterday showing as blue pockets, hardened by the night's frost. My footsteps barely crunch, the snow is so hard. The very air seems hard, stiff with cold. The snow catches the early light like dust. The whole valley is silent. Truly silent. The far side rises, dark and emphatic, like an undiluted block of watercolor paint.

I take a pee behind a tree, and by the time I'm back inside, the kettle is already rattling. Coffee in a filter. More resinous pinewood into the stove, which makes me want to roll a cigarette, then down to work with the hot mug at my elbow. The coffee is scalding, but at this altitude it won't stay hot for long.

The cabin is where I'm working these days. Its owner lets me use it for a nominal rent, in exchange for taking care of it, and when I'm on a roll sometimes I stay the night. It feels and looks remote but is only a few miles from the center of Santa Fe, in the mountains of New Mexico.

After an hour or two of early writing I stop to meditate. I face the wall and run my current koan through my mind. After a while something steps out of left field, an unexpected shift. All efforts with the koan are suspended. No effort was needed, it turns out. I gave up what I thought I needed to do, and the koan found me. Its silent, empty, vibrant world wakes up all around, and I'm filled with not only a quiet joy, but awe. It's as if the old master in the tiny story has stolen up behind me and put his hands on my eyes, over my ears, on my heart, and allowed me for a moment to see the world as he sees it. He has touched something that at first feels like an immemorial wound, and I want to cry out of sadness mixed with relief. This is real, I feel, and a kind of hollow opens in the heart of all things.

It's another old koan with the great master Seppo,* who sat for thirty years before coming to an awakening that resolved his life, and I realize I hadn't even noticed a question buried in the middle of the story: *What is this?* Perhaps I am tasting an answer now. This: this openness, this empty, silent stillness in the midst of things—could this be what he was asking about?

---

* Chinese: Xuefeng, 822–908.

After a while I step outside again. The world is at peace, because all things are doing exactly what they must. Cause and effect are functioning perfectly, as of course they must. The sun breaks free of the valley's lip, and smoky light streams down into the trees, striping the snow with the blue shadows of the trunks.

I go in and spoon out the oatmeal that has been belching on the little stove.

Three months ago I finished another novel up here, which is now entering the mill of the publishing business, and now I'm at work on the old family book again.

SIX A.M. ANOTHER WINTER MORNING in northern New Mexico. A Saturday. It's bitterly cold today. I should have worn my long johns, I think as I cross the yard outside our house in the dark. The mud is hard as cement.

The house hangs on a hill above downtown Santa Fe at 7,200 feet above sea level, about a thousand feet lower than the cabin. If I weren't so intent on trying to keep warm, and felt inclined to look around, I'd see a night sky prickling with the fierce stars of New Mexico, as D. H. Lawrence called them. But I'm hunched in my jacket, trying to protect myself from the savage cold. I've only gone a few steps and already the air is sucking the warmth from my bones. The neighbor's motion-triggered light switches on and a cloud of breath blooms before me. At the bottom of the drive I stamp my feet, blow into my hands, jam them in my trouser pockets, which are warmer than the coat pockets, and wait for my ride.

On the facing hillside you can make out pools of light among the trees: houses. The city lights spread across the dark land.

Up the road, a mud wall flickers and begins to glow: the

beam of a car coming. Now I hear a growl, a point of light appears, and another: headlights.

For a second, a buzz of concern: *Have I got everything?* I'm wearing my little backpack and think over its contents: wallet, phone, koan folder. All I need.

But the concern is enough to draw out another worry: *Have I got everything I need?* We have been living in New Mexico for two years now. Clare has a job cataloguing a vast art collection in town, a good match for her skills and interests. She also finds time for her own artwork, and we have the camaraderie of close friends, both from our earlier time in New Mexico and among other young parents. The boys are attending an alternative school—this being Santa Fe—where the kids sit on cushions on the floor and get drilled in Latin and Chinese, and basic Euclid and Pythagoras, and study the speeches of famous leaders such as Lincoln and Churchill. Once every term, classes stop for "Climbing Week," when the kids rope up and scale an enormous cottonwood tree overshadowing the playground, filling its boughs with their dangling bodies like exotic fruit. "Good for their nervous systems," the headmaster reassures the parents, who stare anxiously up into the tree. It all suits our boys. They are curious and lively, their eyes often lit up with enthusiasm and glee as they head to school. Most evenings they ask me to walk with them one by one, and we go up a hill near home or stroll the neighborhood talking about whatever is on their minds— discoveries in algebra or the humorous vagaries of their friends' behavior. I've also got a part-time job, at the Institute of American Indian Arts, across town, teaching literature and writing to Native students, and magazines keep hiring me, and life goes on, and the cost of living is lower here.

But still, I often wonder when we will actually go back to England. With the boys entrenched, sometimes it seems we've given up on the idea. Is that a good thing? Is it bad? Right? Wrong? Sometimes it bothers me.

Then I remember I'm on my way to the zendo, to my new Zen teacher, Joan Rieck Roshi, who is John's "dharma aunt," meaning she studied in the Japanese home of our lineage, Kamakura, side by side with John's own teacher. He has "passed" me on to her for now. It just so happens she lives less than an hour away. It's a chance in a million. There are only a handful of teachers from the core of this lineage in America, and we happened to move quite close to one of them.

Every Saturday Joan holds a morning of meditation. For this morning, at least, I can shelve the worries. I'll figure them out later. And anyway, all is not lost: I have finally made real progress on the family novel. It's a touch long, at just over three thousand pages, but I'll cut it back. Good or bad, producing the mountain of material has been cathartic, and I tell myself I have it down on paper now, that's the main thing. *Relax. Have a broader perspective. Aren't you a Zen student?*

I'm in the middle of these ruminations when a small blue pickup stops in the road. No need to pull over. It's early, and it's New Mexico.

The passenger door resists my tug at first, then squeals and gives.

Sherry has the fan blowing hot and hard. A tremendous shiver runs through me as I rub my legs. We greet each other with a quick hug and get going. Forty minutes down the freeway.

Sherry has been a student of Joan Rieck Roshi for twenty

years or more. She began her Zen training when her son was still small. Now he is at college in the Bay Area. Meanwhile Sherry is a hiker, traveler, rock climber, lean and fit, kind and intelligent, and a committed Zen student.

Over the years we would make this drive together well over a hundred times. Up to the brow of La Bajada Hill, down the long slope to the lower plateau that reaches to the foot of the Sandia Mountains near Albuquerque.

The land turns a color between suede and blue as dawn grows. By the time we exit the freeway, the cottonwood trees in the valley of the Rio Grande are still dark, but the sky has the lucent hue of the inside of a seashell.

We park outside an old adobe house on the main street in Bernalillo, a small town, quiet at this hour, ten miles north of the big city of Albuquerque. Actually it's always quiet, a broad old western street lined with low buildings.

A trace of anxiety: sitting. Sitting itself, even for just two or three hours. Will it be hard, painful, boring, excruciating, enlightening? It's often a little scary to face oneself without distraction.

Sherry and I leave our bags at the end of the hallway, get ourselves a cushion each, and go into the zendo and sit facing the white wall.

Wooden floor, black cushions, white walls: a zendo. A "place of meditation." Of simple awareness.

Joan and a few others are already installed on their cushions. Some others arrive quietly, but once I'm settled nothing distracts from the deep feeling that's coming on as I stare into the gray depths of my shadow on the wall.

A faint smell of incense. A bell sounds. Three slow pings.

We are already into the first period. No moving. No sound. It's happening already. Zen: you just do it. To begin, begin.

I count my breaths. One to ten. Counting the exhales. A warmth opens up in the chest. Then I remember the koan. I have another koan.

I have been sitting with it all week and will be "presenting" it to Joan later. This is the way we do koan study. Joan will either be satisfied or not; if not, I'll sit with it for another week and try again next Saturday.

It's a famous koan of Master Unmon. "I don't ask about before the fifteenth day; bring me a phrase about after the fifteenth day," he says. None of the monks can respond, so he answers for them: "Every day is a good day."

Every day is a good day is a sentiment I can only admire from a distance. I'm not experiencing things that way, in spite of being some way along in koan study, in spite of help from my teachers and years of regular meditation.

But Joan won't be interested in my understanding of the koan. We may talk about it a little, but only once I have done the more important thing, which is to "present" it.

Every koan is about awakening. That's why we have to have tasted "awakening" to work with them. The theory is that by studying how generations of old masters acted, in the koans, we gradually deepen our own awakening, until something happens that allows us to join them in their ongoing awakening. What this something is is sometimes called "great death," which leads to a "rebirth." It's a different thing from *kensho*: *kensho* opens a door, offers a glimpse, but a glimpse is not enough to bring lasting peace of mind. Not for me, anyway. I have my moments, but they're usually just that—moments.

But it's all rather unclear. The masters are cagey about mapping things out too explicitly. And *kensho* is hard enough to come by. Nevertheless, having had at least a few upheavals in my sense of reality by now, I wonder why I'm still as prone as I am to unease, still a bit dysthymic, and I can't honestly say that every day is a good day. Often, in fact, I think just the opposite. Sometimes I'll catch myself thinking not just that a day is anything but good but that it's positively *bad*, even that a whole *week* is bad, even a month. Even a *year*. Yet I'm a moderately "advanced" Zen student. At least on paper.

Does Zen actually work? I sometimes wonder. After all, I still get elated when power brokers or in-crowders from the world of books send me a friendly greeting, or throw a contract my way, or when a poem comes out in a renowned magazine. And crestfallen when left off a short list: *I've given my whole life to this, and look how they treat me.* Et cetera. A phantom haunting the weeds, as Zen puts it: that's what I am still. An unreal person caught in an unreal world. How much better it is to sit in a zendo and let the unrealities drain off like the toxins of some drug trip, and start to see the bare bones of our actual existence, unentranced.

And on the other hand, I am surely better than I used to be. Less driven by compulsions, less anxious, less regularly dissatisfied. I have more tricks up my sleeve. I can breathe into a knot of worry in belly or chest and watch it melt like an ice cube under the warm stream of my attention. Another kind of awareness switches on, often, one that is calmer and bigger. Somehow the moments of "insight" live on. In a way. Each *kensho* has been an immersion into a reality without time or space where all is well. Therefore in some way I know what Unmon is talking about in the koan. But on no account am I peaceful the way my teachers seem to be.

The bell rings and we all get up and walk slowly for five minutes. It's nice. The floor creaks and sags, and the light in the room is even and peaceful. I keep the koan in mind but allow the attention to relax somewhat. It's good to have done another round of meditation, to be giving this morning to Zen. Later I'll spend the rest of the weekend with the family. All is okay.

The third sitting period is "*teisho*" time, when Joan gives a talk.

The monitor hits a pair of wooden clappers and we all make a small bow and sit down again.

Joan has given hundreds of talks over the years. Maybe thousands. She is formidable. Quiet, slight, silver-haired, gentle, tender, but made of iron. She is a powerhouse, a treasure house, a storehouse of human energy and clarity. Yet modest, unassuming, outwardly unremarkable. This is how mature Zen practitioners should be, they say: indistinguishable from an ordinary person.

As I watch Joan speak, a wave of gratitude wells up. She has given her life to helping people through this training. As I listen to her talk, the room becomes a little box floating in a great space.

Then it's *dokusan* time. We take turns stepping out of the zendo and sit waiting on a cushion out in the hall. When we hear Joan's handbell from the interview room, we strike a small bell in the hall to announce ourselves, and go in.

The first time I presented a koan to Joan, she sent me away, dissatisfied with my presentation.

Since then, in koan after koan, meeting after meeting, she has been challenging me to become less cluttered, simpler, clearer.

Each time it's like having shiatsu performed on the psyche—a double act between Joan and the masters in the koans. I walk out lighter, emptier. If Zen training is a kind of parenting, we are being stripped down more than built up, shown how little we need, not how much.

"Every day is a good day." Today I manage to go in carrying a trust in a broader reality, sure that Unmon's comment is connected with it. I'm ready to "show" the koan. But no sooner have I sat down and recited the koan than a simple question comes at me, something that had not even entered my head to be pondered. I'm stunned, and can't say anything. Then out of nowhere a response arises.

She smiles. It's apparently what was wanted. Then we're both smiling, in fact laughing. Freed—from the mind, from understanding. For a moment everything is palpably alive, and to recognize its aliveness is intrinsically good, because we are part of it.

Another question comes, and without thinking I respond again, all unease gone. Another smile.

We talk a little about it, but now there's not much to say. The koan needs, in a sense, to cease being a koan and become our experience. Then what is there to say?

I leave the room in fizzing peace. Except I'm hardly aware even of that. All I'm aware of is each step I take, the bow I make to Joan from the door, the dusky light in the hall, the creak of floorboards, the quiet in the zendo, the feel of the cushion as I settle again, the light on the wall, the lovely gloom of my shadow. I could almost cry, I'm so grateful to the others in the room, to the couple who own this yoga studio and allow the sitting here once a week, and to Joan, and to the koan.

When the sit ends, we all chat as we pack up, brushing off the cushions, stacking them on shelves.

Sherry and I drive back to Santa Fe, stopping on the way for a takeout coffee. And that's it. I have a new koan for the coming week. I'll keep investigating the broader questions of who I am and what I could be doing to be more helpful on this earth. That's how Zen training happens. It's slow, painstaking, peaceful, troubling, long, immediate. It's a path, not a conclusion. And we only ever find it here and now.

I'VE BEEN INCHING MY WAY through the hundred koans of the *Blue Cliff Record*, the most revered "classical" collection, compiled by the Chinese master Setcho* in 1028.

Joan invited me to come for an extra *dokusan* each week if I could make it, at her home in Rio Rancho, an Albuquerque suburb. I was pretty excited by this. Koan training is unbelievably long. Sometimes I'd fall into doing the math. Of the five koan books, one had about seventy koans, two had a hundred each, and two books about fifty each, but you had to tackle both the "verses" and the "cases" in these, which in effect doubled the number. That made about 470. Then there were some add-on texts about which it was hard to get clear information, but they totaled perhaps two hundred more. About 670 in all. At a rate of one *dokusan* per week, that was about thirteen years, assuming you didn't keep getting sent back. There were repeat koans that cropped up in more than one collection, which you were usually allowed to skip, but not always. And there were retreats. On retreats you might have one or more *dokusan* per day. But many people who finished the koans apparently turned around and went right back through them again. They weren't the same the second time, people said.

---

* Chinese: Xuedou, 980–1052.

But to be making these kinds of calculations at all was not very "Zen" of me—a clear sign of how badly I needed the training. The longer it took, the better. Nevertheless Joan's offer of extra *dokusan* was generous and I knew it.

I often felt that koan training was the heart of my life, my lifeline, the path to peace, to some kind of completion as a human being. I believed it was making me a better dad and husband, less self-obsessed, less distracted and reactive, and Clare tended to agree. From the outside, you could look at it and think it might itself be a distraction from family, work, love, friendship, but in fact it was the opposite—it opened one up to them, to trying to be more generous and attentive, and wanting to be with them more, and relishing their company.

HOW STRANGE, I WOULD THINK as I drove through the residential suburbs of Albuquerque. Here I was on my way to a subdivision near a golf course not far from the Cottonwood Mall, to grapple with an enigmatic little story from early medieval China, with a quiet woman from Wisconsin who used to live in Japan and then Europe and who now lives in this southwestern desert city, who has been through some kind of existential shift I'm not sure I have been through myself, which probably means I haven't, though I have had glimpses of its possibility, which the characters commemorated in the Chinese anecdotes had also been through. By studying their words and actions in a specific way, we have a chance to go through it, too. And it's worth it. That's what we're taking on faith.

Except not only on faith. Both Joan and John are manifestly at peace. Both are ready to give up inordinate amounts of time to help others in this strange training, with minimal ostensible reward except for the joy of sharing it, and both seem to have given up their own agenda in favor of others'. And they enjoy their lives more than anyone else I know. You feel it when you're with them. You see it in their eyes. They're at peace, free, full of quiet energy, acutely intelligent, and loving.

That's another thing. This dharma training seemed to make people uncommonly articulate, engaging, sensitive, intuitive. How come?

So here we are, still doing this ancient practice but in a different context: not a monastery, but within ordinary lay life. At Joan's house we sit on cushions on the sitting-room floor. I present the new koan, which is about a master, Kyorin, who, when asked what Buddha-nature is, answers, "I'm tired from sitting for a long time." She probes me about it. Things come clearer. Ideas evaporate. The master's tiredness becomes a vast world, in which the room, the carpet, the talk, the afternoon light, the sound of a car going by out on the street, all rest in infinite ease. The koan comes alive. It's as if the master in the koan takes over. He becomes everything. He becomes me. All is well, all was ever well. This is what the koan wanted to reveal.

We have a cup of tea together at the kitchen counter. I'm excited. I love Zen, I love Joan, and actually I love life. And just possibly, life loves me, I feel as I sip my tea.

I WOULD GET THIS FEELING around Joan, that everything near her flourished. Her world was one of gentle well-being. It was one of the happiest things I'd ever known. At first I'd feel it in her house, then it would spread to the garden outside, then the neighborhood.

Maybe she would help our family's life to flourish, I sometimes thought. And she actually did.

She had a way of taking care of objects. She would treat glasses and cups as living things, almost, that deserved nearly as much care as people. When she washed dishes at the sink or set cups out on the counter, along with a teapot and an extra thermos of hot water and a saucer of cookies, you'd feel a loving attention fully given to them.

Once when I was washing up, she started drying a saucer, then stopped and handed it right back. There was a smear on the rim I had missed. I felt a little ashamed, since I had been trying to show how attentively I could do tasks, like a good Zen student. Yet her little, ordinary correction made me feel that I, too, was being taken care of.

Once I was meditating beside her on a windy, sunny day, and she had the windows open with the blinds drawn. The blinds were rattling in the breeze, shaking erratic shadows all over the wall in front of us. *Surely she'll want to close the windows*, I thought, *so we can concentrate better.* But she sat right on through. Didn't she mind the fluttering, the clacking? Or did she mind, but not mind the minding? She was still and quiet as a rock. It inspired me to dig in and find my own immunity to the distraction.

Joan grew up in Wisconsin, and as a young woman she entered the Catholic Maryknoll order. When they sent her to Japan as a young sister, she developed a deep appreciation for Japanese culture and spiritual life, and after twelve years in the order, she left it and returned to the States to pursue a postgraduate degree in Japanese culture. The degree required her to do research in Japan, and while back there she asked a friend to introduce her to a Zen teacher. The friend warned her that she ought to finish her thesis first, before meeting the teacher. Zen had a way of taking over. But she went anyway, and sure enough, after starting practice at the San'un Zendo in Kamakura, she gave up her academic aspirations, stayed in Japan, and pursued Zen training under her master, Yamada Koun Roshi.

Many years later when she had finished her koan study, she decided to go to the Jung Institute in Switzerland to explore the possibility of becoming an analyst, but a group of Swiss people interested in Zen asked her to teach them, and she complied. Over the next thirty years she founded and built up the Sonnenhof Zen Center in the Black Forest, together with the German Benedictine monk and Zen master Willigis Jaeger, beside whom she had trained in Kamakura. She also taught in Dallas, Oregon, Italy, Switzerland. She went where she was needed.

She was wise: I'd sooner have heard her take on a problem than anyone else's. Just under the visible surface she was powerful, vibrant, peaceful. Though she would never agree with this, and would accuse me of exaggeration, I felt she was like some master from a Kung Fu movie: wherever you turned, there she was already, calm and balanced, ready for anything. She had no agenda, so her mind and heart were clear. Or was it vice versa? She often quoted her own teachers. Some teachers had a certain glamour, some even fame. Here there was no trace of interest in name or gain. Joan wouldn't even let people call her "roshi"—a term you often hear in Zen circles in America—though she had the right to be addressed that way.

Some of the Zen teachers I'd met earlier in life didn't feel like this. Perhaps I had seen them through immature eyes, but some seemed to relish their influence, or their eloquence, or their place at the leading edge of a new movement in the West. Some became embroiled in scandals. But with John and Joan it felt as though they were just grateful to be with you. Or didn't terribly mind whether you were there or not. Most of your life happened elsewhere anyway, and that was how it should be—your practice was your own thing. Their role was only to guide you for as long as you wanted them to.

If I was having a hard time, John tended to meet me in it, and empathically feel what I was going through, and offer some TLC. Joan was more austere, more apt to say, "Don't get too caught up in it," and send me back to whatever koan I was on.

The first style could be comforting, but the second had its wisdom. It helped me find over time that things did not matter as much as I often thought, even seemingly big things. It helped to call forth my own resources. The purpose of Zen is not to create dependents, but people who stand on their own feet in the midst of life's travails, and remain clearheaded and kindhearted. It trusts that students already have all they need. In fact, they are already the whole universe, if only they knew it.

Both she and John bridged the gap between ancient foreign practice and contemporary Western life. They showed that the practice was not exotic—it was about our lives. Yet it addressed the very existential conundrums I had long wanted to. To see Zen carried forward by Westerners like them was heartening. It made it safe and relevant. I might not have been at peace yet, but I had faith that I might be one day. I was on the right path: they proved it. That in itself brought a kind of peace already.

BY NOW I HAD LEARNED more about their lineage. Known as the Sanbo Kyodan, it had been influential in the West. A number of Western Zen figures had studied in it. Robert Aitken Roshi, a renowned teacher and writer, was among them, as was Taizan Maezumi Roshi, also a prominent teacher in America. They had both followed its koan curriculum with their students. The poet Gary Snyder, one of the pioneering Bay Area Zen practitioners back in the fifties and sixties, had also studied in it, and founded the Ring of Bone Zendo in the California Sierras. Yamada Roshi himself had officiated at that center's opening, in 1983. In time another Zen teacher, Nelson Foster Roshi, had become its primary leader, and he had completed his training under Robert Aitken. Sanbo Kyodan had a significant influence in the United States.

I had heard of these people, yet they seemed remote from the core of the lineage, which, by chance, I had stumbled into. John and Joan both maintained a direct connection with the current Japanese abbot, attending the lineage's annual teachers' retreats, bowing under the yoke of the Japanese masters in order to continue ever further in "clarifying the dharma eye," and thought of themselves as directly part of it.

ZEN TRAINING IS LIKE A bathtub where the plug has been pulled. At first nothing seems to be happening, but the water is surely going down.

We're a plastic boat floating round, bobbing along, past the rubber duck, along the side of the tub. That's interesting but no big deal. The water is going down, but too slowly to see.

Then a moment comes when it's clear the sides of the tub have grown taller. How did that happen? That's more interesting. The perspective is changing.

Then the water is noticeably shallower. Hey, who did that?

The movement of boat and duck around the perimeter speeds up. The cycle around the edge happens just a bit quicker.

Then we glimpse a sudden vortex down at the plug hole. It's a shock. Where did that twisted rope of energy spring from? We might be tempted to stop: now we've seen the vortex. Perhaps we'd heard rumors of it, and now we've seen it for ourselves and know it's real. Isn't that enough?

We're in Zen training. It's by no means enough.

The tub continues to empty. The journey, the process, is far from complete.

Suddenly there the vortex is again, a silver braid spiraling into darkness. This time we're tugged right into it, with an alarming, heart-stopping jolt. An intense energy strikes us to the core. And we bob out again.

But the boat has been broken by the jolt. We're flotsam on the surface now, and the water continues to drain. Then, with a gulp of the drainage system, we get caught once again in the eddy. We don't realize it's happening, then before we know it we're sucked right down into the whirlpool, through the mouth of the drain, down and down.

Total darkness. Life as we knew it gone, devoured by the plumbing, sucked away into the core of the pipes. Somehow, through that impossible keyhole, that eye of the needle, we pass into ... beyond ...

That's what Zen training is for: to suck us out of life as we know it, out of our self as we know it.

All along we thought it was something *in* the bath we were waiting to have sucked away, but it wasn't: it was the water itself. And it turns out we ourselves were the water all along.

Dogen said that ordinary beings have no illumination in their consciousness, but Buddhas have no consciousness in their illumination. Awareness has to be extinguished, all trace of a witness gone, for the path of Zen to flourish.

Absolute Zero

I WAS LIVING IN TWO WORLDS. Sometimes at the zendo, or on retreats, or doing my daily sits at home, getting lost in a koan, my heart would open. Once, I was at Walmart buying a new safety net for the boys' trampoline, and while I was waiting in line my eye fell on a large-screen TV. It must have been tuned to MTV. A boy band was singing, all dolled up and trying to make an impression, and it seemed such a futile thing—to be pacing around a stage in fancy costumes in an effort to convince people they were worth watching. A shiver of recognition ran through me: Wasn't that what I had done, with books, readings, a visible career—striving to persuade an unknown audience that I was worthy of notice? Then my eye wandered down to the cardboard packing case on which the TV stood. The humble cardboard was even-colored, with a tender fineness in its texture. Now *that* was beautiful. I fell in love with it on the spot and couldn't take my eyes off it. It carried a truth the image-conscious lads on the TV couldn't come near. I found myself close to tears.

Other times I'd be lying in bed at night with my sons on either arm, and the New Mexico rain pattering outside, coaxing the desert into giving off its thick scent to the night air, as waves of simple love rolled through, making the night seem endlessly deep. The scene in the bedroom would become timeless, vast, or else very small—it was hard to say—but connected to a long, invisible chain of human experience. Then I might start to initiate the process of extricating myself from the sleeping boys, only to feel Saul's little fingers tighten round my wrist, and the more I pull the more they tighten, clearly intent on detaining me. There might be an instant of impatience—*What, still not asleep?*—and a thought of things I wanted to get to. But then I'd roll over to find his eyes wide open, gleaming at me in the dark like deep wells. And immediately there'd be the recognition that nothing could matter more than this moment, this resting child, his eyes full of sleepy love, and this mingling of breath and bodies and bones.

And there'd be a more general lesson: Could anything matter more than the present moment? Somehow that was where life itself was always waiting to meet me, if only I could remember.

Moments of reckless love, now and then.

But then back I'd go into my day, my study, and work would be waiting, and there'd be no message from the agent, or there would be a message and the news wouldn't be good, or occasionally there'd be good news out of the blue—an advance, a short list, an offer from a magazine, whatever. Then more bad news: poor sales, a decision not to publish. And so on. I was a weather vane in the wind. Good news, bad news; I'd spin this way, that way. Satisfaction, self-worth; disappointment, shame.

My teachers weren't like this. They weren't nauseating paragons of blessedness, but they still moved through life's vicissitudes with grace, like machines engineered to operate without friction. They could walk into a room and you wouldn't even know. Except you started to feel slightly better. They could sit with you in silence and you felt they knew you, without a word being said.

They had both done what Buddha had said: found the path out of *dukkha*. Often translated as "suffering," *dukkha* is closer to "dissatisfaction," its implicit metaphor being of a wheel hub misaligned on its axle. There's friction. It doesn't turn freely. Both John and Joan had no friction with life. No doubt they'd deny it, but they turned freely.

But not me. In spite of all the practice I'd done, the study under them, the faith I'd given Zen, throwing in my lot with it, I couldn't deny I still had mood swings. I still got "caught," as the Zen people put it. I looked at my teachers and saw their peace, and knew in some ways it derived from their having worked with similar kinds of existential insights to ones I'd undergone, yet they were not like me. Their energy was deep and potent, fluid and easy. They did not get upset. For all my "progress" in the training, I still floundered and flapped in my little puddle of mild dysthymia. I was blessed with a glorious, humorous, talented, grounded wife, with a family, with a career that, while not spectacular, was quite steady and provided us with an income as well as me with some real fulfillment. I had teachers, a community of fellow sitters, a modest, cozy home. What more did I want?

I didn't really want more. I just wanted peace. Zen had landed some hammer blows to my skull, yet the deep ease of the masters eluded me. I was too tough a nut: a few cracks to the shell, but each time the shell reconstituted.

I was a whiner, still, after everything that had occurred. When I was doing the PhD, the research had been too hard. When, on a wing and a prayer, I made a living as a travel writer, it should have been poetry. When at last I settled into two poetry fellowships, collections and prizes under my belt, it should have been fiction. And when the novels won contracts, awards, accolades, it should have been different novels. To my bones an ingrate, an anhedoniac, an insatiate.

Now it was the same with Zen. I couldn't quite pull it off. The dybbuk of discontent on my shoulder always had the last laugh. The genes tweaked out a final twist in the spiral, and the joke was on me.

Dogen said, "Even if you have attained the way, you have merely put your head through the gate." He was right. I had stuck my head through several times, and always withdrawn it. I didn't have the genes for inner peace, I thought. My sister and brother both had impressive careers and healthy homes; Clare was a sought-after mediator, and David was a renowned correspondent on BBC TV News. They had both settled early in life into families of their own, and lived deep and competent lives. I was the troubled one, the traveler, with the unpredictable career, tangled in the frayed hems of the shawl of competence, never quite able to grab the thing and wear it; often stable, happy, philosophical, then dropping into cycles of mild depression, demotivation, shame. I'd work hard at projects, then do something not necessarily to derail but to compromise them.

"Little Big Man," Dad used to say of me. Contrary: that

was Henry. Washing his hands in the dirt, drying them in the stream. Dysthymic: mild, but chronic.

Oy vey. Dad wasn't like this. Some people. What can you do?

BUT THERE IS ONE THING you can do with them: sit them on a cushion and tell them to shut up. And be still. Which was what my teachers did with me, again and again.

Was it still about trust? I trusted John, I trusted Joan, but not enough? Not enough to say: my life is after all not my own?

The teacher-student relationship is complex. Over the years Joan gently guided me, and sometimes not so gently. When I was full of myself, she reminded me that I had to try to live generously and kindly; when despondent, that I knew of a world of peace. She pushed me into seeing life as an ongoing exploration, and every moment as an opportunity for investigation. But perhaps the main thing is simply the teacher's presence in your life. They have given their life to the teachings, and to passing them on. They may have their failings, and a good teacher knows it. Yet they are there to keep you training. Again and again, to call you back to it.

But in spite of the constancy Joan and John had shown me, I still had trust issues.

Deep down, I still saw women as providers of comfort, pleasure, security, through their unknowable bodies and clear-sighted hearts. But any moment they might turn round and dump you. And men were still deniers of worth, thieves of self-respect, purveyors of shame; they put you down, then tried to recruit you for their power trips.

ONE MORNING I WAS SITTING on the kitchen floor in our house in Santa Fe, hunched over a puddle of clear liquid about nine inches in diameter. The liquid was tears. For the first time in years, I was weeping without restraint. A reservoir of old grief had been tapped, touched, opened, the cork blown. The well of grief rose, and the tears streamed from nose and cheek uncontrollably.

Through the example of Joan, I had started on some Jungian dream therapy. Long ago she had worked on her dreams at the C. G. Jung Institute in Switzerland, and said it had helped. By chance I had recently met a maverick dreamworker from Vermont, brilliant, controversial, confrontational. A former mailman with an MA in philosophy, Marc Bregman had stumbled into a workshop led by the Jungian James Hillman long ago and never looked back. He had developed his own potent form of dream therapy. Dreams were guiding us. We had to surrender to them and receive their guidance: that was the basic message. Nine times out of ten, they wanted us to open to our long-buried wounds. That was the way to healing of the soul.

There came a point where I could no longer deny the invisible membrane of distrust beyond which I couldn't go. I didn't know what it was, but my dreams knew. They showed a path through it. Their path was grief. Pain that I had forgotten, but the soul hadn't. My soul would let me go no further down the path, not until I had paid my toll in tears.

Marc did sessions cross-country, by phone. They were no less powerful for that. He used my dreams to reduce me to tears, nudge me to the brink of a grief I hadn't known how to acknowledge, and, with barely a prod, push me over.

He regarded dreams as uncanny bringers of semi-divine insight into our psychology and behavior. "Have you ever had an affair?" he asked in our first session. So the dreams were onto me. The period of our marital strife a few years back had centered around it. It was long since over, but there it was, right off the bat, lurking still in the psyche.

I had learned that the secret to a happy relationship was not believing that it must be with the right person, but that your partner *was* the right person. And any valences of the soul not being met—that was okay; they could be touched in other ways than sex-love partnership. The mystical urge for union, for example, was best met through finding a guide, a teacher, a master, not by illicit grappling in a motel. The midlife crisis could become a crucible of growth, of alchemy.

Yet I was still distrustful of men, still siding with women, still hoping to resolve life through a mightier blaze of success. In short, still full of myself: that's what he said the dreams showed. I couldn't deny any of it. Then, gradually, the dreams started to break the crust, and teach a deeper trust.

Threatening men kept coming after me, until I gave in to them, whereupon I found they had only been trying to love me. My trust in that love slowly began to grow. In one dream I was having *dokusan* with John and put my head in his lap, and the world as I knew it came apart. In another my father rowed me across a Scottish loch to a castle on an island. The king was having a banquet and invited me in. Like the prodigal son, I knelt before him and rested my head in his lap and wept, and he put his hand on the back of my head: I had come home, to an archetypal father who forgave all. I shook with archetypal humility, penitent and grateful.

In my dreams I was killed again and again. Arrows pierced my body, bullets disposed of my brain, fires burned me up. It was all about death of the ego, Bregman said—and my heart started to grow stronger.

I KEPT HAVING DREAMS ABOUT skydiving, and though it wasn't part of the therapeutic approach, I decided to take them literally. I went all out for a drastic change in perspective.

Accelerated free fall, they called it: AFF. Meaning you jumped on your own the first time. From ten thousand feet. Why do it by halves?

I had no idea what was happening the first few seconds, then for half a minute I floated two miles above the New Mexico desert, with an inexpressible sense of safety. Then only one mile above it. I pulled the cord and felt the massive tug of the parachute.

The jump actually worked. I worried less afterwards.

I took up intense ashtanga yoga. Yoga had been part of the TM regime, and I'd done it on and off for many years. I'd always loved it. Now I got more diligent, and unearthed a vibrant peace within the body that brought its own fulfillment.

Then one week I was in New York to meet with an editor. In the friend's apartment where I was staying, I had been working on the manuscript of the by now ancient family novel, cutting it back so far to around fifteen hundred pages. In the tight little kitchen one morning, I accidentally knocked a chopping board to the floor. It glanced my shin as it fell. Sudden pain, a loud knock when it bounced on the floor, and suddenly I couldn't find any bearings to orient myself by. The blow knocked out some piece of structure-creating consciousness. I became light as a feather, with no center of gravity. In spite of the pain, it was joyous, weightless. I had no mass.

It was intense enough that I called Joan.

"I've lost all my bearings," I moaned into the phone.

"What do you need bearings for?" she replied.

A series of small things, an unseen descent: one way has to give up, die away, so another can emerge.

❧

DAY THREE OF A *SESSHIN*. You have a writing assignment in England and timed it so you could attend this retreat with John. As usual it's at Cold Ash, the retreat center on the Berkshire Downs, just west of Reading, where all his *sesshins* are held. You stay in a small room with a crucifix on the wall and a basin in the corner. You can see the hills thirty miles south on a clear day.

Things are beginning to settle. You've passed through the physical discomfort of the first day—sore knees, a crick in the neck you thought you'd left behind but which revived on arrival. The second day brought some emotional disturbance. You wondered about the family book: did it have a chance of working out, and actually what were you doing on this retreat anyway, shouldn't you be working on the book right now, it's still a mess, a tangle of canvas and rope. And so on.

Then, hard on the heels of the first two days, this morning, the third, you wake up so clearheaded, so fresh, awake, and lively to the new sensations of the day—the soft dawn filtering under your curtain, the rich *shush* when you turn on the basin tap, the delicious creaking outside your room as someone walks down the corridor—that you forgo even your morning cup of tea. You don't want to disturb the sumptuous peace with anything, not even tea.

The zendo seems so beautiful your heart almost breaks—the black cushions, the gray twilight, the single star of a candle on the altar. When the bell rings for the first period, its note is as clear-throated as a nightingale's. The faint dawn breeze from an open window brushes over your bare hands. You taste it in your skin, sweet as ice cream.

A thought comes up: *Hey, you don't normally feel like this.* For a moment the thought catches you, and you start pondering the meaning of these sensations, before remembering that there's a better way to go: no thinking, just experience them.

It's somewhere in the middle of the morning that the tussle begins. John would normally be giving a talk now, but he has instituted a change. The third day is a "quiet day." No interviews, no formal talk. The whole zendo is humming. In the periods of walking meditation that perforate the sitting, the monitor goes around opening the windows. The thin curtains flutter madly, scattering armfuls of shade across the floor, and it feels as if you're moving over the surface of a windy lake. Then, toward the end of the walking, *snap* and *clack* as the monitor goes around again, closing the windows and curtains. Then *click!* from the wood blocks, and everyone paces briskly back to their seat, flowing like a mountain stream. Then stillness again in the twilight as we settle on our cushions.

Why is it so beautiful to be in this darkened room? The other people—some thirty-five of them—feel like pine trees in a forest, silent and still, stirring now and then. You hear someone breathe deeper, then fall silent. Someone shifts a little on a cushion: a whisper from the fabric.

Then it starts. Somewhere in your body. A ripple of tension. And another. Soon a wrestling match is going on inside you.

Elbows and knees pressing inside your ribs as if a pair of toddlers are hard at it, grappling with each other. What's happening in there?

Over the past few years you've felt two people living inside you. One is the usual old you, with his struggles, hopes, dreads; the other is different, at peace, made of gentle promise. He loves to sit. He loves other people. He loves helping. He doesn't care about your career, except insofar as it helps the family. He doesn't look ahead. You've even said to Joan that you feel like two people are living in you, at which she smiled and said nothing.

Now it's as if these two entities are having at it, in hand-to-hand combat. You can't believe you're actually sitting still. But you are. If you move even a little, the fighting stops. Like two animals shy of being noticed, they won't wrestle unless you keep absolutely still. They go into hiding. Resume stillness and they're at it again.

This goes on all day. It's exhausting. It feels like a deep, unscratchable itch. You long for it to be over, but that doesn't help. You know what you have to do. You have to be still and let them do it.

It continues all through the next day too. Then, during the evening sit, suddenly peace. A glassy stillness. It's so beautiful you decide not to stop sitting when the day officially ends, but continue into the night. The zendo is quiet and dark, and now you feel the absence where the other sitters were as a softness all around.

It's the last night of the retreat. You sit late, deep into the night of the half-lit zendo.

Your vision starts playing up. Bright lights seem to be shining. This has happened before. You ignore it. The sensation comes on whereby you feel you're sitting in the back of your skull and looking at your vision as on a screen, apart from yourself. Like being settled in the dark of a cinema, with the screen of sight off in the distance.

Then things get weird.

You're in Egypt, in an ancient temple. There's some kind of stone plinth, and the foot of a giant statue. You're in the statue's shadow, there's sandy desert all around, dry air, the scent of dust.

Then you're in a theater. Paris or London in the 1890s. A gold proscenium arch rises high overhead, with the shaded stage pit before you, the glow of footlights. You sense the quiet expectancy of an audience.

A slow joy rises like yeast in dough. It's wonderful to be sitting in the glow of past centuries.

Then you become superconscious of your breathing, but it's no longer yours. It's like watching an animal breathe, as if through a lens. You ask, *Who is it breathing?* There's the rustle of inhalation followed by exhalation. Whose breath is it?

You switch your attention to your sight. The question spontaneously arises: *Whose sight is it?*

And there's hearing: some kind of faint hiss in the room, and a soft rumble perhaps of a boiler in the basement, deep under the floor. Again: *Who is hearing?* It's as if some unknown being has usurped your senses.

As you receive these sense experiences—breathing, seeing, hearing—you try to find out who it really is sitting in the middle of them. What is there, in the space *between* hearing, seeing, breathing? There must be something there, because that's where *you* are. But the more deeply you examine this space in the middle, the harder it is to identify who's in there.

Suddenly it's clear: there's no one there. Just empty space. Breathing is happening, but there's no one breathing. Where there ought to be a breather, only space. There's hearing, but no one hearing. Where there should be a hearer, just space.

It's this again: *no one*. Like on the mountain in New Mexico.

Except it's not the same. This time it's a flattening. Breathing, hearing, seeing: they flatten against one another, two-dimensional. Whatever was in the middle is squeezed out. Somehow, as a result of that, where "I" should be, there is nothing but space.

A rush of joy. Why joy?

Because it's like putting down the heaviest burden, a weight as absolute and dreadful as Jehovah. It was a lie all along. One tweak in the angle of vision and it's gone. No *me*. Something else—the heart, or space, or existing itself—floats up, weightless, free. Boundless and empty. Non-existing, perhaps.

But how could nonbeing be blissful? You don't know, but it is.

This is what the famous "just" of Zen means. Zen often says: *Just sit. Just walk. Just eat.* But "just walking" doesn't mean: keep your mind only on walking and don't think about anything else. It means: there *is* no mind to put on walking. There *is* only walking. There truly is *just* walking.

Right now, it's *just* seeing, *just* breathing, *just* hearing.

What relief. What heaven, to be gone!

"Gone, gone, gone beyond, gone utterly beyond," says the *Heart Sutra*, a core scripture of Mahayana Buddhism. Beyond what? Beyond all.

Space collapses. The wall, the cushion, the night outside, the carpet, the sound of the rumbling boiler down in the cellar—everything is equidistant, no distance at all. One great intimacy.

The wall and the boiler's rumble turn into a pair of loving palms. The wall—that flickering barrier of light and shade so familiar to the Zen student—and the room, and the thoughts and sensations that arise, the sounds, all these are one single act of love. It's love that brings the world into being. The floor, on which you slowly walk through midnight hours in the zendo when you get up for some walking meditation, is itself love. The walking, too, is performed by the same simple love, all because there is no one walking. There is only walking.

I SAT THROUGH THE NIGHT with a river of energy coursing through the world. The whole world was love's plaything, a cork bobbing on a silent torrent.

I broke for a cup of tea in the early morning, then quietly went back and took my place again in the zendo, long before the official sitting began.

A CONCERN ARISES: I HAVE to see the teacher.

In Zen, confirmation is essential. All masters had their insights and experiences checked by their masters. That's how Zen is passed down. You bring it to the teacher. Zen stays deep and clear by not letting us self-approve, even when the very notion of "approval" seems absurd. But this was the final morning of the retreat. By lunchtime it would be over. Would I have a chance to see John?

When the others came and joined in the sitting at six in the morning, I asked the monitor if I could get in to *dokusan*, which would mean jumping the queue. He said fine. So in the last sitting period before breakfast I was ushered in.

The light in the *dokusan* room seemed golden, as if the two of us, John and I, were sitting in the Bronze Age. The sounds of birdsong from the trees outside resonated as if we all lived—birds and us—in one big tank.

I didn't know where to begin and was just about to start trying to explain myself when John picked up the handbell and shook it. He told me he'd see me later, he really would, but for now he was seeing students working on the first koan.

It was the first time I'd ever been dismissed so soon.

I went back to my place. As soon as I sat, peace dropped like a mantle. Again, nothing but hearing—the clear, echoing sounds of early dawn, when light is creeping under the threadbare curtains.

Such peace. Like living in the aftermath of a long war.

There was breakfast, then John's morning talk, then more *dokusan*. After the talk the monitor brought me back up to the line outside the door of the interview room. Two people were ahead of me and it was already eleven. John's *dokusan* could be long and slow, and I knew it was touch and go whether I'd get in before noon, when the retreat ended. I passionately wanted to, but a major part of the training is patience. To sit outside the door not knowing if we'll get in, learning to calm the urgency, remembering that all is fundamentally the same whether we get in or not, is a training in itself.

Finally it was my turn. I made my bows, settled on the cushion before John, and sighed.

He smiled and asked me what had been going on.

He looked at me and his face seemed so close that it was part of consciousness itself.

I started to talk about what I'd been experiencing. He hummed assent.

Then he said something. He named a state I'd heard of that had been a remote prospect of training, highly unlikely ever to be tasted by me, certainly not in the foreseeable future. I'd have to be a different kind of person. I was surprised when he said it and was sure he must be wrong.

I had been sitting with a strange koan the past day or two, about Master Kyozan,* in which he and a monk do a kind of charade. The monk makes movements with his body and arms, and each time Kyozan responds by drawing Chinese characters with brush and ink.

I hadn't been able to make head or tail of it, but while I was sitting with the koan, it hit me that if everything was empty, then even the cherished "experiences" I'd had over the years were also empty. I'd once heard a teaching about there being eighteen kinds of emptiness, and the eighteenth was the "emptiness of emptiness"—in other words, there is not even emptiness. In a sense, if there were, then it wouldn't truly be empty.

So what had I been doing all these years? What were the koans, the masters, the "experiences," and the *dokusan*, the talks, the meditation even? What was Zen training? Was it all just a charade, like the two characters in the koan making their strange gestures, a hopscotch going nowhere?

I was trying to put the pieces together. That long-ago experience in New Mexico: Was that the same as this? As my mind struggled to construct an understanding, suddenly that former moment was immediately present. Time vanished. That time and this had never been separate. Then what had I been doing through all these years of "Zen"?

---

* Chinese: Yangshan, 807–883.

As I heard John speak just now, I felt as if I were perched on the edge of a great cliff. Before I had time to think about whether I might step off, a thunderbolt dropped on the crown of my head.

FALLING OFF THE CUSHION. LYING on the floor. Weeping. Everything gone. All the hard work of holding together the world as Henry knew it—gone. No more Henry, no more world. Nothing. No more Zen. Truly, nothing. True nothing. Everything annihilated. Nothing left. Nothing at all.

It's hard to know what exactly happened, but when I look back on it, there's simply nothing. Not even awareness of nothing. A gap. But not even a gap. Blackness. But not even that. It's hard to know what to call it. Death, perhaps. "Death" seems the aptest term.

One impossible fact: nothing at all. Not emptiness, which might still suggest space with nothing in it, but *nothing*. Nothing to see, no one to see, no seeing.

It was like a boot kicking out the lamp that had illuminated all things. Not vast space: that was still *something*. Not everything being one: that was still something. Not no-self: somehow there was still an awareness of that.

This was reality at last. Nothing. Not even a witness.

The ultimate joke.

TEARS FLOWED THROUGH A WONDROUS universal dark.

At a certain point John had to leave to go down to the zendo for the *sesshin*'s closing ceremony. I could stay in the room here if I liked.

I was still lying on the floor, shuddering with sobs and laughter. He put his cushion under my head, leaving me on the floor, inarticulate and shaking.

The world rearranged itself like epochs of continental drift, all happening here and now. Huge pieces of the world moving about. The *dokusan* room flew under the basement, which bobbed up into the sky. The trees across the car park whizzed past the windows. Everything was a merry-go-round.

Zen has its own name for this. There's no shortcutting the process. In order to be reborn, first we had to die.

When John finally came back, I was still lying in a daze.

He asked how I was doing.

"Just fine," I said. I rolled over and stood up, and the whole room got up with me.

"Everything in between has been erased," I remember saying.

He smiled. Then told me that Zen said oddly little about this. Joshu once asked a master about the Zen death in a koan, and the master told him not to prowl about in the nighttime, but to come back in the daylight.

"We'll have no dying here," I jumped in.

He agreed, and added that another master had said the whole world was turned upside down.

We lit incense together. The whole world bowed before the altar. The walls of the room, John's face, the doorway—all were born just then.

When we came downstairs to the dining room where the lunch party for the end of *sesshin* was beginning, as luck would have it the first person I met was one of the senior students for whom I felt great admiration. We hadn't talked much, but I had always thought I could sense the depth of his Zen. We embraced in a long hug.

At the celebratory lunch, when we were each asked to speak a few words, all I could say was "Thank you, thank you," over and over again.

John said, "Normally Henry's an articulate guy," and everyone laughed.

FOR THREE DAYS AND NIGHTS I hardly slept. I trembled with gratitude, in a new world.

Great peace. That was all there was. Dogen called his temple Eihei—"eternal peace." I trembled with peace.

It was only a beginning, but finally I had given myself up. I didn't mean to, but I did, and without any god or divinity or magic intervening.

It couldn't have happened without my teachers. John became a new kind of father to me. Something new had been trying to be born, and now it was. At the same time, Joan, who had shepherded me through so many koans out in New Mexico, ceased to be the best dharma aunt and became my dharma mother.

I could have said: How fortunate. I had two teachers and they worked in a kind of stereo, keeping me on my toes. But now it seemed this entire earth was one single teacher.

Unmon said, "Medicine and disease correspond to each other. This whole great earth is medicine. Where is your true self?"

I knew the answer now. I couldn't have named it, but I could show it, clear as the end of the nose on my face.

ALONE IN MY MOTHER'S APARTMENT in Oxford, the day after leaving the retreat, stunned by newness, I was caught off guard by a gust of gratitude toward my parents. They had given me life.

It was the most obvious thing, yet for so long I had failed to see it: without them, I would not have had this greatest of all opportunities: to be a human being. At last I had become no more nor less than what I was: human.

My existence was a gift, and its unspeakable generosity had been hidden from me, by nothing but a mirage of grasping and aversion, by a basic ignorance that consisted in taking a mirage as real.

The system had been uprooted now, and in its place a sweet spring kept welling up, gushing with joy.

A few days later I realized that this momentous event in my life had happened by chance on my mother's birthday.

TWENTY YEARS OF MEDITATION, AND now for the first time I felt like I had just been born into the world. I was alive. That was all. Alive.

THE NEXT DAY I WAS in London. The trip to England had been funded by a newspaper that wanted me to write about a feted new restaurant in Bayswater.

As I sat drinking tea with a friend who was putting me up in the city, his face, his presence, the words we spoke, the table at which we sat, the rotund teapot, the emphatic mugs that waited for us—all were beautiful strands of kelp that grew up from an ocean floor. When I went upstairs and meditated in his study, on a cushion lifted from a chair, as soon as I sat on the floor the whole house, and the street outside, and London itself, opened like a flower.

That evening I took notes in the cavernous new restaurant. I didn't want any alcohol, but the host kept plying the table with wine, and a collection of little tastes of various vintages collected at my place. They were beautiful. In the past I might have felt an obligation to try them, but there was no trace of that kind of obligation anywhere, not in the whole universe.

I SAT WAITING FOR JOHN in a coffee shop the following day. He had kindly offered to meet for a debrief after the retreat. As the time of our appointment approached, I realized I badly wanted to buy him a gift, and dashed outside.

The café was in a little row of shops. There was a wine shop. That wouldn't work. A newsagents. An estate agents. Then a card-and-knickknack store. I paced in, scanned the shelves, noticed some candles, and settled on a large altar candle and a card. I just had time to pay and write my thanks in the card and get back to the café as John arrived.

We huddled at a table and he gave me counsel. He said this new experience was a process and I should let it unfold. A teacher couldn't do much. One teacher had likened his role to helping a butterfly out of a cocoon. If you touched the wings, you might damage them. It happened by itself.

John leaned close over the table so our odd conversation would not be overheard.

"Look at Case 77 of the *Blue Cliff Record*," he suggested.

It was another koan famous in the Zen world. A monk asked Master Unmon, "What is meant by the pronouncement to go beyond the Buddha?"

The question is an allusion to a line of scripture, an irreverent flourish typical of Zen, about the need to leave any notion of "Buddha" behind. In answer, without hesitation, Unmon said, "*Kobyo.*"

A *kobyo* is a rough country rice cake. Something of comparable culinary status to, say, scrumpy, the rustic hard cider of the English West Country. Or mac and cheese.

There happened to be a piece of shortbread on a saucer in front of me. It was a marvel, more precious than any notional Buddha or divinity, because it was here. It had arisen. Or rather, there it was in the very act of arising. But it didn't matter what we said or did. John and I were not just *in* one ocean; it was as if sitting on either side of the little table in the West London café, with the wind heaving through the big sycamores outside and the blood-red London buses lurching up the avenue, the sky dark and low, a promise of rain in the air—as if the whole moment, with all that constituted it, including John and me, *was* one ocean.

We were already far, far beyond the Buddhas. All of this was utter goneness, functioning with infinite fecundity.

I walked John to his train home, and as I watched him move away across the shining station floor beyond the ticket barrier, I knew he was not leaving. For the first time I felt he had truly found me, and I him, and now we could never lose each other.

I REALIZE THAT LAST SENTENCE may sound nuts. I began this account so rational I had no way of receiving the revelation that hit me on the beach when I was nineteen years old. Am I ending it so irrational I've lost all regard for the way things are?

Zen may undermine false assumptions, but its goal is to help us live more helpfully—not in servitude to an imaginary tyrant called "me," but in the service of others. In the core of "ancestral Zen," this happens through the collapse of the prior notion of who we are. It's hard to believe that what is then revealed might be a universal reality that includes all beings, that this could be a palpable and intimate experience rather than a grand idea, but that's how it is. It's because the tradition is about living this reality, rather than positing it as a metaphysics, that Zen training takes so long, and why it is worth grinding through hundreds of koans with a teacher, and then doing so all over again. Nothing matters more than finding that our "real self" is absolutely inclusive. And learning how to live it is the journey of a lifetime.

❧

BACK IN NEW MEXICO, I went to see Joan as soon as I could. I sat down in front of her, sighed, and told her something had happened. She looked at me, and I at her, and tears welled up in me.

"Ah," she said.

I wiped my eyes and spoke a little.

She nodded. All she said was: "Good."

She smiled a little. Then said something about not needing to talk much about the deeper experiences.

A war was over. It wasn't clear if I had won or lost—but presumably lost. An infinite, marvelous loss. The contents of the war, its causes and rationales, its bitterness and rage, had already become vague memories. It was a great absolution.

She told me about a correspondence her teacher had had. A friend wrote to inquire about the teacher's experience of awakening. He wrote back describing it with three words: *"Eihei. Eihei. Eihei."*

Great peace. Great peace. Great peace.

"Great peace" is possible even for troubled, "sick-souled"

people, as William James called us. We should not despair too soon.

I WALKED ABOUT IN A daze of gratitude for days, weeks, months. At first I assumed it would all wear off. But gradually it dawned on me that it was never going to. This last shift hadn't been so much an "experience" as just that—a real shift. Years on, it still hasn't really faded. Zen had actually done the impossible: it had changed me. Over time, I stopped being able to tell whether it had "worn off" or not. It no longer mattered.

But in those early days, it was like being born again—or not again, but for the first time. Finally I knew what my life was. Not in some metaphysical or ontological sense, but in terms of the old Zen language. When one monk "awoke" under the promptings of the sixth ancestor, Huineng,* after weeping, sweating, trembling in shock, he is said to have declared, "Now I am like a person who knows for themselves when they drink water whether it is warm or cold." Another old master said of his awakening, "Now I know: eyes horizontal, nose vertical."

It doesn't sound like much. But they aren't talking about knowledge, but rather about experiencing life for the first time, from the inside out.

Back home I was bewildered by gratitude—for Clare mostly, and for the boys, for their very existence. I was baffled at the wonder of everything existing. It was an overwhelming marvel.

This kind of state, according to the old way of thinking, would obviously wear off after a while as well. Yet year after year,

---

* Japanese: Daikan Eno, 638–713.

if anything, the wonder and gratitude grew, the space of the heart welling up daily with love. It confounded all conditioned expectations. But that's what this practice is for: to deliver such a blow to our conditioned construction of reality that the factory itself is knocked out.

In Japanese they say: *mu ichi motsu—mu ju zo.*

"Not one single thing—an inexhaustible treasury."

They also say: *shin ku—myo u.*

"True goneness—wondrous being."

To drop into bottomless, timeless, spaceless zero—that is to emerge as wondrous being, from which nothing is excluded. A world beyond things, where, although phenomena appear as before, it's impossible to say whether there are or aren't things. It no longer matters. As Master Nansen* said, "This is not mind, this is not Buddha, this is not a thing." Instead, each tiniest phenomenon is beloved, is love itself. In spite of being limited, mortal, multi-flawed beings, we are nevertheless capable of finding timeless love in the depths of our being.

I'm talking like this but remain an atheist. This has nothing to do with any notional divinity.

THE DRAMA WAS OVER. THE whole thing called "my life" had been just that: a drama, a story. A dream. I had woken from it. It had ended.

Yakusan, in the ninth century, likened awakening to a snake shedding its skin and the true body being revealed. The whole "skin" of our imagined life sloughed off. I was born in the real world now, not the world as I had thought, but as it was—beyond

---

* Chinese: Nanquan, 749–835.

description, marvelous and ordinary at the same time, limitless yet just exactly as it seemed.

"What needed to be done has been done," as Buddha said.

SO WHAT NEXT?

That emerged over time.

Things began to crumble. I remember being caught one morning wondering if I should shave. Right away I realized that the real concern was not the state of my face, but what other people would think of me. Would I look tidy to them? I resolved there and then, with a burst of warmth, not to shave or cut my hair. It didn't matter how I looked. I had found what seekers through the ages had sought. There was a resolution to human life. It wasn't easy to find, even if we had the good fortune to stumble across teachers who could point us down a path to it. But it existed, and it was true. All it took was to give ourselves up.

Previously, the teaching of the various *kensho* experiences hadn't penetrated deep enough. Now it was as if the very *I* who experienced them had been dug out at the root. No one had had them. There had been no one to have them all along. I was free at last to be who I was. And who that was I couldn't say. Yet I knew.

THERE'S AN ENLIGHTENMENT POEM BY Yamada Koun with the line "All my karmic sins were extinguished as if in a bolt of lightning."

An ancient ax strikes the cranium. Suddenly it appears: the bare fact of nothing at all. All this living, all this Zen: all along it was nothing. Nothing to see, no one to see, no seeing. Next thing you're on the floor, face wet with tears and laughter, every last nook and cranny of your self gone, therefore fully absolved.

The strange thing was that anytime I chose to look, it was still going on. A black hole in reverse, a sun, a nuclear fusion seething away—but where? I didn't see how anyone could say. What *it* was, everything was. One touch and it sucked away the universe. Another, and all things were born.

The mother and father of everything, the fertile void: so loving, so powerful, so all-aware—what a thing it was. Yet it was no thing.

I HAD BEEN LIKE A beast stuck inside a haystack, pushing and thrashing, not knowing if it was getting anywhere. My teachers cajoled me, but not even they could tell me the way out. Eventually I burst out of the far side, into daylight, or moonlight, or something in between, in such a way that I could never go back under the hay.

But what had I really been doing during all these years of practice? Through the simplicity of being still and quiet, something had been growing. Every now and then it showed itself, then withdrew again. A beast, sure enough, burgeoning within, the ox of Zen's famous "Oxherding Pictures."* Finally it sloughed

---

* There is a map of Zen training known as the Ten Oxherding Pictures, first developed in ninth-century China, which runs as follows: (1) Setting out to find the ox. (2) Seeing the tracks of the ox. (3) Glimpsing the ox. (4) Catching the ox. (5) Taming the ox. (6) Riding the ox home. (7) At home, ox forgotten. (8) Ox and self forgotten. (9) Reaching the source. (10) In the marketplace with gift-bestowing hands. *Kensho* equates to the third picture, and the "Zen death" experience to the fourth. The path continues until the practitioner is freely and selflessly functioning in the most ordinary way in ordinary life.

off the sleeve of self and world. In the weak daylight of England the true ox arrived, and it wasn't going away.

I WROTE TO JOHN.

> The world has turned back to front, inside out, upside down. Things I had thought bad are not bad, and things I'd thought good aren't good either. I realize I have never known people I've known for years.
>
> I long to sit long hours while the thing that has been born grows stronger. I am fully awake yet don't know who I am. A fuse has blown, there is only silence.
>
> I feel so grateful to my parents for giving me this life. I'm overwhelmed with gratitude to Clare and the boys. And to you and Joan. I see how much of this life I have lived to gratify "Henry." It makes no sense at all, and never did. A long childhood has finally ended, and a new one has begun.
>
> Thank you, thank you.

LATER, IN A CAFÉ, ANOTHER time, I asked John how he had known. I had entered the *dokusan* room and started telling him what had been going on, and he called it at once. I hadn't been so sure.

"It's a strange thing. Have another look at Dogen's experience," he told me, referring to the thirteenth-century master who first got me started on Zen back in Natalie's kitchen in Santa Fe. Dogen described his awakening as "body and mind falling away." After it happened he went to see his teacher, Rujing,* and said, "Body and mind have fallen away."

---

* Japanese: Tendo Nyojo, 1162–1228.

Rujing immediately agreed, confirming it.

But Dogen told him, "Don't be too hasty. This could be temporary."

Rujing responded that he wasn't being hasty. He knew. He could tell.

"Even though Dogen wasn't sure, Rujing knew right away," John said.

So this was what Zen existed for: to bring a human being to a condition that, impossibly, resolved everything. And to pass it on.

I QUAKED IN AWE FOR the most ordinary things. Sitting on a cushion, gazing at a wall. Daylight growing in the early morning. The sound of a car out on the street. I'd dropped through the floor. The earth swallowed me whole.

Gradually it became clearer how this reality got obscured: it was through thinking and then believing the thoughts. It was a subtle process, but ubiquitous. But once this dark, radiant fact opened up, we had an alternative. It was possible to see the obscuring process in action, and cherish it without being caught by it. It, too, was empty, after all.

FOR A WHILE IT WASN'T so easy to work. I sat for several hours a day letting everything steep in zazen.

The Korean Son master Chinul* talked of "nurturing the sacred infant." First Zen training allows the infant to be born. Then it nurtures it and helps it grow. It's real, yet Zen is silent on this part of the journey. It seems the whole effort is to bring this

---

* 1158–1210. Son is the Korean form of Zen or Ch'an.

birth about and trust that when it does, we have been sufficiently trained that the infant has the space it needs to grow. Then it gives us a path of action to follow. The action is service, the whole world its theater of operation.

Meditation was different now. I knew what Yakusan meant when he said that to meditate was to "think not-thinking."

"How do you do that?" a monk asked.

He replied, "Non-thinking."

Non-thinking: a luminous clarity that didn't seem to fade no matter what I was doing, even when asleep.

I DON'T MEAN TO BRAG about any of this. A real danger in practice is to seek, then become proud of, our "awakenings." The Tibetan master Chogyam Trungpa dubbed it "spiritual materialism," and it's just another form of self-serving egotism.

I'm writing this account because I want people to know what Zen still carries in its DNA, its "bloodstream," as Bodhidharma called it. Zen can "work" even in a lay life. Even an angst-riddled, atavistically ambitious, self-thwarted heathen can become more resolved and at peace—more so than he ever deserved—and more committed to being helpful.

But perhaps this now sounds like an even worse kind of bragging, one imbued with false modesty, or even evangelism.

On the other hand, these kinds of experience do happen. Zen acknowledges them, as if, with a weary sigh, saying, "Yes, this is how people are, it happens." The danger is that it can become something to attain, or to have attained. The tradition has mechanisms for working against this, but the best of them is simply a deep enough experience to sweep away the whole sorry business.

"Kick out the bottom of the black lacquer bucket," goes an ancient Zen saying. Lose every last bit of consciousness.

Do that and you're still not even halfway down the path.

THIS IS WHERE THINGS GET harder to write about. As long as Zen hasn't really kicked in, there is still conflict within, still work to be done. Once it has delivered, and the errant postulant has been sucker-punched, and notions of "life" have blown their fuses, the practice becomes harder to articulate.

Yakusan entered the hall one night, amid the assembly of monks, and in the ill-lit zendo announced, "I have a single phrase. But I won't say it until a bull gives birth to a calf."

An impossible birth, clearly.

But one monk called out in the dark, "The bull has given birth to a calf. Why don't you say it?"

Yakusan shouted for a lantern to be brought so he could find the person who had spoken. By the time they got the lamp together, the monk in question had disappeared back into the crowd.

Book Burial

DAD IS DEAD NOW, OF prostate cancer. He'd had the disease more or less invisibly for fifteen years, and it got him in the end.

He died a happy atheist.

"What do you think happens, Dad?" I asked him in his hospital bed in the final few weeks.

"We go out like a lightbulb," he said, with a groan of relief.

He was relieved to be in hospital. He hated not being able to walk, and in hospital it mattered less.

"It's all a dream anyway," I told him. "That's what Zen says. Not what it appears to be."

"Oh, I like *that*." His eyes lit up.

YOU NEVER KNOW A PARENT's body like you do when they're dead. Dad's, for example: I always knew he had a strong nose; we all did, it was common knowledge. But now, lying dead in hospital, almost naked, pale and slightly bloated, stiffening like a fish out of water an hour, the great blade on his face rises sharper than ever—a fin with an identity all its own, a wing still cutting its own path through the world.

I nudged it a few days back while shaving him, when he was still alive. Plumped on the hospital pillows, he enjoyed having his son lather his face. He had held off letting the nurses shave him because I had done it before, and already he considered it Henry's job. "Henry shaves me," he said.

He was like that. Constructing the way things were, making shapes as he went along. I used to think that was what all fathers did, but it was what he did.

It was the heel of my hand that nudged his nose. I must have hurt him. But he was stoical about it, a man whose sense of self all his life had been bound up in his nose. Never a moment would go by but the nose would have its say: a toot, a snort, sniff, sniffle. A scratch, a discreet probe with a fingertip.

If I did, he didn't let on, only stiffened on the pillow.

"I'm sorry, Dad."

"No, no. Just carry on."

He didn't so much mind lying in bed as hate not being able to walk. Six weeks after it became clear he would no longer walk, he was gone. No walk, no life: that was his way, too.

I held the cardboard bowl of warm water the hospital nurse had given me under his chin and proceeded with the awkward operation of shaving someone else, making backward movements, undoing the mirror-induced habits of a lifetime.

Now it's four days later. All the drama and struggle are over. A faint silver stubble again covers his jaw, but he's gone.

I shave him one last time, more carefully now, maneuvering

the blade through the passage between top lip and nose, letting it crunch gently through the coarse stubble that spreads from the rim of the bottom lip down the chin.

Then we wash him, two male nurses and I. No one else in the family wants to, afraid of what it might be like. But it's fine, nothing gruesome.

His body is stiff all over, the room quiet. Just the wet sounds of our damp sponges.

It occurs to me that I should feel something, cry the way I have in recent weeks with him, but I don't. It's odd—implausible and too soon—that he should be dead and we should be washing his corpse. But here we are doing it. Our breaths come and go tremulously as we dress him in clean clothes from the bag his loving wife packed for the hospital.

IT DIDN'T RAIN THE DAY we buried him. There was light cloud and brief blooms of sun.

The rabbis of Golders Green, in London, had been fast. The body was sent from the Oxford hospital up to London the afternoon he died, and came back the next day in a cardboard box, abluted and purified for the next step in his soul's migration. But we waived the twenty-four-hour Jewish prescription for burial, to give us time to organize the funeral, and kept him in a fridge at the undertaker's for a few days.

My father and stepmother had been paying dues to the synagogue for decades, even though they never went. So it was the synagogue that swung into gear as soon as they heard of his death.

The rabbi who did the service was a Lubavitcher. He brought along a box of old volumes of Talmudic commentary, heavy tomes that looked like Victorian ledgers, and as the earth went in, shoveled by the mourners, he lobbed these weighty texts in. They thudded on the coffin lid, then onto the earth as it started to cover him.

"It helps the soul," he explained. "It feels less estranged in its new circumstances if it has some religious books with it."

Ever the people of the Book.

ONE TIME I HAD ARRIVED at the hospital ward to see my stepmother at the head of the bed, bending over Dad, holding his hands, talking fervently, quietly.

I hung back by the gap in the curtain. They didn't notice me. I couldn't hear what they were saying but could feel the fizz in the room. They were still in love. They were like the lovers they must have been long ago, when they met in hotels or borrowed apartments and knew their time was brief. Here it was again, the clock ticking against love: never enough time.

I said a few words at the funeral—we all did, his three kids— and I said that it seemed clear that, beyond all the merits of his scholarly labors, his convening of conferences, his editing of Soviet texts, his clandestine services for MI5, his books and articles and lectures, what had been the center of his life was this: this love with our stepmum.

He'd once told me that he was unhappy after the divorce from our mother; he didn't like living alone. He said to my sister and me, "You don't want your dad to be alone, do you?"

And we hadn't answered because we didn't think he *was* alone: he had us. Yet we saw him only once a fortnight, and we couldn't really conceive of the rest of his life when we weren't there.

I had understood from afar that the new marriage was happy. As a child I hadn't wanted them to be happy, because that would mean they'd stay together, and I couldn't imagine any way of healing our family except for Dad coming home. Not that Mum wanted him back. Early on, I had got lazy and stopped imagining other solutions. It was either/or.

That was one reason I had been writing the family book for decades: because I hadn't known what else to do.

Every time I worked on it something happened, the world became tender with hope. And the day had finally rolled around when the book was finished. At the time, I was uneasy. As the prospect loomed of the book actually being published, I feared for my parents, and for my children. It was fiction, yes, but also no. The book had taken so long to write, and its ever getting published had been such a remote possibility for so long, that it was a shock to realize it might actually happen. Would my parents read it? How would they react? Would it hurt them? What about my siblings, and my stepsiblings? And our more distant relatives? Might it shock and hurt a lot of people? Might it ruin the blossoming love between our boys and their grandparents? Could they cut their grandchildren out of their lives? And would the anxieties of literary life jerk my old self out of its grave once again, to make empty demands on everything like a zombie on speed?

In my corner stood a powerful literary agent. A taciturn man, he was effusive over the book, and started preparing a list of publishers to send the manuscript to. He foresaw big things for it.

But I realized I had moved on. The literary game was over for me. It was suddenly an easy decision. The risks weren't worth it. I shelved the book. If I could have disposed of it so easily, I'd have thrown the manuscript down into Dad's grave along with the volumes of Talmud.

As it happened, my current publishers, with whom I was still under contract, didn't like it anyway but felt bound to honor the contract, and paid us regardless. It was the best of both worlds: the wider family was spared the trouble, and our household got some compensation for all the grief the book had put us through.

I STOPPED WRITING.

The value of it was no longer apparent. Even if you managed to midwife a fine poem, what did it matter? Better than reflecting and recording this world was to become intimate with it while you could—that was its own reward and fulfillment, and needed no record.

There wasn't just the worldly side of writing, but the engines of the inner creative process too, the forces that generated phrases, paragraphs, verses, images, structures. They had been constantly at work since my teens, a grim power that cared for little else. It cherished and enjoyed beauty but was amoral. Not anti-ethical but non-ethical. Its standard was aesthetic power, period.

That was what I had lived by: a compulsion, a calling, inherently repetitive in its dynamic, a kind of addiction. Literary productivity promised fulfillment and sometimes delivered. It could be good to write. It gave you a chance to digest life, to practice a craft, and it offered a way of interpreting life, of being a participant in its creation, not just a recipient. But even a crumb of success, for me, had led to overconfidence, tall but flimsy, a creative arrogance, enduring long enough to get the job done, again and again, and destined each time to crumble into the ground of shame from which it had risen.

Now this whole dynamic had ceased.

More and more I realized that my on-and-off conviction in my own ability as a writer had concealed many blind spots in craft. Perhaps I hadn't been particularly gifted, just arrogant, with distinctly less talent than many writers, and had had *more* than my fair share of success, not less.

Oddly, this idea brought relief. These days I liked being less good than others, less known. Life was sweeter in the lowlands of modesty and failings.

QUIET. NO WORDS. THE FLYWHEEL of hope and angst that had driven the writing lost its momentum. The need to write had risen from a node of unease on the ribs, and it was empty now. The world was one luminosity. What could a book matter?

The quiet was a gift. It came from my teachers, who received it from theirs, who had received it from theirs before them. It passed from generation to generation. But it wasn't exactly up to us or our teachers. It had a life of its own. That's how Master Keizan* described it in his *Transmission of Light*: as water poured from vessel to vessel.

I UNDERSTOOD NOW WHY LEGEND claimed that 1,500 years ago Bodhidharma had transported the teaching across the Yangtze River on a single grass stalk. How slight and slender is the ferry, the craft, by which the teaching is transmitted. On one blade of grass. It almost needs no craft at all. Yet it does. It needs this frail human frame. It came to China sure enough on that single stem, and the great Ch'an tradition flourished, and

---

* Keizan Jokin, a Japanese master; 1268–1325.

spread to Japan as "Zen," then on further, to the modern West, to us.

❧

I STARTED WORKING FOR A friend's hospice organization, doing simple chores and errands for people who were dying, sitting with them at their bedside while they slept, chatting quietly when they were awake. Occasionally I'd be there through the night.

I started going to the prison south of town, where a couple of us taught yoga and meditation to inmates who wanted to learn. Then I'd go home to the family.

No need to achieve: all was achieved already. The great project of this life had been to realize that. Dogen said, "The great Way is intrinsically accomplished; the principle of Zen is complete freedom." All that came next was service, love, trying to be helpful and open.

I sat a lot each morning and evening. It was like walking through a pine forest, the earth soft underfoot, the canopy high overhead, and a quietness, a limitless twilight among the trees that went on forever: neither light nor dark, both light and dark. Time, day, night, and epochs opened like petals, and the "mind-flower" bloomed.

SOME TIME AFTER THAT CRUCIAL retreat with John, I met with the abbot of the lineage, Yamada Ryoun* Roshi, a Japanese master then in his late sixties, who had been sitting Zen for over

---

* Pronounced "ryo-un," in two syllables.

fifty years at that point and who decided to start coming annually to America to lead a retreat.

His father, Yamada Koun Roshi, had been the teacher of more than a dozen Western Zen teachers, among them Joan Rieck and Robert Aitken, who had studied together in Kamakura. In the years before his death, in 1989, Yamada Koun had apparently grown uneasy over the "dharma clarity," or lack of it, in some of these Western teachers and had initiated the training retreat for teachers that his son was still hosting annually. Most of the teachers eagerly attended each year, but a few among the American cohort did not. This had inevitably generated some remoteness from the original lineage, and in some Zen circles in America the continued existence of Sanbo Kyodan even went overlooked, almost as an awkward fact best ignored. After Koun's death, there had been a new abbot for fifteen years, Kubota Akira Roshi, and after him Yamada Ryoun had taken the reins. He was now trying to ensure that the lineage's core teaching was conveyed to these shores as clearly as possible, by coming to lead his annual retreat on this side of the Pacific. As a by-product, perhaps this might also help to heal whatever rift there was with the wider American sangha.

The first retreat was held in the suburbs of Toronto, in a big old center that was the home base of the Scarboro Missions. White-bearded old missionaries home from their forays overseas chatted quietly through lunch at tables in the corners of the dining room, while some sixty-five of us, gathered from around North America, silently glided among them, in between long bouts seated on the floor of the chapel on our cushions.

It was the first time I had met people from the wider lineage. A few had come from far afield: from the Philippines, from En gland and Japan. Naturally, there wasn't a lot of chat during the retreat, but before and after, groups of us huddled together at tables, strolled down to the nearby cliffs overlooking Lake Ontario, and got to know one another.

I found them an impressive group: people whose priorities in life lay beyond themselves, who were working for the good of others. You could feel a lightness and bonhomie among them, a kind of health in the air that was a little new to me, which I guessed came from doing work on behalf of others.

On that retreat, the first time I met privately with the abbot for *dokusan*, as soon as I sat down before him, the light in the little room turned strange—radiant, pregnant—and just as I was about to start speaking, I felt something like a hand reach inside me and find the vibrant space that had opened up there. The hand not only knew what it had found, but also knew it had been recognized. I could not only feel it, but feel the hand's recognition of my feeling of it. A buzzing joy emanated from the mutual recognition.

In his deep, quiet voice Yamada Ryoun said something about sensing that there had been a deep experience.

I thought I understood then that the experience must have happened to him too, and to John, and to Joan. It did pass itself on.

At that moment, the abbot became another of my teachers. Thereafter, I would see him at his annual North American retreat, and if it was ever possible for me to make it, I was welcome at his zendo in Tokyo too.

I MADE A HABIT OF sitting through the night, usually on the last night of a retreat, not as a feat of endurance but because it was easy. Something was alive in me, and when I sat it could fulfill itself and grow stronger.

I spent a week sitting on the streets of London. I began near the great religious buildings. They seemed sympathetic amid the teeming commerce. St. Paul's, Southwark, Westminster Abbey. I sat gazing into their gaunt stones in nearby alleys. I had rain gear but rarely needed it. Sometimes it was embarrassing at first. There'd be tourists and ordinary Londoners going about their business, and there I was, dropping to my knees, blowing up my little cushion, and positioning myself oddly, facing cross-legged away from the street at a wall. What did they make of it? Gradually I would put it out of mind and tune into the sense experience of just being there.

On the second day I ventured away from the cathedrals. Hyde Park Corner, Marble Arch, Trafalgar Square, the big bridges. I'd walk in between sits and randomly select a new spot, and drop in for a few hours. Outside the Bank of England I sat through several rush hours like a busker, except facing the wall, away from the pedestrians, hearing the river of footfalls behind me.

I guess it was a species of mortification, to be still in front of so many moving people. I didn't care. Somehow it felt like a debt that had to be repaid—to my father, to my mother, to the dharma I had received, and to the great city.

KOANS WERE DIFFERENT NOW. I felt I knew the world the masters were living in, and it wasn't what it had previously seemed. During my earlier training I had felt as if every koan had shot through me from another realm, using me like a hand puppet to "present" itself. But now it felt as if the screen between me and that realm, weakened by so many koans, had given way. I was standing in the same realm as the koans. It was clear that that realm and this realm of everyday life had never been separate from the start.

John had once given a talk about a Zen dialogue where a monk asks Joshu, "What is Zen?"

Joshu: "It's not Zen."

Student: "Why is it not Zen?"

Joshu: "It's alive! It's alive!"

John had asked us all rhetorically, "*What* is alive?" The table, road, car, wall, no less than the bird or the cat, a thought about lunch tomorrow, a spoon on the table, the humming fridge. In Joshu's world you might reasonably ask whether anything was *not* alive.

Zen is the opposite of withdrawal from the world. It's a radical acceptance of life, the pain and suffering no less than the beauty of the dawn skies, of the sea in rain, the mountain dark under morning clouds, and the shopping list. Unless a path leads us back into the world—reincarnates us, as it were—it's not a complete path. For Zen, this life, this world, is the very absolute. Making a cup of tea, fetching milk from the fridge, standing outside on the front step, watching the remains of a storm drift across the dawn sky, and hearing the *drip-drip* of rainwater into a puddle from a roof are miracles. The miraculous, in the end, is the fact of anything existing at all.

That's why the koans all speak the language of ordinary things. Dogs, bridges, mountains, rivers: the concrete things of this world are their very fabric.

A monk once asked Joshu, "What is my teacher?"

Joshu said, "Clouds rising out of the mountains, streams entering the valley without a sound."

The monk said, "I wasn't asking about them."

Joshu said, "Though they are your teacher, you don't recognize them."

THERE IS A HUMP WE can get over, a corner we can turn, and it's getting less mysterious by the week as research in the field of contemplative neuroscience keeps after it. Psychology has a harder time with the contemplative shift. Freud and Jung both assumed it was part of the unconscious, since it wasn't part of everyday consciousness, and since we couldn't find it without relinquishing the hegemony of ordinary consciousness. Yet it's the polar opposite of "unconscious." It's consciousness gone exponential, all-inclusive.

Neuroscience has been having a better time of it.

Richard Davidson, a well-known leader in the field of contemplative neuroscience, has headed the Waisman Laboratory for Brain Imaging and Behavior at the University of Wisconsin–Madison for years. The lab uses imaging technology to study the effects of meditation on the brain. He himself is a Tibetan Buddhist practitioner, and I got to know him a little during periodic visits he made to Santa Fe, where he would teach at Upaya Zen Center.

One time I asked him whether Tibetan Buddhism recognized an experience of thoroughgoing nothingness, with no seeing, no seer, no seen.

Sure they did. To my surprise, he said that just such an experience was a deep goal of Tibetan "Dzogchen" practice: to clarify the nature of mind, ubiquitous throughout space and time yet completely empty.

We were sitting in an adobe teahouse in Santa Fe on a drab

afternoon, and his eyes shone clear and dark. He was open and deep. You could feel it. It was a good conversation, and I was happy—and he too, I felt—to discover this shared reality beyond schools.

I asked if his lab had ever caught such an experience on a brain scan as it happened. The odds seemed overwhelmingly against it.

"We can see its echo," he said. "We can see when it's happened."

He described some of the changes in brain function and neuroplasticity that accompany it. The midline networks of the brain where narrative activity happens—an essential locus of our sense of self, since the self is basically a story, the story of "me"—go quieter, he said. Less narrative, less self. In meditators who have gone through a deep experience, the midline is silent.

It made sense. The aftermath of the experience is endless. Every moment is that very experience unfolding. Time rolls on, but it also doesn't move an inch. All time is always here, once we've knocked the bottom out and found the "groundless ground."

I FOUND I COULD TELL whether someone was living this experience. I could feel what condition a person was in—whether reaching out or holding on, or at rest, at home, within.

The after-effects of that experience were a long time withdrawing. I'm not sure they ever did. Instead everything kept unfolding from that original moment.

But what it left was not some exultation. Rather, as the exultation receded, a glow, the embers of an old fire that been extinguished, remained. What remained was a great space, a vault like the dome-roofed sky, a glowing cavern, an old stone cathedral, a mosque like a pine forest, columns receding into the distance, bare spongy floor underfoot, and deep twilight that was the ideal climate for the trees—semi-moist, fungus-fragranced—where they could live for unimaginable ages far longer than any known life spans.

But whether that space was inside a person or outside, it wasn't possible to say.

It wasn't something. But it wasn't nothing either.

Utter goneness. Yet not nothing. But still, not something.

No Other

LATE WINTER IN NEW MEXICO again. Nighttime. Snow is falling, large, damp flakes that flicker down like wet leaves through the light of an outdoor lamp.

In a low-lit bedroom an old man is softly moaning. He is in some kind of distress, but it's hard to tell how severe, as he expresses himself so quietly. He is ninety-two, his white hair so thin it's like down. It must be two or three in the morning. I've been resting on a couch near his bed. I decide not to disturb him. Is he dreaming or awake, or have the two become indistinguishable for him?

When morning comes and he opens his papery eyelids, the irises are fine and radiant as a butterfly wing with light shining through it. I pull the drawsheet in the bed to turn him. Normally when I do this, he holds out a skinny hand to help and clenches the steel rail of the hospital bed that has been moved into his home. Today he doesn't. It hits me: the air in the room has changed. A stillness has entered, fizzing with business of its own.

His wife bends over him, holding his hand, and speaks in a loud voice. He doesn't respond. She tries again, then bustles out, saying we should let him sleep more. I murmur agreement.

Phone calls are made, a daughter arrives, a son is flying in from the Midwest. A priest comes, large, bustling, friendly. Other people show up, hospice workers like me who spent time with the old man over the previous months. Huge bunches of daffodils appear in the room. What must they look like to his eyes? Blazes of buttery golden light. Springtime in his childhood. Who knows if he even sees them.

The presence of stillness in the room grows stronger. His wife is moaning beside the bed. He was a military scientist in life, a dutiful man. When I had to feed him he never complained, and would meet my eyes with his diaphanous gaze as I lifted the spoon to his lips. He never lost his Catholic faith, and perhaps that is helping him face death. Perhaps it doesn't strike him as death.

The room fills with a new peace. A relief in the air. His wife has ceased to moan. She is crying silently. The priest gets up from his chair and intones a sonorous prayer. The rest of us sit still, as if deep underwater, almost as if breathing were an intrusion.

He has died. The lead hospice worker glances at me with a faint, curious smile, her cheeks marked by tears.

I go outside into the morning. The sun is shining through the piñon bushes, the earth is coated with light snow. I inhale the pine-scented air and pull out my car keys.

Time is tight. Later this morning the abbot is flying in from Tokyo to lead a retreat here, and I am responsible for meeting him. I just have time to go home for breakfast and a little time with the family.

AS I DRIVE BACK ACROSS the wide Galisteo Basin, the desert slowly emerges out of a velvet dawn and turns watery blue. Just as I reach the top of a long hill, the wing of darkness over the earth withdraws and the Sangre de Cristo Mountains spring into view. The gaunt lump of mountains receives the first blush on its face; at their feet, the last street lights of town mingle with the sun winking off windows and roofs.

I feel like weeping as I look at the smooth morning hills, at the city glinting like rubble in the distance. It's one of those vistas that seems mythical. It still gets me every time. Like an archetypal ramp to a citadel, the highway reaches straight at the blue mountains, massed with metallic cumuli, and the whole sky and land are in motion like a living organism. A burst of exhilaration seems to rush through the land, and I remember a long-forgotten mystery: Why did Dogen say that mountains walk? I'm glancing at the answer now: as I move across this plain, it's not "me" moving, but all things, all things as one. In this placeless place, mountains aren't mountains. They are real in a way the word "mountain" will never capture. They're alive, and wildly free.

AT HOME ARE MY WIFE and boys. So easily our family might have fractured. But the marvel at the heart of Zen broke in and healed disaster. I feel so grateful to be able to go home. It's the only place I want to go.

We're still living in the same small, ramshackle house on a hill. I rumble along the rutted dirt road, then up the driveway. It's early, but the boys are already out on the ragged trampoline.

They stop bouncing when they see me coming and emit the predictable cries for me to come and join them. I ought to be tired after the long night, but today it's as if the heart is inside out, and a tender energy rises through everything: through the low weeds by the door, the chamisa bushes, the apricot trees still without leaves but studded with buds, the stack of firewood by the wall, and the children's faces and cries.

"Look what I can do," the boys shout, and show me their latest twists and flips, before I spill myself onto the contraption and start using my body weight to catapult them, shrieking with delight, high into the sky.

"Whoa!" they cry after an unnervingly big launch, and kill their next bounce by rolling onto their backs giggling.

In the house their mum is preparing breakfast.

"Pancakes?" I ask.

"It's a school day, but I thought what the hell," she says.

She is a tall, beautiful woman and I still can't quite believe my luck that we are together. We kiss and I make coffee.

"He died," I tell her. "This morning."

"Oh, honey." She hugs me and suddenly the brightness of the old man's death is here again, in our kitchen. It feels like nothing so much as love.

Zen offers a way to give up, so love can break in.

I call the boys in for their pancakes and the kitchen fills with excited chatter.

"Hey Dad, Dad, I did a backflip . . . a side flip . . . a front flip . . ." Their faces beam up from the table.

When I climb back into the car to go to the airport to meet the master, a fume of smoky sun is spilling down the mountainsides. This land is so big. Yet it's light as a feather.

THESE PAST FEW YEARS MY teachers, Joan, John, and Yamada Ryoun, have started training me as a beginning teacher. With hesitation, with the recognition that my own training would be endless, that I was still working under their guidance to get a little closer to living up to the ancient road of Zen, I acquiesced. I didn't really feel I had much choice. My parents had given me life, and my teachers gave me—another kind of life.

Having finished all the koans under Joan's guidance, I embarked on further training, a "koan review," under the brilliant Filipino master Ruben Habito Roshi, a former Jesuit and, since the early 1990s, a professor of comparative religion at Southern Methodist University in Dallas. He was married to the renowned scholar of Chinese literature Maria Reis, also a Zen teacher, and they would both welcome me into their household for a few days at a time. Somehow, with seemingly inexhaustible energy, Ruben would find time between other commitments for one or two or sometimes more long *dokusan* per day, unleashing his passionate Zen wisdom from a multitude of angles, firing koans at me, expecting instant mind-free responses, wearing down any lingering "stickiness" of mind, again and again blowing away the dust, as he put it, quickening my sluggish Zen activity, battering the encrustations of self-clinging, opening new vistas of unencumbered dharma. He once called it "romping through the universe together." It was exhilarating, dynamic, vivifying. I quickly grew to love him too. In time, over a few years, he led me through all five koan books again.

MEANWHILE YAMADA RYOUN ROSHI HAD invited me to join the lineage's teacher training retreats. He was a remarkable man, both a master with an awesome reputation and at the same time a significant Japanese business figure. His English was fluent, after long stints in the United States and London, and his command of the koans without parallel—he had spent nearly forty years training with them, first under Yasutani Roshi,* then his own father, Yamada Koun Roshi. If you could get to study with him, it was the opportunity of a lifetime.

At the annual teacher training retreats there would be awe-inspiring seminars where powerful masters did "dharma combat" over a koan, until gradually the circle settled down to the most salient truth the koan opened up. Finally the abbot would make sure all teachers were clear on the koan's main points. The purpose of these trainings was to help us maintain this teaching, so new in the West, so easy to let slide into conceptual approaches, or "dead Zen," as the old masters called it. Zen is a waste of time if it's not embodied in dynamic lives of service. The koans are less to be "understood" than lived. But it's very easy for koan training to go astray. It needs a firm hand and a deep, clear eye.

The first time I went to one of these retreats—an intimidating experience in itself, especially as the most junior of the "senior students"—when the time came for my *dokusan* with the abbot, I entered the little room full of memories of our radiant encounters at the retreats he had given in America.

---

* 1885–1973.

Hardly had I sat down and uttered my opening play than he was shaking his head and reaching for his handbell, the signal that he was ending the interview. He shook the bell and I had to leave.

Dizzy and stung, I spent the rest of the sit trying to understand where I had gone wrong. Gradually the dismay dissipated, and the next day I went back in, sure that now things would go better.

He listened for a moment, then again the hand went to the bell. I heard a brief phrase about my being caught in delusion, and that I must throw it away, and I was out the door. That was the last time I would see him for several months.

Not only was I obviously not ready for the big league; the fact I felt upset about it only underscored how unready I was. I realized I had better give up on any ideas of being trained as a teacher after all. Slowly, comfort and peace returned: it wasn't about teaching. What an idea. It was about practice. I quietly took my place at the back of the zendo and let the next koan swallow me whole.

One of the other teachers, an older Christian nun who worked on the cancer ward of a children's hospital, asked me how things were going, and I told her.

She smiled. "Remember what Mumon says about the way the lion teaches its cubs," she told me, referring to a verse where Master Mumon describes how a lioness will bat her cubs down a bank so that they have to climb back up, growing in strength, initiative, resilience.

"Seems it always has to be like this, at some point in our training," she added, nodding her head, perhaps at memories of similar times in her own training.

Sure enough, the next time I attended the teachers' retreat, a year later, the master and I met in a kind of radiant present, and he decided to authorize me as an assistant teacher, initiating a slow progress through the different levels of responsibility in the lineage.

At the same time, the worldwide network of good, kind people involved in this lineage became friends, brothers, and sisters in the dharma.

THE ABBOT HAD UNIQUE POWER. Most times I did a retreat with him, some new vista would open up, pulling the ground out from under my feet. Training with him was another beginning. Time after time, he pushed me to experience things in new ways, pushed me into new glimpses of the living dharma, all by the skill with which he handled the koans and his deep, long examination of human nature.

During one retreat, a koan suddenly broke me open, and the whole world became my flesh. The identifying process of self redomiciled to the wall in front of me, so that I was the wall, smiling back at Henry. The power of the abbot's presence had blown in like a wind.

That night I didn't sleep, and was taken on a journey by Joshu, down into catacombs where I met hundreds of dead people dressed in dusty gray and brown outfits, to all of whom I owed a great debt. Joshu wanted me to know it. They had carried themselves through their lives, unfolding over centuries, in order that I could have mine. Were they former lives I had lived? But I didn't believe in reincarnation. Yet the vision left an intimate sense of responsibility.

I don't want to sound highfalutin or grandiose. Suffice to say, whatever the circumstances, powerful gusts blew in in new ways, destroying more assumptions and preconceptions, revealing new dimensions of wonder, peace, and simplicity. But more than any of these things, the relationship with the roshi was growing into one of love and indebtedness. And the more it did, the more indebted I felt to others too—to my wife, my children, and all my teachers. It was no exaggeration to say they had all saved me.

JOAN, MEANWHILE, HAD BEEN RETURNING to her center in Germany two or three times a year to lead retreats there. She decided she would stop going, and in order to withdraw from that commitment, the last three times she went she took me with her. We co-led the retreats so the students would have a chance to get to know me. When she ceased going, I would continue to go twice a year and they could carry on their training with me if they wanted to.

The retreats were large, with sixty or seventy people, and the Sonnenhof Center, a big old converted chalet-style farmhouse perched on the side of a mountain in the Black Forest, was a magnificent place for meditation. Joan had established and built it up herself, with a lot of help from the students and her colleague Willigis Jaeger.

At first it was daunting to meet people in the *dokusan* room. Not only was there the challenge of finding ways to be helpful with people's practice, but as a British half Jew, I had my own struggles with being in Germany at all. It was a nation I had more or less avoided all my life.

I talked it over with Joan and realized that I was actually holding a prejudice. That meant there was a chance to open up another chamber of my inscrutable, tricky heart, whereupon a tide of forgiveness flooded in that I didn't know had long been dammed. Meanwhile the sense of having to live up to something as a teacher lessened. Unless I was natural and genuine, I was unlikely to be of much help. The dharma I'd received from my teachers began to show itself unbidden. The less I did, the more it could do. The teaching was about anything except me.

SOMETIMES A FEELING WOULD COME up in meditation, a quiet clutch or burr in the chest. Finally I saw that it was unease about being a teacher. Surely I couldn't be a solid enough meditator to be guiding others. In perfect circularity, I took the very fact that such unease was arising as proof that I hadn't attained the unshakable ease proper for a teacher.

But one evening as I was sitting, the thought occurred that an occasional misgiving was only to be expected when adopting a new role. Perhaps my teachers after all knew better than I did. What if the very idea that something was wrong were merely an ancient habit? Perhaps everything was all right. Not that there weren't manifest problems in our world, but that the old, customary sense of being in error myself was an atavistic inheritance, out of date now. Things were as they had to be, the good and the bad. We had to do what we could to make them better, that was all. And anyway, I would never stop being a student.

THE FURTHER YOU GO IN Zen the less you understand. That's how it is. You end up feeling a bit like Socrates, who said he knew only one thing, namely that he knew nothing. Although in Zen you don't even know that.

Over time, passages of this book started presenting themselves in my morning sits, and during the night. I didn't mean to write another book, especially not a book about how I stopped being a writer. That would seem the height of tautology, not to mention self-absorption—above all, in a book that claims to be about a path to becoming less self-absorbed. But eventually I caved, and started to pick up a pen and jot down the paragraphs as they came.

(Ah, well. You hold the consequence in your hand.)

One reason for writing it was that I was concerned it would soon all be gone. "I was here—once and no more." Before the land disappeared entirely, I wanted to make a record of the old road I'd found and followed, in case it might help anyone else searching for a path like this.

The poet of Cold Mountain, Hanshan, who lived in ninth-century China, wrote of Cold Mountain, where he lived: "I have forgotten the road by which I came." He also said: "Cold Mountain? There is no road to Cold Mountain."

I wanted to try to map the road by which I came, all the same.

THROUGHOUT MY TRAINING I'D THOUGHT I just wanted to find again the "one bright pearl" I'd glimpsed on the beach at nineteen, the Golden Fleece the youth failed to bring home, and the inner torment he felt about that being the very measure of his failure. I would never have guessed back then that bringing home the fleece was the lifelong endeavor at the core of Zen: how to *live* the one bright pearl, have it be the bedrock of our lives. Zen can't be a matter of self-interest. To "drop body and mind," as Dogen put it, is not the end. What matters, then, is how we enact a bodiless, mindless life in the world, even as we are embodied along with all other beings, with them at the forefront of our caring, and all trace of awakening erased.

Zen: the only way to keep it is to give it away.

IT WOULD BE FALSE TO suggest that all troubles ceased, period. Now and then I carried on with the dreamwork to move through some difficulty. I entered a phase of somatic trauma release work with a gifted local psychologist, Bill Smythe, releasing some old patterns of anxiety that surfaced in the body. And I was blessed to be gifted some mindfulness training by the meditation adept Shinzen Young. All of these broadened the base of my practice and teaching.

All I had really wanted, all along, was to be taught to love this world, and now I had. Even if there were another, better world, I didn't want it. Zen opened an unknown wellspring that gushed like the watch fire of love, the Roman candle in the heart I first tasted many years ago on the beach in South America: a fount of love that never ceased welling up. As Juan de la Cruz said in the sixteenth century:

How well I know that fountain which gushes and flows
though it be in the dark of night.

After which there is nothing to do but share and serve.

In the end it's all a fairy tale. In the end, all Zen saves us from is ourselves. It may be a little inaccurate but not unreasonable to say that in the end, all Zen is is love.

Mountain Cloud

I RECOGNIZED MOUNTAIN CLOUD ZEN CENTER right away—it was the place I had been to decades before, for mindfulness days with Natalie Goldberg. In its quiet stretch of valley on the edge of Santa Fe, it was still beautiful and still strangely deserted. It had an air of quiet expectancy about it, as if waiting for something to arrive, to happen, to fill it perhaps with love and life.

It was Will Brennan who brought me up there. He was a longtime Zen practitioner, a former schoolteacher turned plumbing engineer, and was a kind and mild-mannered man. He had completed his koan study under various teachers, and we had occasionally met at Joan's sits, where he was continuing his training under her guidance. He was one of the founding members of Mountain Cloud, and he offered to show me around one Saturday afternoon after we drove back from a morning sit with Joan.

Pinewoods covered one side of the little valley, while sparse juniper and piñon dotted the other. Beneath the soil there were ridges of red granite, geologically the southern end of the Rockies, which broke out here and there like the spine plates of a stegosaurus. Known as dragon rocks to the old inhabitants, they offered sanctuary to hefty old piñons, which sank taproots deep into crevices and over the centuries built up domes of topsoil rich enough to foster the growth of other trees.

Small gulches and arroyos branched up into the valley sides, in scenes of breathtaking beauty—canyon landscapes with boulders overlooked by lonely pines, all in miniature.

Amid the scenic beauty stood the main building of the center, a large-beamed hall of rammed earth skimmed with adobe, built to the golden section. You walked in and the heart softened. The chest warmed. It was human-scale, yet with a subtle grandeur. It reminded me of when I set foot on the Acropolis: how the buildings were not large, and matched human senses and affirmed them. They felt good to be among.

This place had that quality. There was a dining room, a patio, a small wood-fitted kitchen like a galley on an old sailing ship, a bedroom, and an interview room, and tucked amid the conifers nearby were four cabins with bunks. It was all like stepping into some old dream that got suspended, into a fairy tale where the castle had been frozen in time.

The center hadn't had a regular teacher in twenty-five years. Its original teacher, Philip Kapleau, a man from the same lineage as me, had been called away a year after it opened. Through the years since his departure, it had not flourished—underused, barely maintaining itself with rentals, just managing to keep the roof patched and the gutters in good repair. Two or three of the old students kept on sitting here, rolling in one night a week, year after year. One of them was Will. The place felt not derelict exactly, but vacant. It was perfect, yet without life in it.

It turned out it had a troubled history. Philip Kapleau had been a revered American Zen teacher yet had never actually been authorized to teach by the lineage. He left Japan when still only halfway through his koan training. Not only was his self-appointment to the role a breach of trust and procedure; it was unhealthy. The teaching passes on through humility and surrender. To bow to circumstance, not to set oneself up in any way, is crucial if we are to have any chance of receiving the liberative beauty of the teaching and passing it on.

In addition, Kapleau had become well known through his part in helping to edit and translate a famous Zen book, *The Three Pillars of Zen*. The volume was the work of three men—Yamada Koun Roshi, Kubota Akira Roshi, and Philip Kapleau—and was an edited anthology, not an authored work, yet when it was published in the United States, in 1965, Kapleau's was the only name on the cover. His relationship with the lineage soured, and he became one of the many lone-wolf self-appointed gurus dotting the landscape of Western spirituality.

Over the years since his departure from Mountain Cloud, the center had kept going by renting itself out as a venue for different activities. The original founding group had fallen into some acrimony and dwindled down to the two or three who never gave up.

Will wanted me to get to know Mountain Cloud. He asked if I might come and sit with the remnant of the original founding students who were still sitting once a week. I did, and soon I was asked to serve as their teacher. A number asked if they could study with me. Will, in fact, became my first student, a man ten years my senior and every bit as clear. His willingness to bow under the lowly eave I had to offer was a sign of his exceptional qualities as a practitioner. That was the beginning of my induction to the center.

Other old students started showing up—Jan Unna, a deep, peaceful presence, a lawyer turned therapist; Bill Bruce, a brilliant craftsman-constructor, with a deep knowledge of the center's infrastructure; Nancy O'Connor, a gifted editor and writer and longtime student; and Pancho Burke, a kind of local bushman who spent three days a week tending to the spiritual needs of inmates in solitary confinement at the nearby state penitentiary, and who understood the land at Mountain Cloud like the back and palm of his own hand. New students started showing up, too.

We initiated a schedule of regular sits and retreats. I offered talks and one-on-one interviews, and more people began to come. Over the next few years the community grew. I never doubted that the center could come together. We were able to restore and maintain it, and built a community garden and a network of paths threading through the beautiful land. At first we considered it a big night if ten people came. Over time more and more people started appearing, both for the weekly events and the retreats, and the various small groups that had been using the center either coalesced into ours or else left, and the center started to lock in and function as a place where people could find their way to the old road of practice—the path of silence and stillness that leads not into a void but into the heart of life.

THESE DAYS, THE CENTER CONTINUES to flourish, becoming an increasingly large all-generation family. We have added a new accommodation building, financed by support from various benefactors, and young residents now live here, helping to take care of it, hosting daily sits. The garden has become a focus of community life, and we have at least twelve annual retreats, as well as a weekly class for newcomers. Occasional visiting teachers and speakers come. We have formed a special program, the Rio Grande Mindfulness Institute, to introduce mindfulness into the beleaguered public schools of New Mexico. An active board and an operations team run the place. Everything we do is designed to support the teachings of the dharma. The place is just possibly starting to function as its founder would have wanted.

And now Yamada Roshi was coming, this very morning, shortly to arrive at the little local airport, not just to lead a retreat but to perform a rededication ceremony at the zendo, to ceremonially reopen it after its long years of underuse, now that it was vibrant again.

A FINE, CHILLY, CLEAR EVENING. There's a hill behind the center, a steep, loose climb of chunky red dirt and rocks. On its broad brow you can see down onto the flat roof of the center among the trees, and beyond to the plain that stretches out west from Santa Fe. Two silver lines show faintly in the distance: the lanes of the freeway, catching the late sun on a hill. The Sandia Mountains, beside Albuquerque, show as a dark blue silhouette on the skyline.

I sit down on a rock. I like it up here. Someday I'll build a deck up here and live in a tent, I think. (There might be some marital discussion about that.)

There was a master back in tenth-century China, Zuigan,*

---

* Chinese: Ruiyan; 830–900.

who used to sit on a rock each morning and call out to himself, "Master!" "Yes," he'd answer. "Awake!" he'd admonish himself. "Yes, yes," he'd agree.

The light has softened. It's good to be in a landscape like this. I used to live for this kind of view. Big landscapes were a way of escaping oneself. You could get lost in them and become small. Here you can see the laws of the universe in the land: the angles in the skyline of the distant Jemez Mountains, the line where the covering of trees ends, the crack in the land gouged by a river, and the way light affects the view at different times of day. Beauty is only physics, after all.

It comes to me that I also like this small hill because if I look behind me, there the Sangre de Cristo Mountains are, towering up more than a mile in altitude above this spot. This is a good place for me. It reminds me of my level of Zen insight. The few moments of grace I've been blessed with are mere hillocks beside the great mountain range of the dharma my teachers roam, far beyond the knoll where I sit. Yet I don't mind. I'm okay with where I am. It's enough. My hope is one day to be able to pass on the teaching I've received just clearly enough that others after me can fulfill it more amply.

CARS START PULLING UP AMONG the trees below, and shortly before six o'clock many vehicles are tucked among the pines, parked this way and that where they can fit. It's time to go down and check in with the abbot. I took him to his hotel this morning, where he wanted to spend the day resting and puttering around downtown. Later I picked him up, with his robes rolled in a bundle, and brought him up to the center. He has been changing into his robes in the bedroom, preparing himself for the evening.

The ceremony of dedication is soon to begin. We go over the procedure together, then I lead him through the crowd that has gathered tonight—more than a hundred people, more than we can really fit, but somehow everyone has squeezed in, crammed in all over the floor on cushions, mats, and chairs. We have to pick our way through to the front, where two mats have been left out for us.

The timekeeper waits a moment, then strikes the large bell. Its sonorous chime signals the start of the evening together. A hush fills the old mud hall. Meditation begins.

Epilogue

S O IS "ENLIGHTENMENT" REAL? I'VE no idea, but:
Experiences wherein space and time disappear and all is revealed as one infinite consciousness; or as utterly without form and void; or where we ourselves vanish into empty sky; or where no trace of anything, including any witness, remains—real.

Experiences that leave indelible, beneficent changes in the psyche—real.

Becoming more filled with love, more concerned for others—real.

Lasting, positive character change, meaning less aversion and anger, less craving and clinging, more ease with the arising and passing of things as we live with less domination by self-centeredness—real.

Perhaps we can claim the personality can get just a little

bit better through practice, that's all: small improvements, but they're enough.

SO WHAT'S IT ALL BEEN about?

First, maybe Peter Matthiessen was right about "early openings": they can cause trouble. If a seed germinates and splits open, it had better have loam waiting for it.

Second, some of us are going to need other kinds of help, along with meditation: dream therapy, cognitive therapy, somatic work, yoga, whatever it may be. The more the different approaches understand and respect one another, the better.

Third, one common misunderstanding of meditation in the West is that it's an individual undertaking. I fell for that, and fell foul of it. In fact it's collaborative and relational, at least if you want to make real progress.

Fourth, while for some it may be helpful to find a live-in community that has adopted the customs, festivals, clothing, eating styles, and calendars of non-Western cultures, for many that is not what we need. There is no inherent incompatibility between Western culture and meditation practice. The core teachings need not be presented as exotic, since they aren't; they are about the human mind, heart, and body.

Fifth, my teachers have not been Deepak Chopras or Eckhart Tolles, that is, spiritual voices who stand alone, apart from any lineage, for whom the establishment of formidable commercial empires has been part of the mission. Much as I personally appreciate those popular public teachers and their books, I'm grateful my own teachers aren't like that. I was a lone wolf too long myself, snarling with distrust. That was part of the very problem. Considering that there are lineages of practitioners who have been studying human consciousness for millennia and passing on their findings, why not receive the wisdom of their cumulative experience? My life wasn't "saved" by Zen, but by my teachers. They were the ones who had taken the trouble to submit themselves to Zen's long, arduous training under their own masters so they would have something—the best thing—to offer others. And what that is doesn't come independent of relationship. It is in a sense the core of relationship, and to present it as an isolated thing that we discover in an isolated way is to miss the most important point of all. Zen is almost nothing but communal.

Sixth, there is a process a human being can go through that results in an extinguishing of certain aspects of ordinary consciousness and leads to what is traditionally called "prajna wisdom" in Buddhism—wisdom that is "supreme" or, in another translation, "before knowing." In other words, a wisdom that is not knowledge but rather a state of being. That "wisdom" should be something different from knowledge makes sense, since in this process knowledge is revealed as one of the very screens obscuring what the training uncovers. All that we know vanishes, is seen to have been a mirage, a smoke screen. Flexibility, a sense of support and love, a willingness to surrender one's opinions, to be open to others as they are, a sense of deep freedom, of things having fallen into place, of being part of something unnameable yet vivid, and of being part of the family of humanity, of living beings, of all creation, which inspires one to be of service—all these are symptomatic of the shift. But it's not a shift from one state to another; it's more a shift from a state to a process, ongoing, ever new. Moksha, nirvana, epoche (the suspension of beliefs for the Greek philosophers), redemption, liberation, realization, great death, theosis (unifying with God), metanoia, awakening: perhaps these are different labels for similar portals.

Perhaps the "self" that spiritual traditions attempt to pacify, tame, or even annul is a kind of potential, the seed of a second growing up that a human being can go through. Through infancy, childhood, and adolescence we develop a self that functions in the world. There's a first wiring of the neurology in the earliest years, then a second wiring in adolescence. In time, often around midlife, or sometimes earlier, we start to wonder whether our view of life is complete, if there could be more. While some may understand that kind of inquiry in theistic terms, perhaps what we are really doing is tasting the possibility of another stage of development, beyond self: not a metaphysical or cosmological excursion, but rather a deep incursion, into experience here and now. Some neuroscientists speak of a third wiring of the brain, an optional one, a shift that the great wisdom traditions foster. In my case, since my teens I'd been picking up the scent of a trail that might lead to this shift, alternately following then balking at it. Finally I was ready, and fell in with good guides, and with their help stumbled to the brink of an abyss, to a point of no return where there was only one way to go.

Seventh, since that moment, life has been different. More peace, love, joy. More grief too, when appropriate, which I take to be healthy. I don't want to sound beatific or saccharine, and for sure there are still bouts of anxiety and irritation, but they are much rarer and briefer, and bite less deeply. The Buddhist notion that we already contain the seed of "Buddhahood" seems plausible now. However one may understand a term like that, it surely denotes an inbuilt capacity for compassion, peace, love, energy.

On that score alone, as a guided path of meditation training, Zen can surely help.

Lastly, my assumption all through training was that Zen does specially address the kind of experience I'd had at nineteen on the beach. That was both true and not true. Zen deals with whatever a person brings. Bring that kind of experience and it will deal with it. Bring something else and it will deal with that too. Zen actually has no agenda, no content.

Can there be a serious, viable human activity that has no agenda? It sounds like nonsense. Except for this: the world of the masters is one in which all is as it is. Western logic is founded on the "dilemma": a thing either is or is not. No thing can be both *A* and *not A*. India, by contrast, came up with the "tetralemma": a thing either is; or is not; or both is and isn't; or neither is nor isn't.

This same formulation is actually found in the teachings of the Greek skeptic philosopher Pyrrho, who traveled to India with Alexander the Great in the fourth century B.C.E. Pyrrho said, "We should say of every thing that it no more is than it is not, or it both is and is not, or it neither is nor is not."

He may have picked up this formulation on his travels, during which he met with "naked philosophers" on the banks of the Indus: most likely wandering Buddhist ascetics.

It means that we can't hold any views at all. We can't even hold the view that we can have no views. Plato said, "Destroy all hypotheses," which sounds similar, except that he held to that view, and in time it would become a dogma of the Athenian Academy.

In a way, Buddhist training brought me back to my old love of the Greeks and their pursuit of *eudaimonia*, or true well-being. Scholars such as Thomas McEvilley and Adrian Kuzminski have

shown that the old divide between East and West, separating
the ancient wisdom of Asia and Greece, was never as solid as we
used to believe. There was much confluence and mutual contact
during the sixth century B.C.E., when both Greece and India
were parts of the Persian Empire. There is textual evidence that
the satraps and princes set up a large lodge in Babylon for "visiting fellows" drawn from across their empire, who would come
for two-year stays. Poets, physicians, and philosophers were their
chief interest. It's possible that cross-cultural interactions at these
stays ignited the pre-Socratic philosophical revolution on the
Aegean isles.

Zen is soteriological. It therefore must be conceded to have
an agenda of sorts. It seeks in some way to "save" us, if only by re-
lieving us of the baggage of our assumptions and preconceptions.
But it saves us not from malign superhuman forces, nor into the
arms of a heavenly being, but simply from ourselves. Its tagline
might be: "How to get saved from yourself." It seeks to free us
from a mistaken perspective generated by a misunderstanding
about our sense of self: namely, that it's a thing, that *me* is a fixed
entity. On the other hand, it doesn't seek to replace wrong views
with right ones. Rather, it seeks to free us of all views. Therefore
it is valid to say it has no agenda.

I grew up in a time of dark-clad men on the sidelines of
school life who were paid to remind us that unless we believed
their messages of blood, capital punishment, maleficent Jews,
and cannibalistic rites, we were going to burn forever. These days
it seems unfair, even cruel, to heap so much guilt into young
hearts. For my first decades I already lived in the fires of hell, one
stoked from within my own body, which blistered and fissured
in my skin. Hell was already here, as an eczema sufferer. Unless

I acquiesced to the schoolmen's dogmas, I would never get out of it.

Then grace fell on me. Without agreeing to believe in anything, on a beach far from home, I found Gensha's one bright pearl. It took years to meet someone who recognized that I had, and who knew a way to make it more than a passing glimpse. My Zen teachers led me right back to here and now. Except to a new kind of here and now, one that didn't belong to me, but rather to which I belonged.

So it is true that Zen has no agenda. Were it to have either agenda or content, it would be violating its own freedom.

Yet that innate and infinite freedom is not Zen's. It's not anyone's or anything's. It belongs to no one, never has and never will. It doesn't even belong to us. But it's ours to find.

ACKNOWLEDGMENTS

I'VE BEEN BLESSED TO HAVE had mentors, guides, teachers, supporters and allies of many kinds over the years, many of whom have gone unthanked, unacknowledged, and often even unnoticed. I'm sorry. This is not the place to attempt to record all kindnesses shown me, but I can at least try to thank those who inspired, supported, or propelled the journey recorded in this book. I know I'm liable to forget some; please accept my apologies if you happen to be one of them. Too little, and late—but thanks anyway to:

My mother, Rev. Dr. Ann Shukman, my father, the late Dr. Harold Shukman, and my stepmother, Barbara Shukman; Padre Gustavo, Speedy, Flora Papastavrou, Mahesh Yogi, and Dr. Sasha Piatigorski, brilliant scholar of Central Asian wisdom; Reverend Hewitt Wilson, Juan San Emeterio, hotelier-sage of old San Juan, Jack Everett of Shutway Quarry at Sheepscombe, master of chi, bamboo, and the peace pipe, and Wynne MacIver, who nudged me toward silence long before I knew I needed it; Natalie Goldberg, George Bowman, Aidan Hart, Thich Nhat Hanh, Daido Loori, Shinzen Young, and Joan Halifax, shaman, anthropologist, and uncompromising dharma guide, who all offered incomparable counsel, example, and guidance; my stellar brother, David Shukman, and gifted, insightful sister, Clare Ramos; Mish and Martin Dunne, in-laws who buck every stereotype; Ghislaine Agostini, Mimi Kaye, Adam Jacobs, inspiring step-siblings; Mary and Eric Lloyd Wright, who lead by kindness in the Santa Monica hills; Dr. Vickers and the staff of the Radcliffe Infirmary, Hilda Saenz de Deas, Malcolm Deas, and the late ever-caring, ever-kind Bill Haining.

The Zen teachers named in the dedication already know to what extent they have been able to do their lathe-work on this stubborn beam of wood: Joan Rieck, John Gaynor, Ruben Habito, Yamada Ryoun—thank you all.

To early readers who kindly gave time and thought to these pages, many thanks. That would be: Bettina Lancaster, Christy Hengst, Helmut Hillenkamp, Bill Bruce, Rodger Kamenetz, Bill Broyles, Susan Heard, Granville Greene, Chris Hebard, Alex Heard, Henry Richardson (who read some early pages long, long ago), James Ishmael Ford, and Clare Dunne. And thanks to Will Palmer for the excellent copyediting.

Others who have guided, helped, or shown undue patience and kindness: Rory Carnegie, Flora McDonnell, Tias Little; Will Brennan, Lucie Brennan, Jan Unna, Nancy O'Connor; Katie Widlund, Tor Travis, Pancho Bourke; Peg Froelich, Rachel Belash, Gudrun Hoerig, Chris Wuest, Bradan Beech, Jay Coghlan, Kathryn Stedham, Abigail Adler; Margie and Steve Hughes, Chris Worth, Susan York and Philip Kapleau, and all who helped to create and maintain Mountain Cloud over the decades; Pete Wallis, Sandy Chubb, Meg Vaughan Fowler, Shirley du Boulay; Tom Melk, Sarah Potter, and Philo Martinez of Corkins, who generously hosted several productive stints in the high country; Stefan Laeng, Kaz Tanahashi, Peter Cowdrey, and my late great-uncle Steven, overturner of received history.

Mentors and comrades of the page to whom I owe whatever may be readable here, thank you: Douglas Dunn, Sam Willetts, Robert Boswell, the late and beloved Jay Ramsay and Tony Hoagland, Neil Rollinson, Robin Robertson, Anne Stevenson, Pico Iyer, Stewart Wills, Hamish Robinson, Jonathan Carr, Dave Swann, Rob Wilder, Toni Nelson, and Mc McIlvoy.

For help of other kinds, thanks to: Harvey Karman, Marc Bregman, Albert Ellis, Sue Scavo, Bill St Cyr, and Bill Smythe.

Special thanks to Anne Edelstein for getting behind this project, for the thoughtful guidance in revision, and for bringing it to Jack Shoemaker, to whom all thanks for making it happen; and to Jennifer Alton, Yukiko Tominaga, Jordan Koluch, Hope Levy, and Sarah Jean Grimm at Counterpoint.

Additionally, thanks to: Johanna Sindelar, John Braman, John Thorndike, Gudrun Hoerig, Sarah Giffin, Sean Ruane, Maura Noone, Sanjiv Manifest, Sandy Anderson, Dave O'Neill, David Hinton.

Thanks, Peter Weiss. If we hadn't sat down for a cup of tea that September morning at the Teahouse, who knows if this would have come to be.

Finally and most of all, thank you to my immediate family: Stevie and Saul, for your endless inspiration, and Clare, for your immense patience, support, and love.

HENRY SHUKMAN is originally from Britain and lives in Santa Fe, New Mexico, where he leads Mountain Cloud Zen Center and is codirector of the Rio Grande Mindfulness Institute. He is an award-winning poet and writer and an associate master in the Sanbo Zen lineage. Find out more at mountaincloud.org.